RETFORD
THROUGH TIME

Nicola Davison Reed

AMBERLEY PUBLISHING

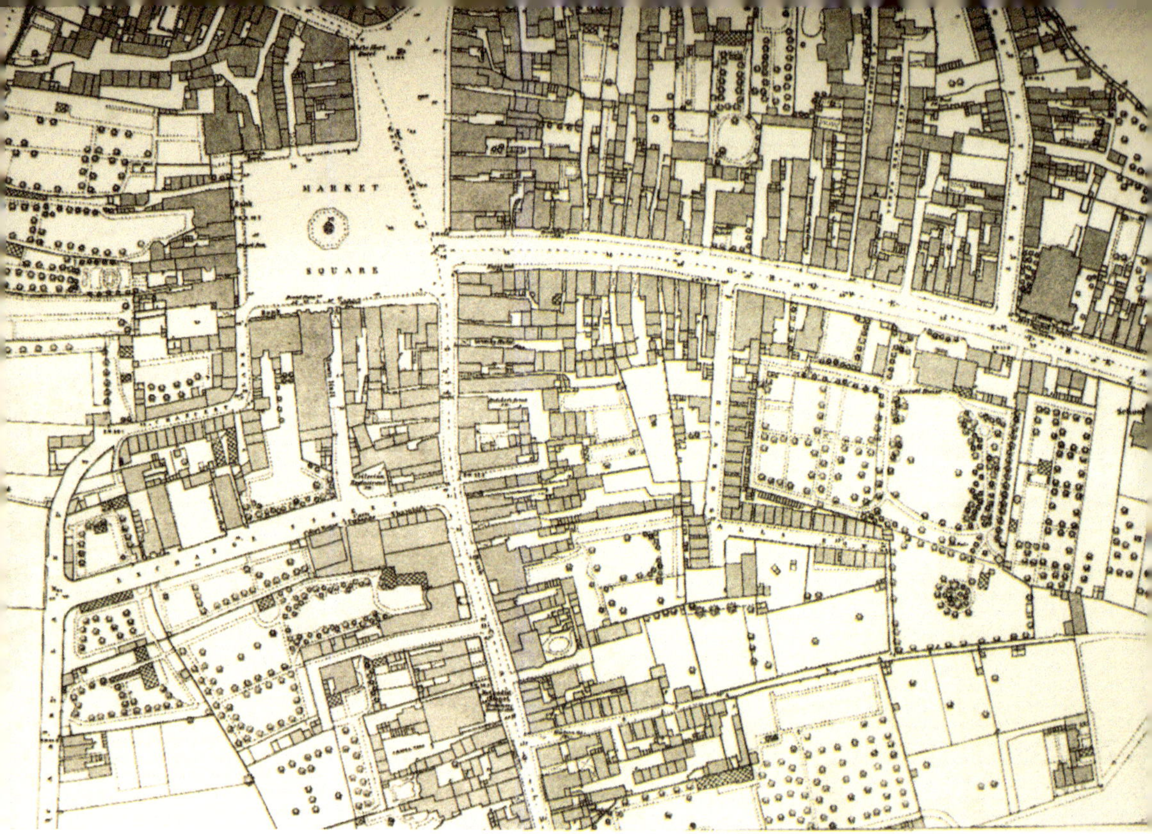

Ordinance Survey Map of Retford Town Centre 1885; provided by Stephen Brown of B. Brown & Son, Osberton Road, Retford.

First published 2012

Amberley Publishing
The Hill, Stroud, Gloucestershire, GL5 4EP
www.amberley-books.com

ISBN 978 1 4456 1188 4 (print)
ISBN 978 1 4456 1196 9 (ebook)

British Library Cataloguing in Publication Data.
A catalogue record for this book is available from the British Library.

Typesetting by Amberley Publishing.
Printed in Great Britain.

Introduction

On the main line of the Great Northern Railway, as it carves through the county on its journey from London to York, lies the town of Retford. Visible from the line, a band of red-brick houses and smoking chimneys emerge, and the belfry of an old parish church rises at its heart. The borough is the centre of the Parliamentary Hundred of Bassetlaw and was the first group of villages to enjoy the pleasures of household suffrage. The next reference to Retford or its immediate vicinity that we meet with is in the Domesday Book, and it is unusually brief and insignificant. It is evident, however, that the place soon flourished and developed, and it came to be looked upon as a business centre for the district around 1246 after Henry III, for 'the bettering of his borough of Retford', granted annual fairs to the burgesses and their heirs.

Other liberties and privileges were given by Henry and his son. Retford was also to have 'a market every Saturday and the amendment of the assize of bread and beer, and the pillory and the ducking-stool, and wrecks and waifs, and a Bailiff'. Robert de Retford, son of Richard de Retford, rose to the dignity of a judge, and was summoned to parliament in August 1295. William de Retford, whom we believe to be his son, was appointed Keeper of the Great Wardrobe and in 1354 was made a Baron of the Exchequer.

The law of the land was merciless and cruel. Men were hanged for the smallest of crimes, but a cleric could demand the protection of the Church.

St Swithun's church continued to be the principal building as the borough suffered three dreadful disasters during this period. A major fire in 1528 destroyed over three quarters of the borough and rebuilding only began in 1540. Another fire struck in 1585 (Worksop raised money for 'the poor men of the late burned town of Retford') and was followed by an even greater fire in 1631, which caused £1,300 worth of damage. The same period saw several outbreaks of severe plague with around 300 deaths in East Retford, while West Retford suffered the loss of over half its population.

On a more positive note, the construction of the Chesterfield Canal brought significant changes. In 1788 Major John Cartwright built the Revolution Mill on Spital Hill, near the Chesterfield Canal. The mill was a steam-powered wool-spinning and weaving mill that employed around 600 people. Today no trace of the ambitious enterprise has survived.

In the 1820s the town only had 220 voters. Easily influenced by bribery, votes often ensured the return of candidates favoured by the Duke of Newcastle. By the 1790s, however, Newcastle's interest was challenged by an independent group and the new constituency of East Retford/Bassetlaw was created.

By 1901 there were 12,340 inhabitants, increasing to 22,000 by 2001. Major private developments (North Road Estate, Welham Road to Tiln Lane area, Grove Coach Road to Bracken Lane area, and Babworth Crescent, for example) were completed after the Second World War. Despite the influx of housing, however, traditional industries in Retford have declined in recent years. Long-established companies such as Jenkins Newell Dunford (engineering) and Bridon Ropes (wire) both closed in 2004. Like so many other small towns, Retford's heritage is now overshadowed by large supermarkets and the service industries. This quaint and charming market town of Retford, in north Nottinghamshire, has historically been at the centre of a number of important communications networks but is now more frequently seen as a blur by long-distance travellers as they speed through on the East Coast railway route. While I was researching this book, a commuter at the train station, perusing the wonderful Welchman images on the station walls, said, 'I have travelled through this town for years and never thought to stop. I never realised it was a market town and how interesting it seems.' Maybe next time this traveller, and others like him, will stop – they should stop; Retford is a town not to be missed.

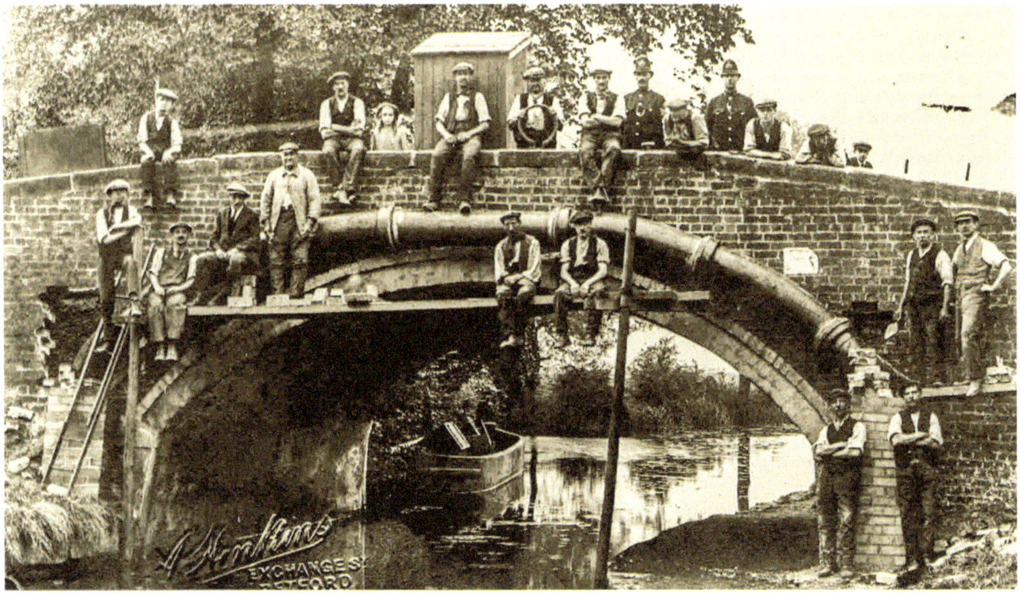

Workmen on Woodcocks Bridge over the Chesterfield Canal, on Hospital Road. Taken around 1920 when pipes were being laid across the canal.

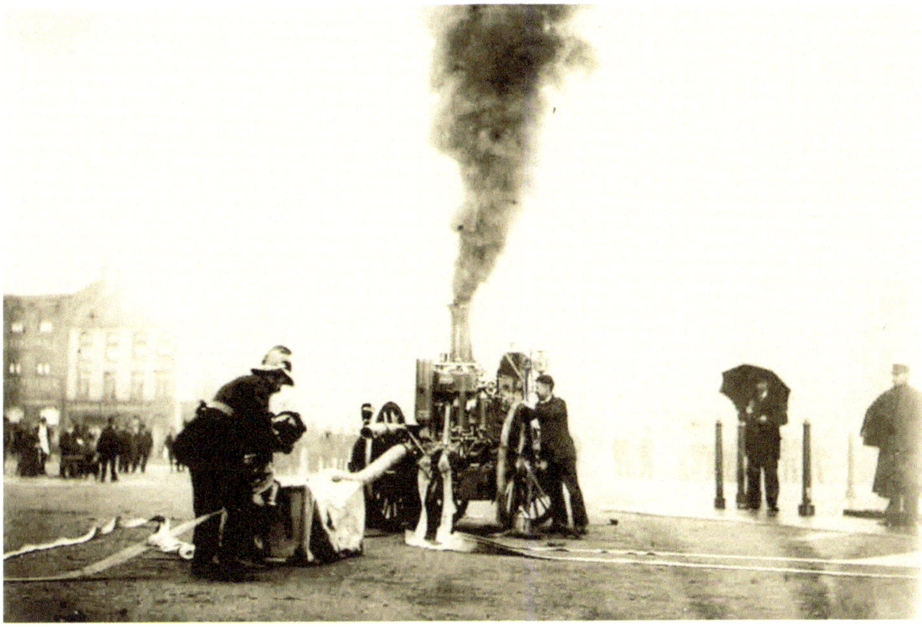

Firefighters in the Market Square, 1897

As far back as 21 BC, large bands of people were organised to fight fires. The first fire alarm system in Nottinghamshire was a 'watch of fifty women' who paraded the town of Nottingham at night. 'Fire Offices' (insurance companies) were formed in the late seventeenth century and they ran their own brigades; the insignia of these offices was a fire mark, some of which may still be seen on older buildings in the City of Nottingham. Early fire engines had manual pumps operated by hand or foot; steam engines followed soon after and were used until 1910. Retford is one of twenty-five Nottinghamshire stations staffed twenty-four hours a day and attending 600 shouts a year, 200 of which the retained service is called out.

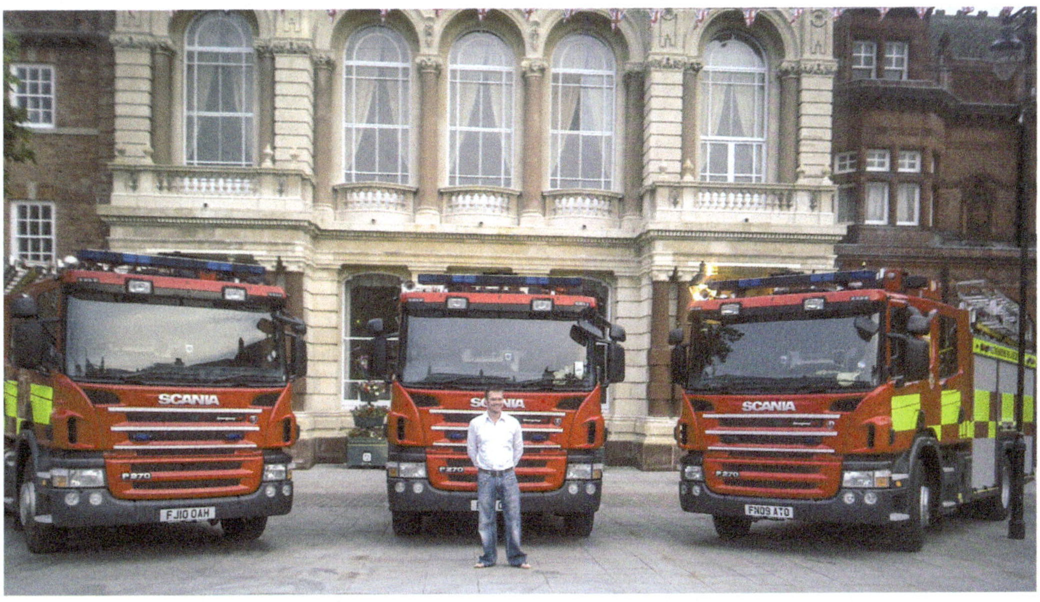

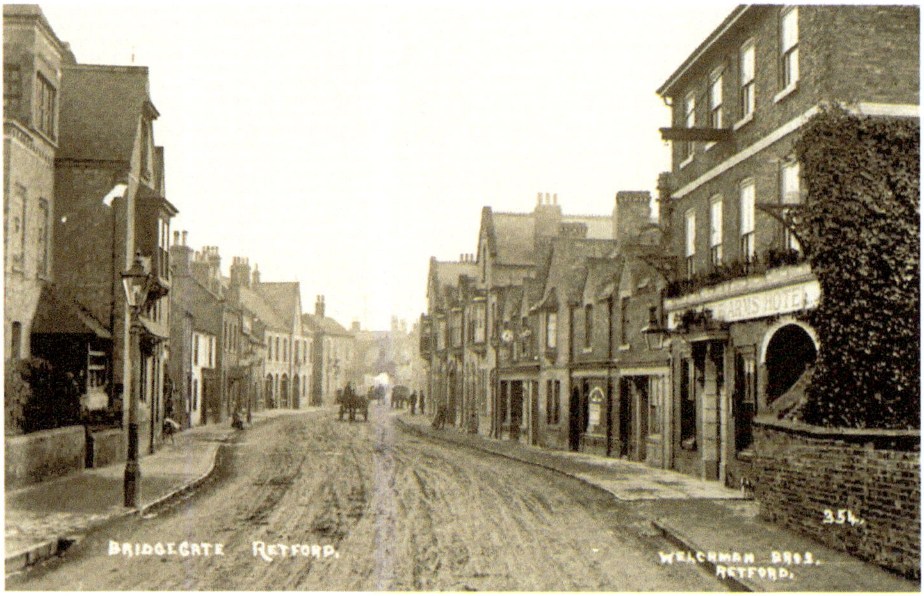

Bridgegate at the Newcastle Arms, 1897

Bridgegate is one of the gateways into town. There was a ford across the River Idle, linking East and West Retford, and the first reference to a bridge here dates from the thirteenth century. The town mills were next to the bridge and, over time, were used for fulling, grinding corn and papermaking. In addition to the built-up area there were around 50 acres of communal pasture on the south side of the town. The Great North Road lay a few miles to the west of the town for centuries, until it was re-routed in 1766 to link up with Bridgegate. Retford now lies on the main through route from London to the North. The road has stimulated the local economy; many inns have since been built to service the passing trade. The Newcastle Arms is an example of this, and is still going strong today.

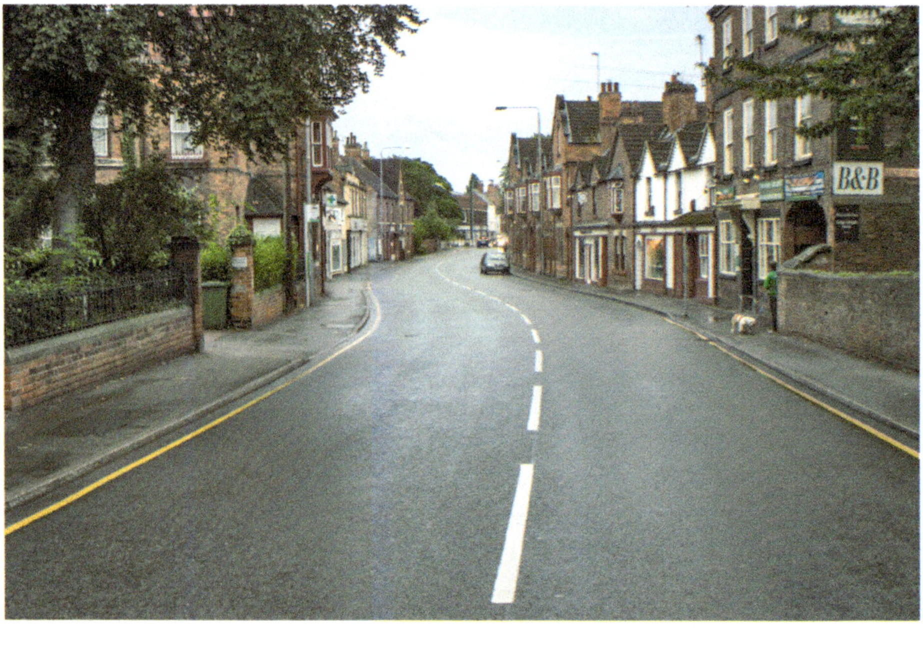

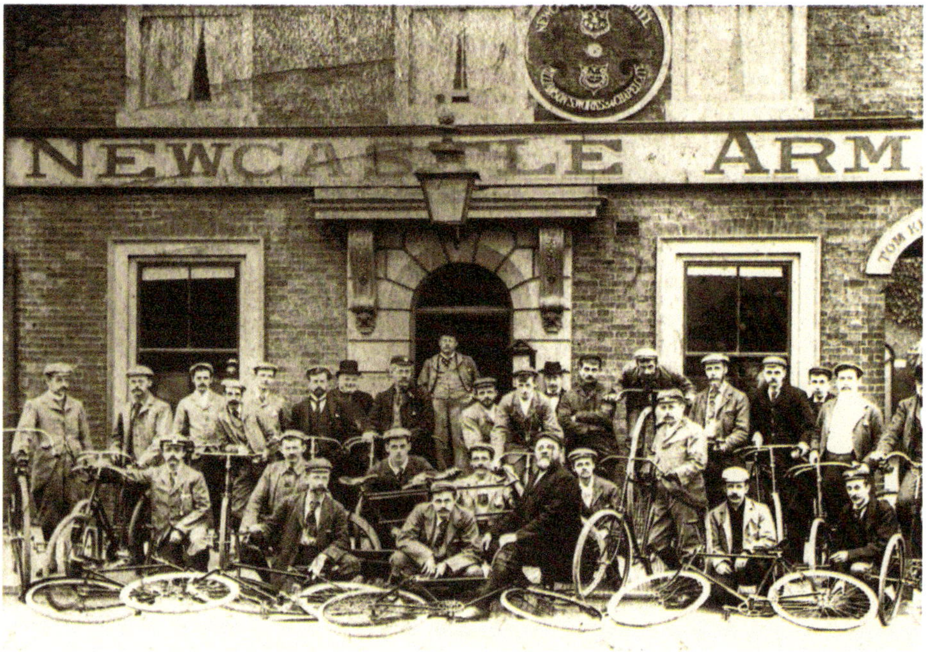

The Newcastle Arms, Bridgegate; Retford Cycle Club, 1900

Historically, there has been a local club in Retford since the early 1900s, and today Retford & District Wheelers Cycling Club meets every first Monday of the month at 7.30 p.m. at the Run Runner public house. All members and those interested in cycling or joining a local club are welcome. In fact the Wheelers' website has a very similar view outside the Newcastle Arms as in the old Welchman image. Today, stables can still be found to the rear of the Newcastle Arms, where coaches and horses were once kept at the time of the A1 road from London to Newcastle. It has plenty of young, new visitors while still retaining many of its older customers.

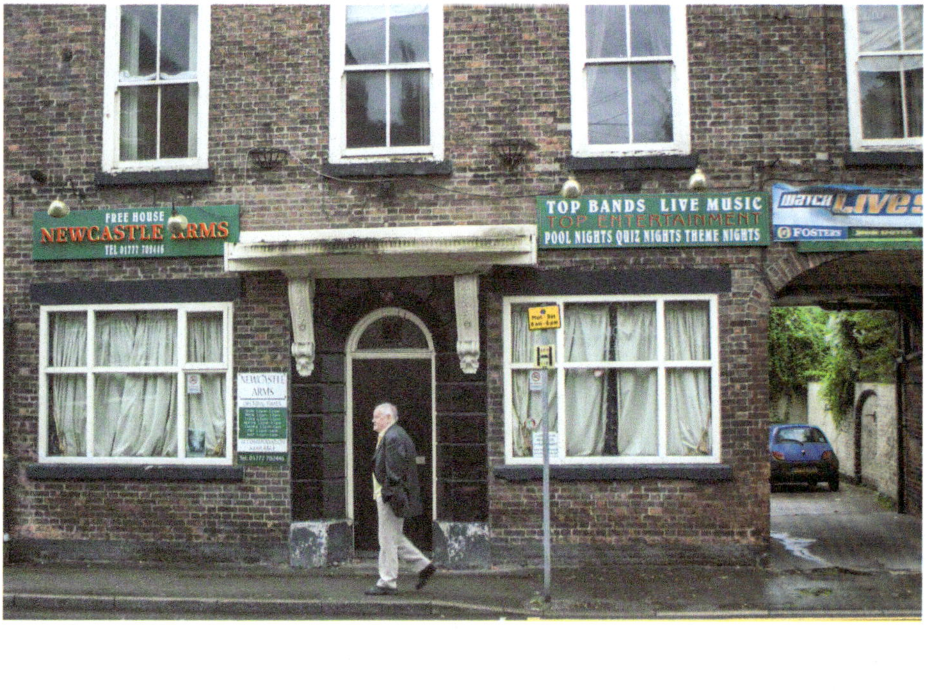

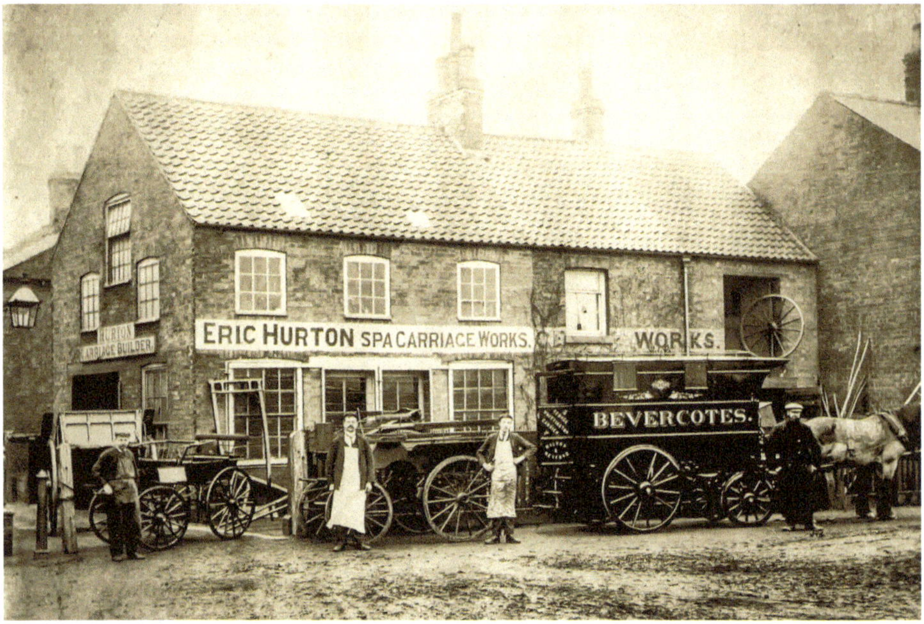

Eric Hurton's Carriage Works, Spa Common, 1910

Eric Hurton's Carriage Works, Retford. Eric Hurton is second from the left. Today the building is lovingly tended and cared for by Norma Nubolt of Retford, who invited me into her glorious home (the homemade buns baking held an aroma to behold!). Inside Norma has this old picture, taken by Edgar Welchman, framed on her wall with lots of other memorabilia of Retford and Grove during the nineteenth and twentieth centuries. Norma told me how Hurton's carriages used to provide funeral hearse carriages as well as the usual carriages to Retford town. Hurton's still exists and is based just around the corner on the next street.

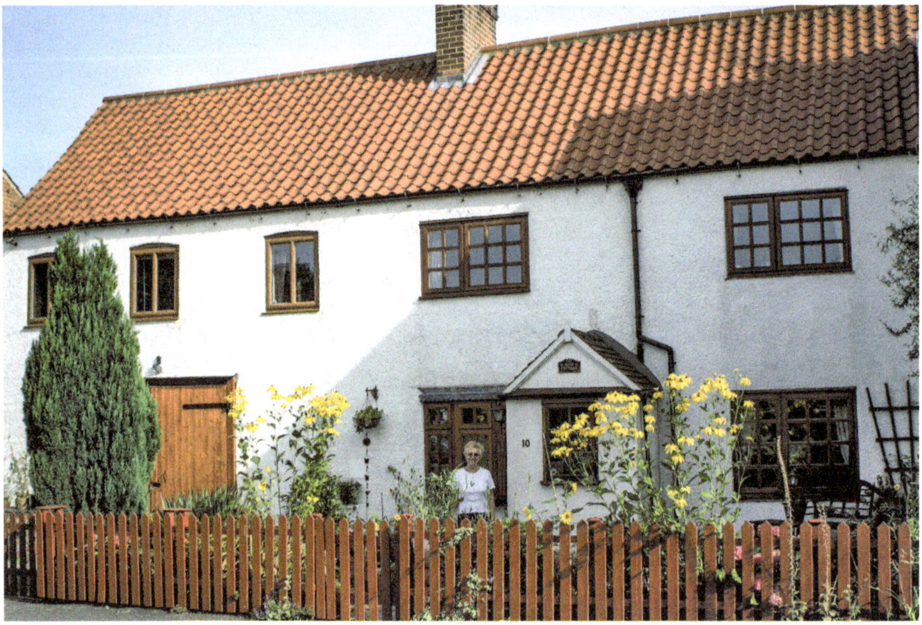

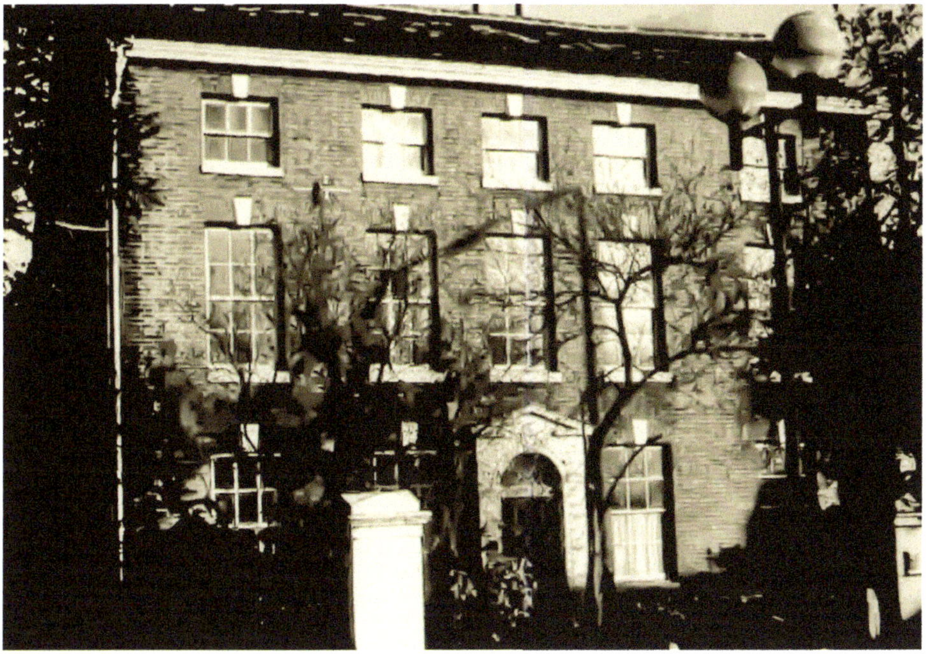

Poplar House, Grove Street

Retford Town has so many wonderful buildings, among which are many fine Georgian houses like Poplar House on Grove Street. Finding an old photograph of Poplar House proved quite difficult; for some reason it did not show up at all in the Welchman collection despite being only a few doors down from his studio. This was the one and only photograph I could find, so please forgive the quality, but I think this house is such a fine statement on Grove Street that it deserves a place in this book. Poplar House was built in the early eighteenth century (when it was known as White Hall), and it is one of the oldest domestic houses in Retford. The rear of the building dates to the 1600s and the roof is made from Lake District slate.

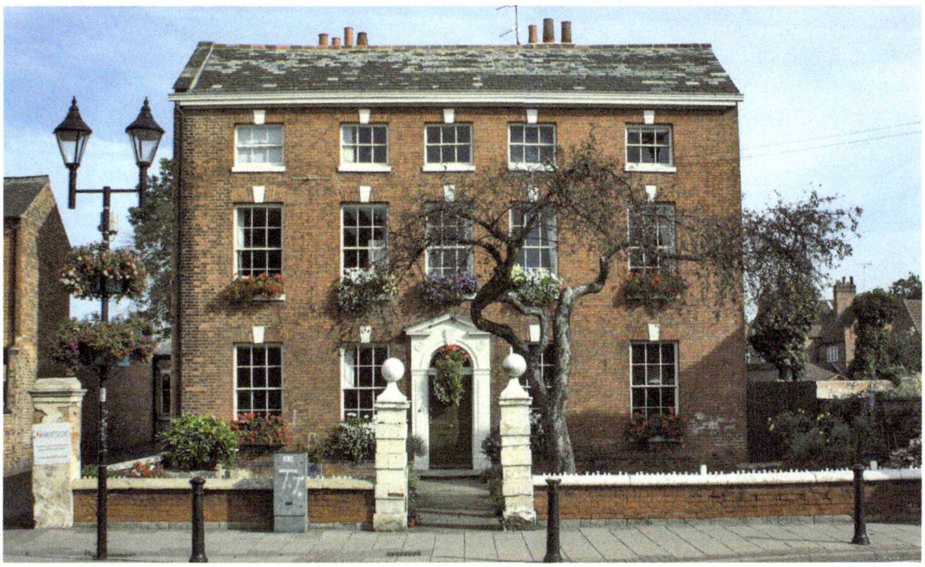

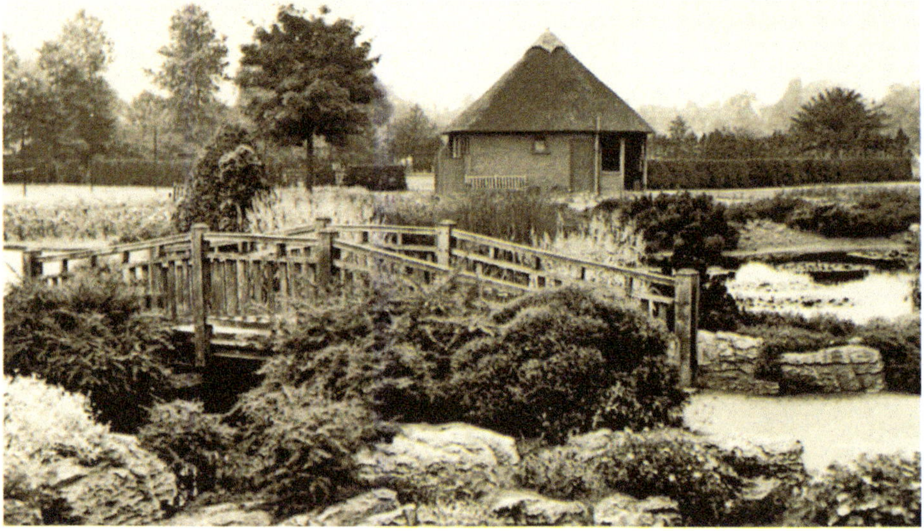

Kings' Park, 1937

Kings' Park opened on 29 June 1938 to commemorate not only the reign of King George V, but also the Coronation year of King George VI. Located in the very heart of Retford, award-winning Kings' Park is often described as the 'jewel in the crown' of the council's green spaces. It was laid out on land donated by the owner of Retford Hall at a cost between £7,000 and £8,000. The works were supported by a public subscription of £2,000. Covering an area of over 10 hectares, the park is divided into two parts by the River Idle. Kings' Park received national recognition in 2007 as winner of Britain's Best Park competition in the Midlands region. This was added to in 2008 when the park not only celebrated its seventieth birthday, but also achieved the prestigious Green Flag Award. The award is reassessed on an annual basis and Kings' Park again achieved the Green Flag Award in 2009, 2010, 2011 and 2012. Locals are very proud of Kings' Park.

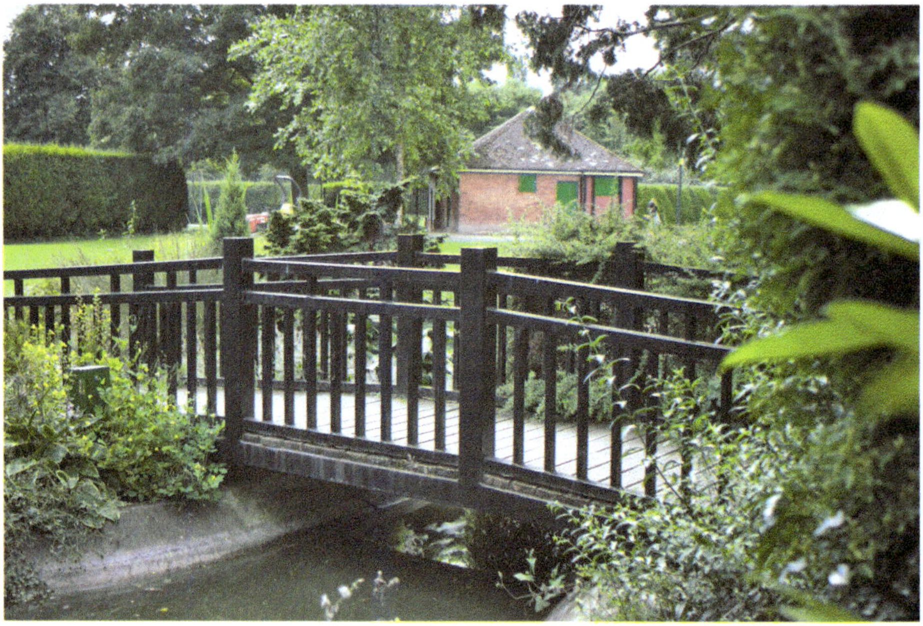

Rush Cycles of Carolgate, 1905

Number 26 Carolgate was owned and run by cycle dealers Mr Sidney Morris and his father Jack. Again, this location has changed many times over the decades and now it is a photography shop dealing with bargain prints and printing services. Several of the shops on Carolgate originally had gardens, but these were all removed when road resizing took place – one of Carolgate's numerous transformations. The pedestrianised area has brought a safety aspect to the street, but a lot of the old charm has been hidden; if one looks up and beyond it is possible to see old Retford peeking through with its Victorian features.

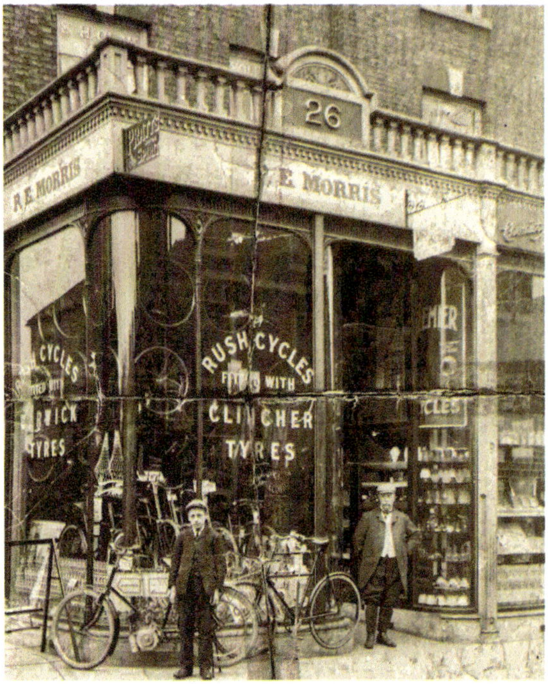

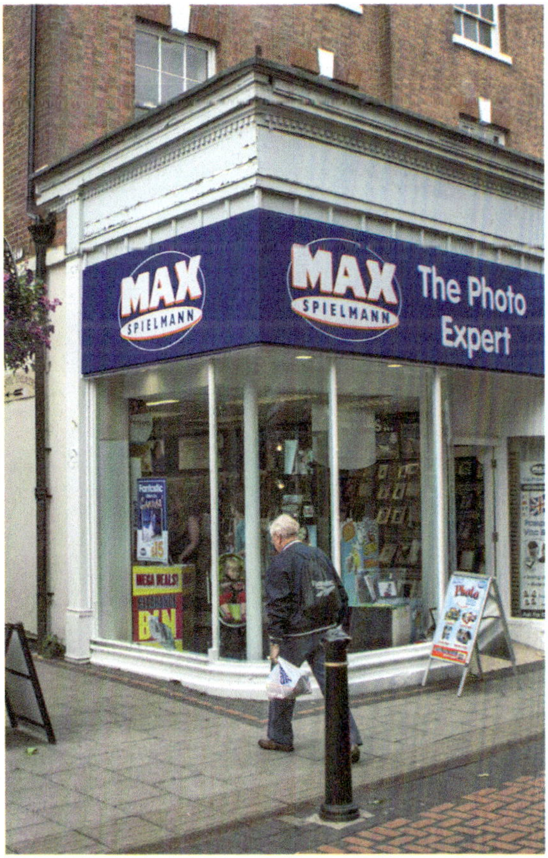

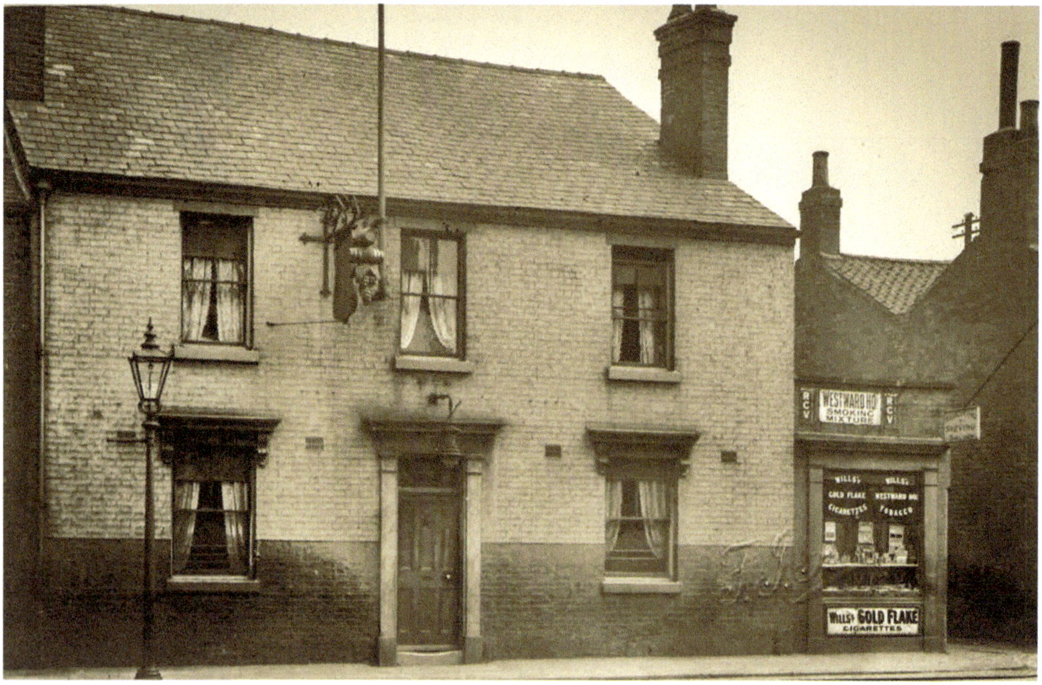

The Clinton Arms, Albert Road, 1920

Unfortunately, this extremely popular drinking establishment in Retford was just another public house to fall victim to the larger, cheaper drinking venues in the town, and sadly had to close its doors to the public. The ex-landlord had created a wonderful pub over the years with a fantastic atmosphere, great bands from blues to cover bands, and open mic nights; it was a sad day for the locals when it closed. Today it is a carpet shop.

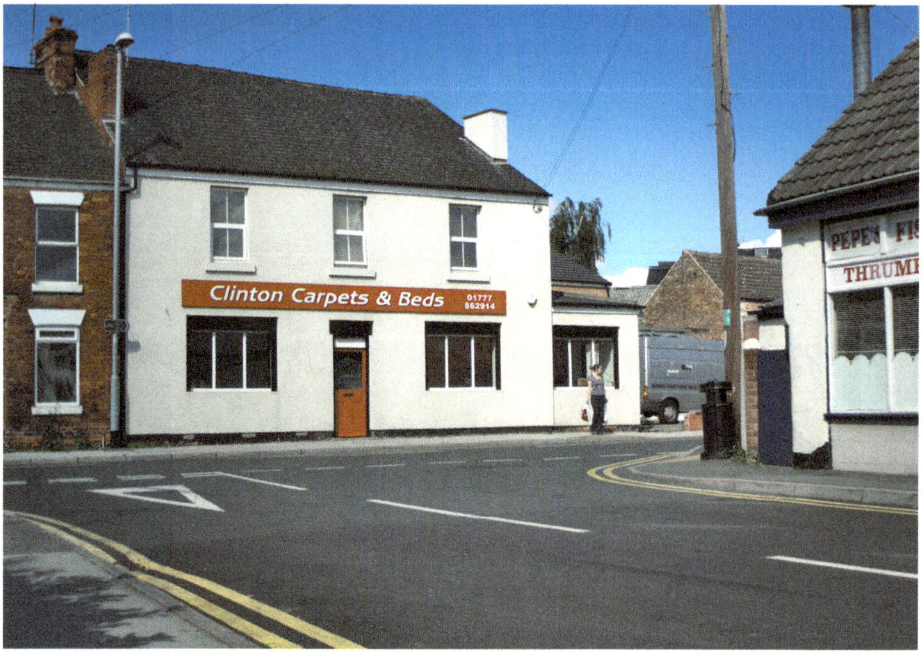

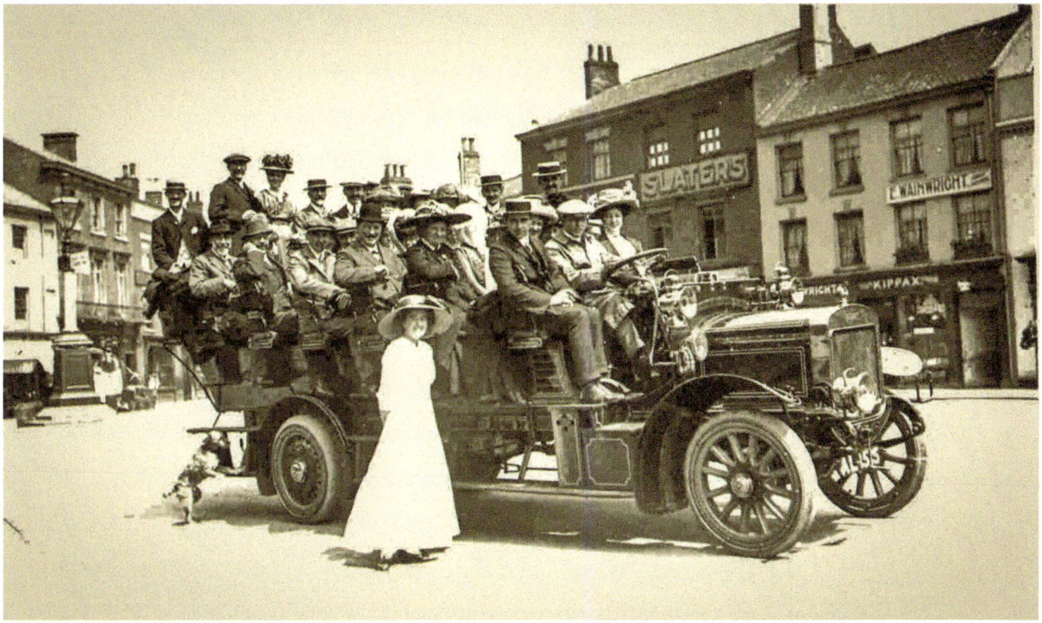

Stagecoach Owned by Mr Bennett of the White Hart Hotel, 1908

The White Hart Hotel is a very important establishment in the town of Retford. Unfortunately it was closed down, as were several of Retford's public houses, but the good news is it has been bought by a Mr Richard Eadlington and his business partner; the two are planning to restore the hotel to its former glory. I wonder if they will hire a bus to take all the staff out on an outing too! In the contemporary photograph the area where the station wagon rests is now a taxi rank and the shops have changed to mainly charity shops like Extra Care, which is very popular in the town, possibly because of Cath and Jane, the welcoming managers. Retford people are known for their friendliness.

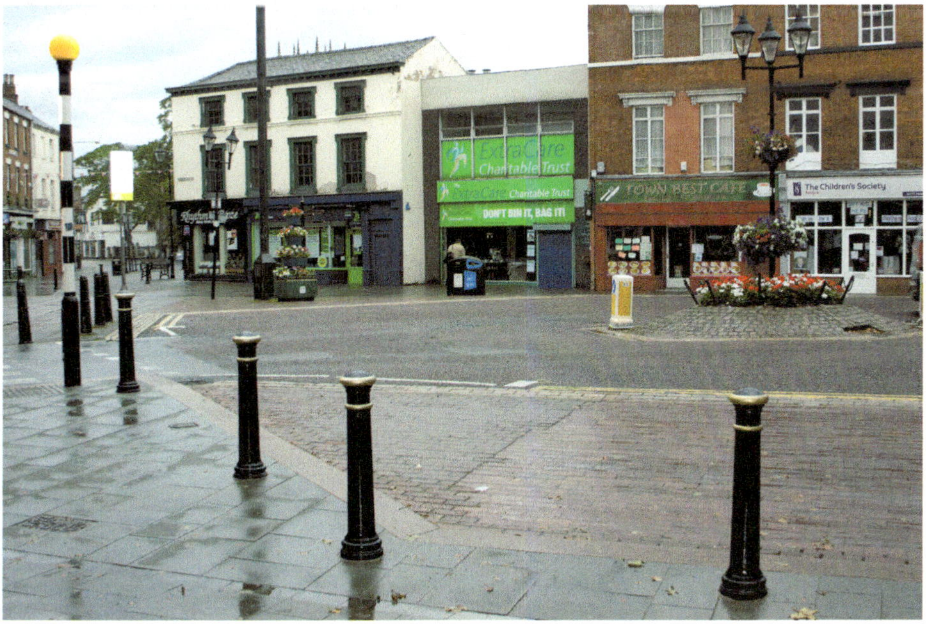

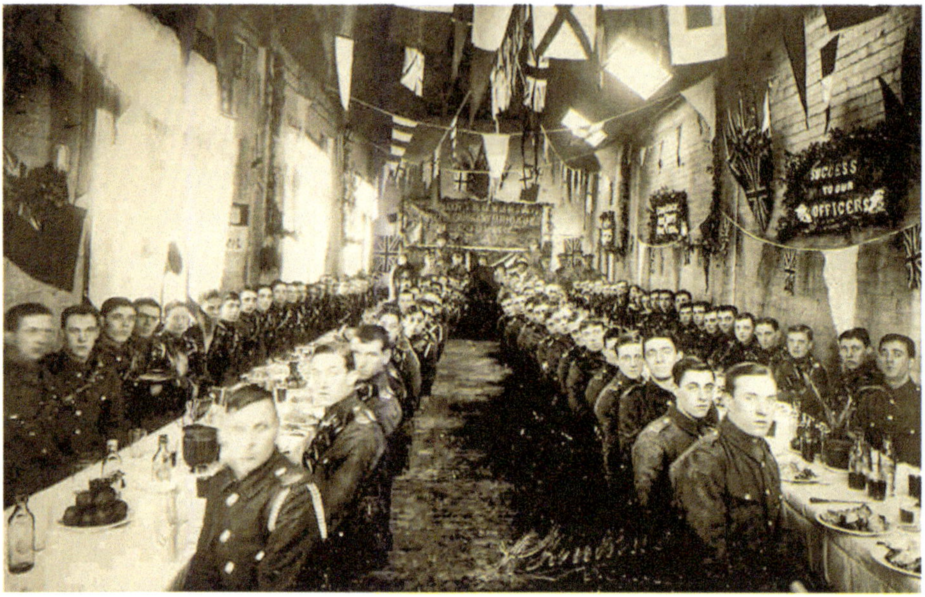

Soldiers Feast at Goodbodys Mill

The mill on the corner of Albert Road and Thrumpton Lane ran from 1843–94. The Retford mill was owned by Messrs Goodbody of County Clare in Ireland. The coming of the railway was the most significant event in Retford during this period; it transformed the town 'from a small rural community into a thriving, partly-industrialised small town, with an important railway junction'. The hamlet of Thrumpton was rapidly developed as a new 'railway town' to accommodate the growing railway workforce. Industrial activities diversified and paper production became increasingly important, involving the mill on Albert Road. Today the old mill is a successful fitness centre and half its original height due to renovation in the 1980s.

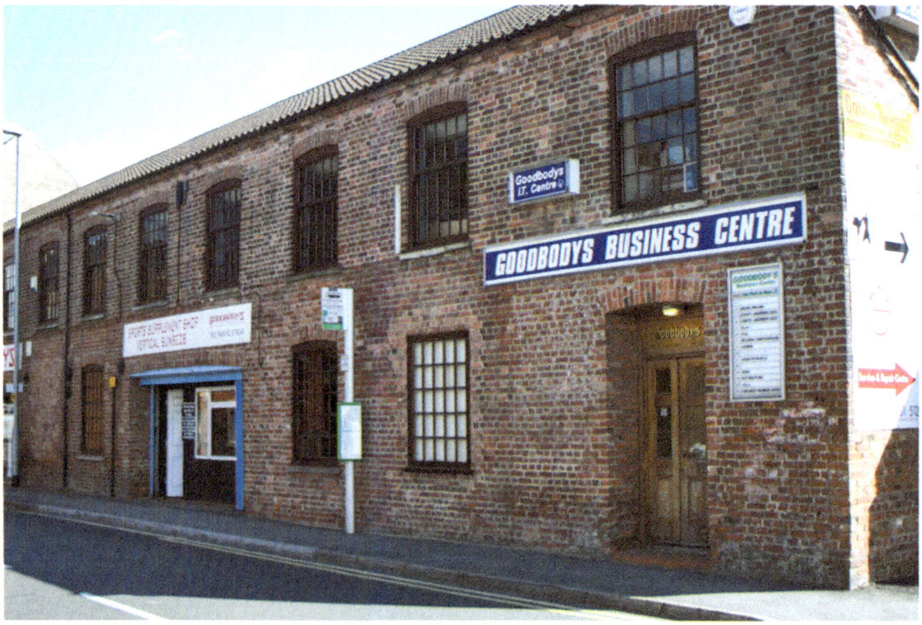

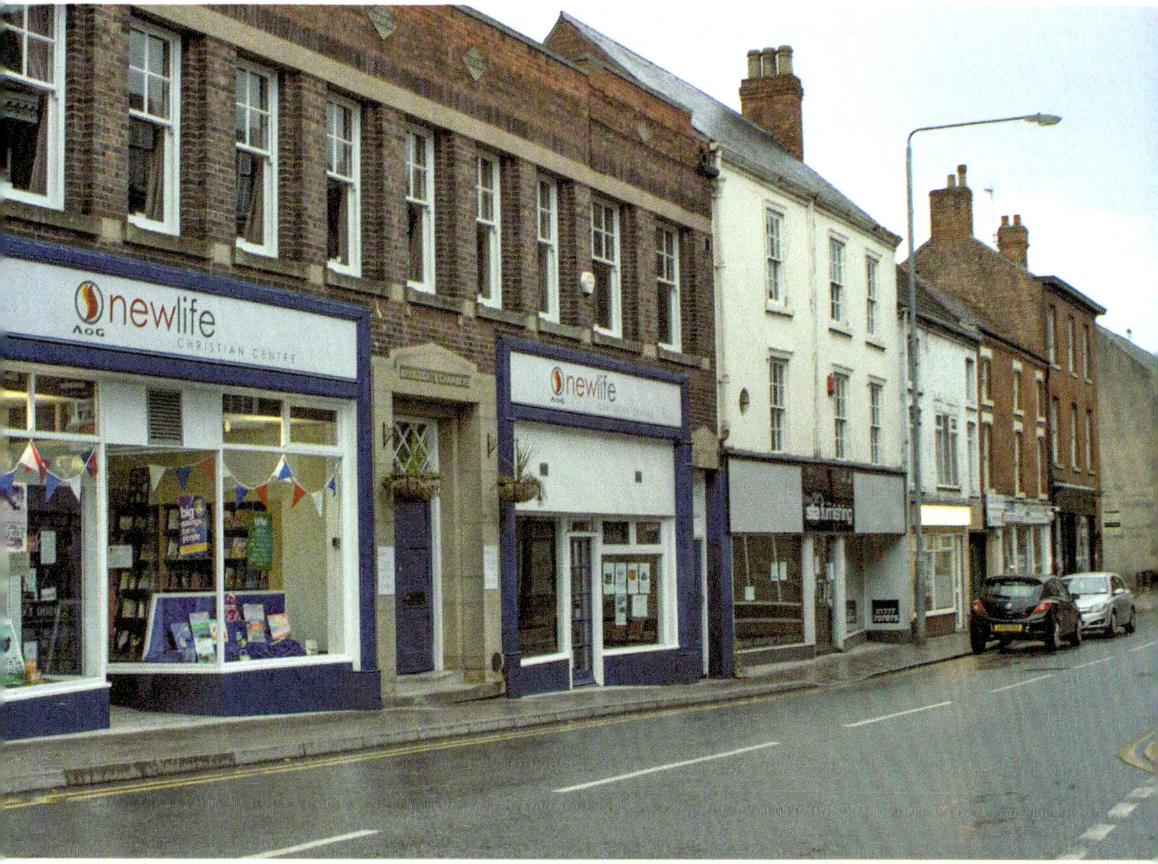

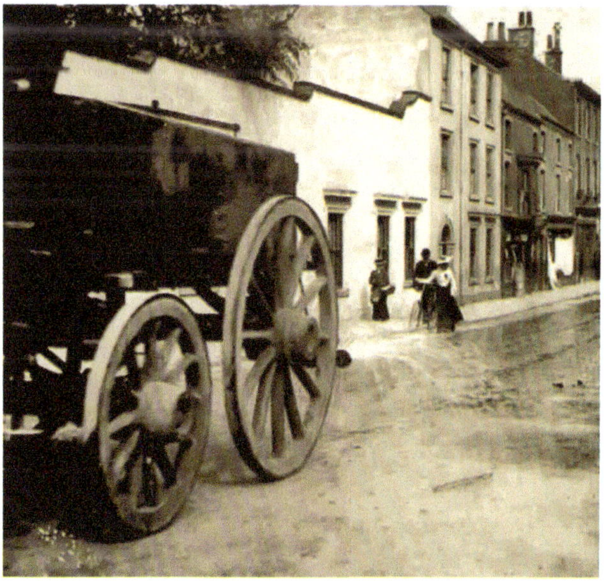

Water Cart on Bridgegate, 1904

The face of Retford has changed greatly; if you look above you can see the links to the past. It took some time to identify the buildings in this image, as a lot have been knocked away, but one way of checking the old against the new is by looking at the chimney pots. Here, the old photograph depicts the water cart used to dampen down the infamous Retford red sand that lined the roads of Retford. I am sure the ladies in the long skirts and the gentlemen in their fine suits appreciated the water cart.

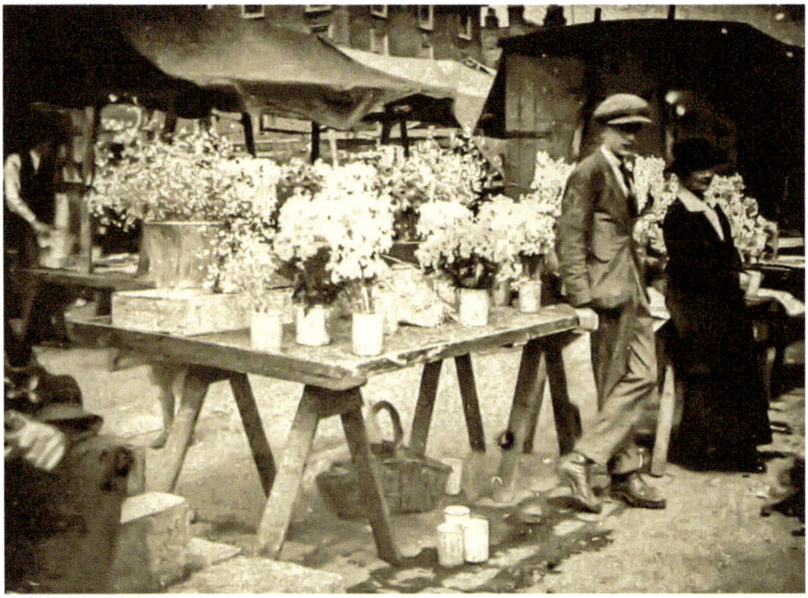

Flower Seller on Retford Market, June 1923

Retford was granted its first charter (the right to hold a fair) by King Henry III in 1246, and this was extended by King Edward I to allow a Saturday market – a tradition that continues today. The very popular open-air market is held in the market square each Thursday and Saturday against the backdrop of the French-inspired Victorian town hall. Also, on a Friday, there is now a thriving antiques and bric-a-brac market. On the third Saturday of every month, Retford hosts a farmers' market, where a variety of locally grown produce including jams, meat, honey and dairy produce is on sale. Bassetlaw Council recently invested £1.5 million in Retford market square.

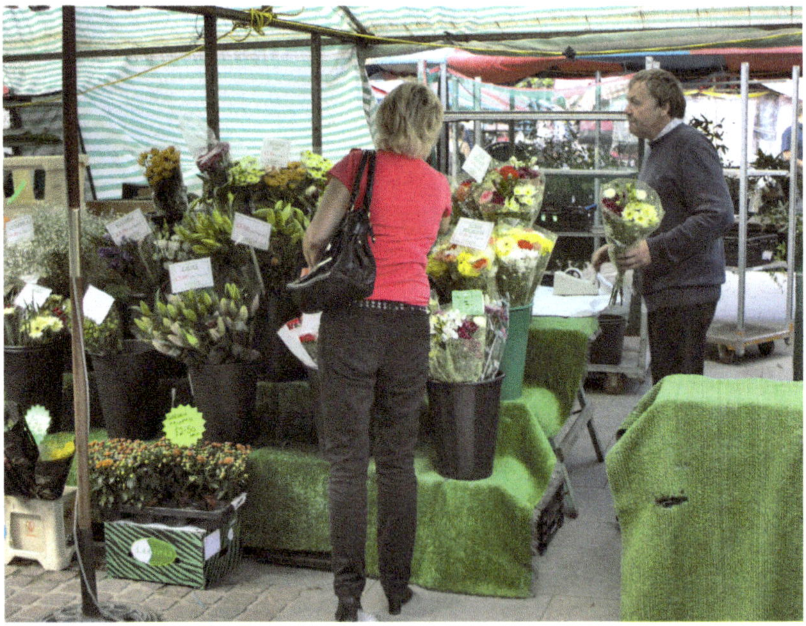

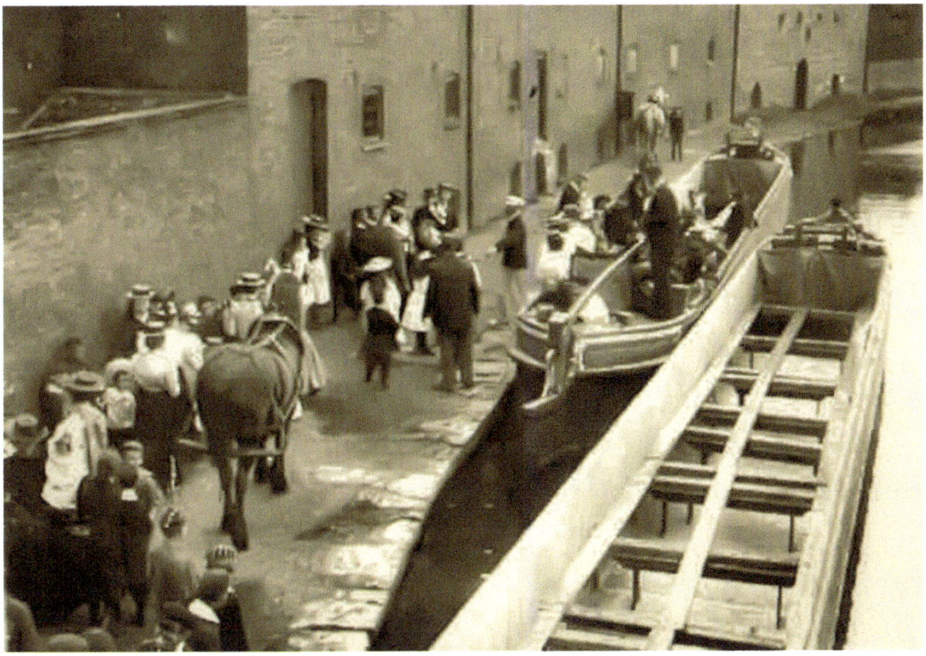

Chesterfield Canalside, 1899

A barge used for rare treats for local school children. By 1766 the first canal-building boom had started and Chesterfield and Retford enthusiastically embraced the idea of a new waterway. The nationally famous engineer James Brindley was asked to lead the project. In May 1775 it was agreed that although the canal was to be narrowed from Chesterfield to Retford it should, nevertheless, be larger between Retford and the Trent so that it could carry wide-beam riverboats. Years of campaigning by the Retford & Worksop Boat Club have now resulted in major restoration of a thriving tourist waterway. Each Christmas the *Seth Ellis* boat still takes children up and down the canal in the floating grotto.

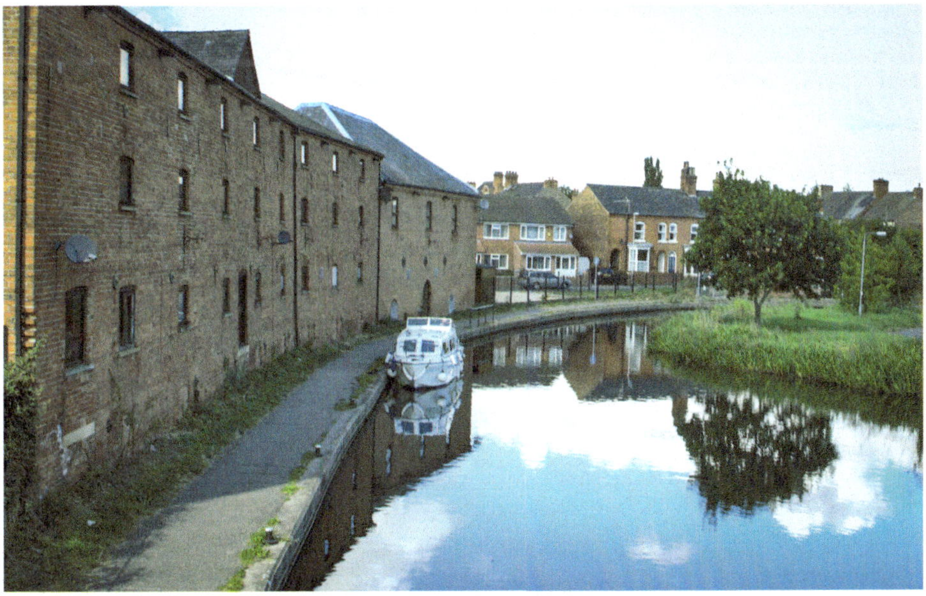

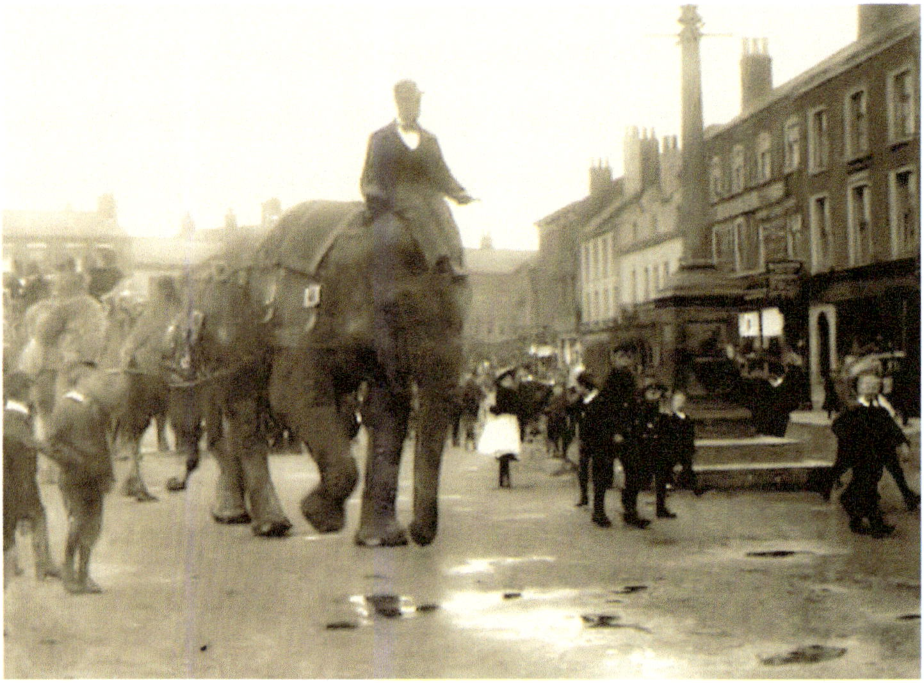

Circus in Town, Cenotaph Market Square, 1894

This image is from the days when the circus used animals for their shows and paraded around the town to generate interest. Thankfully those days are long gone, but the circus still visits Retford frequently. The Retford Cenotaph is dedicated to the memories of groups and individuals lost in battle. It is a very proud addition to the market square, where local people along with serving and retired military gather to honour their memory.

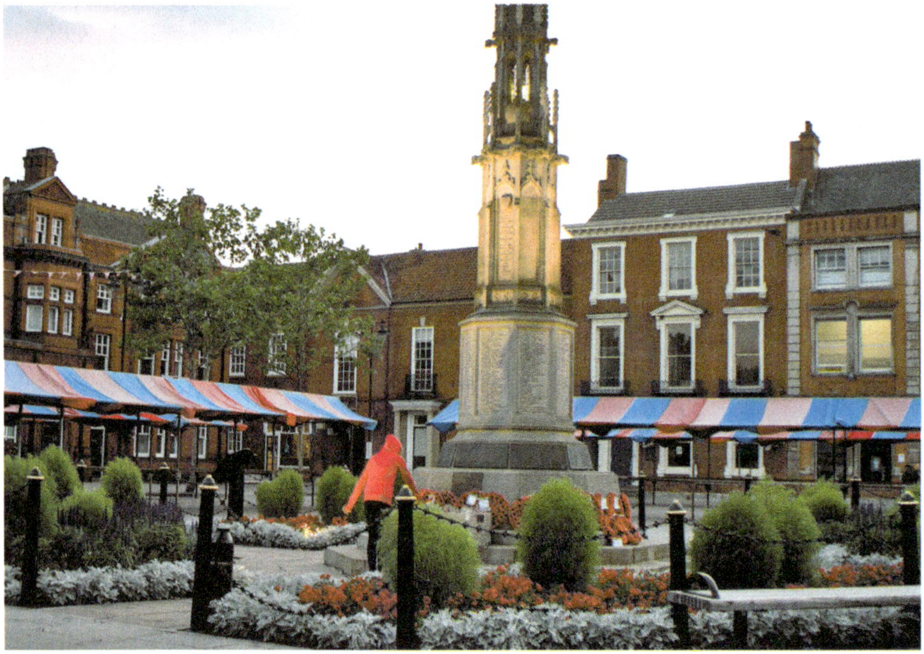

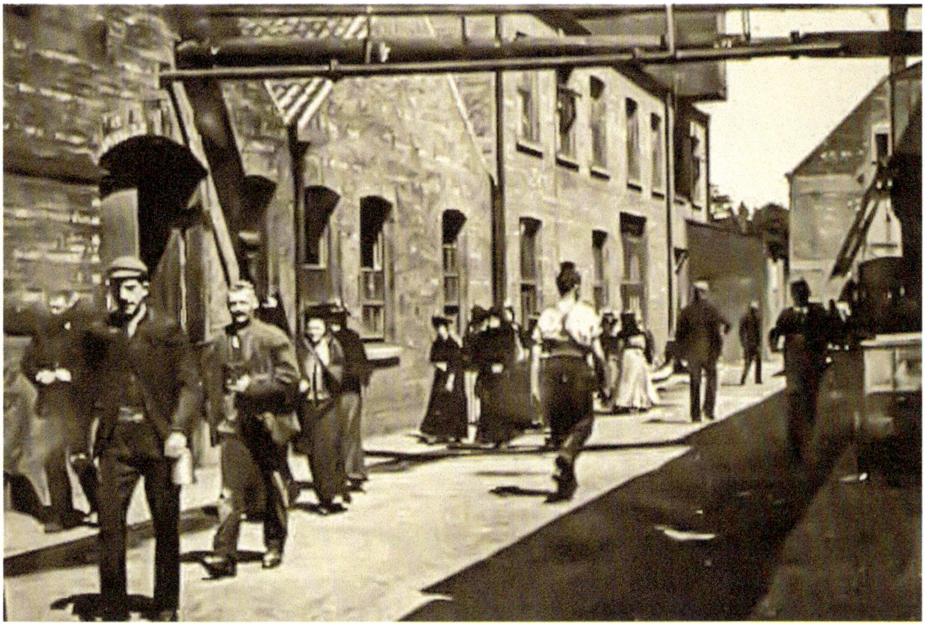

The Northern Rubber Works, Thrumpton Lane, 1894

Late nineteenth-century Retford saw the introduction of new technology and the birth of the Northern Rubber Works (NR) founded by Alfred Pegler, who took residence in nearby Amcott House. It was restored for use as the Bassetlaw Museum in 1986. The factory's proximity to the junction of two important railways helped it prosper. By 1914 the Retford factory was employing more than 400 people, who worked on manufacturing rubber for railways, steamships and mines. In the 1990s NR began supplying sleeping columns for the Nissan Primera car. The factory was taken over by the Icon Polymer Group in 2001, continuing the company's 150-year heritage. The current management team has transformed the business and has demonstrated how UK manufacturing can succeed. Pegler would be proud.

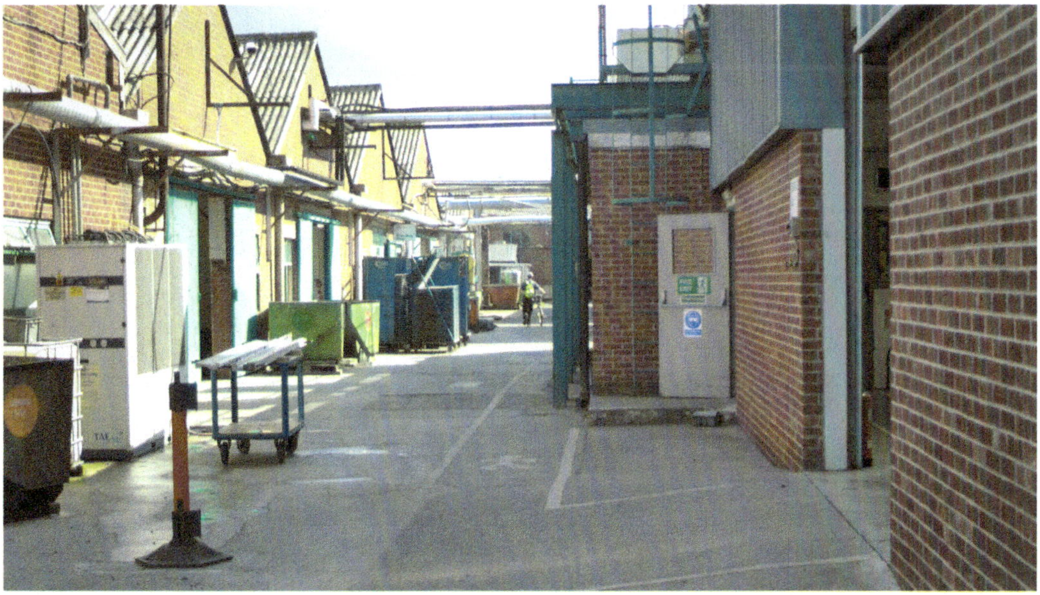

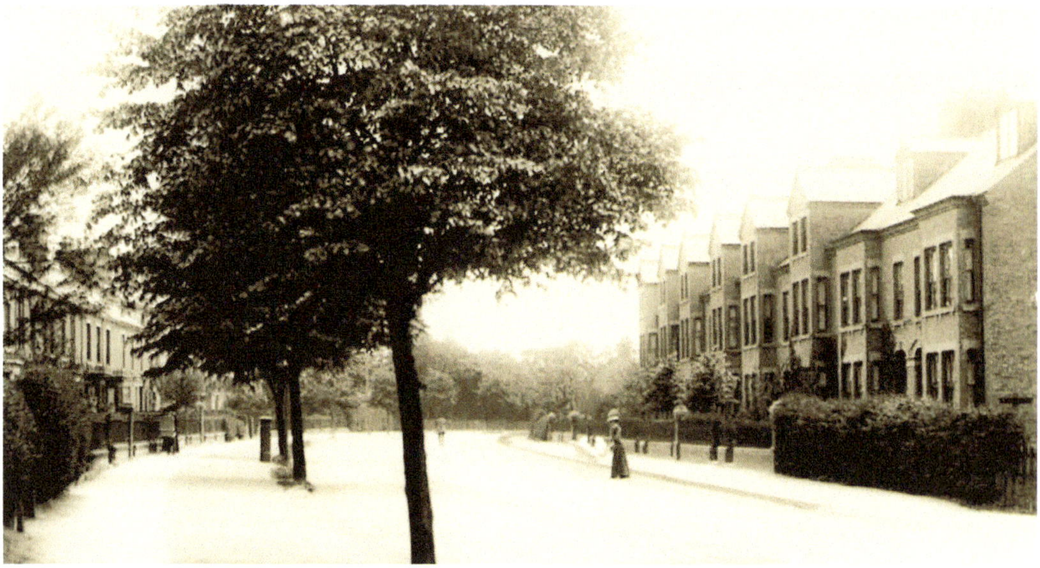

London Road, Retford (Towards the South)

The character of this important road into Retford Town is strongly defined by suburban greenery, particularly in relation to the older properties, which are generally set well back from the road. For example, the larger houses, such as The Elms, Oaklands, Storcroft House and Whinney Moor House all possess extensive garden spaces fronting the highway. The preservation of large mature trees has enabled the area to retain its strong leafy character, and substantial walls constructed in red brick, or well-treed and hedged boundaries, reflect the importance of the houses to which they belong and generate a strong suburban character. London Road is very wide with ample pavement and retains a pleasant charm to promenade on. We can see how the car has impacted on the character of the area. On-street parking and dominant road markings, for example, clutter the wide carriageway. Nevertheless, the historic character remains legible in the overall appearance of the area, reinforcing the area's importance as a gateway into Retford.

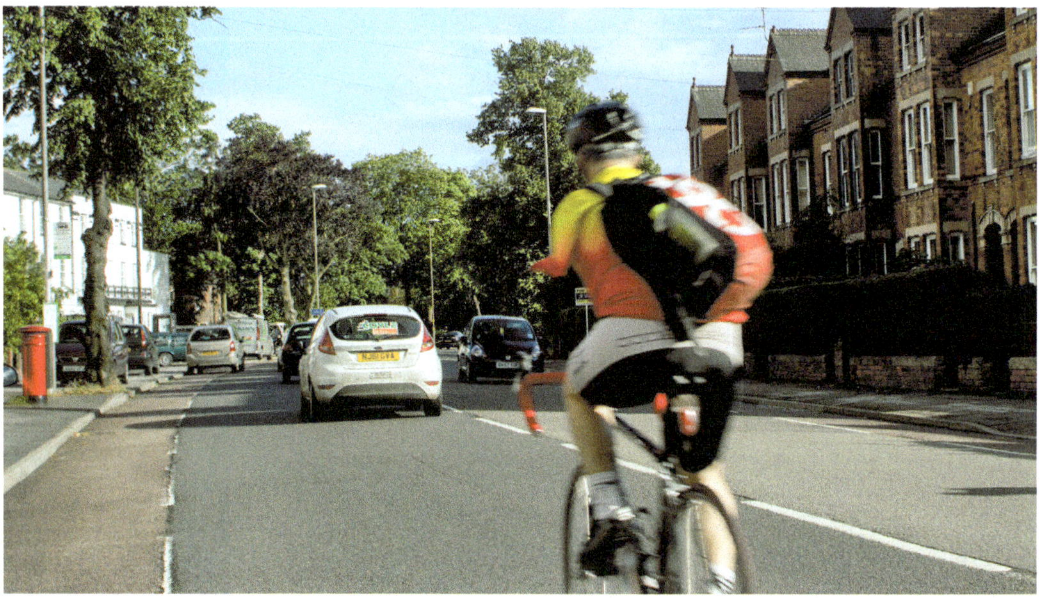

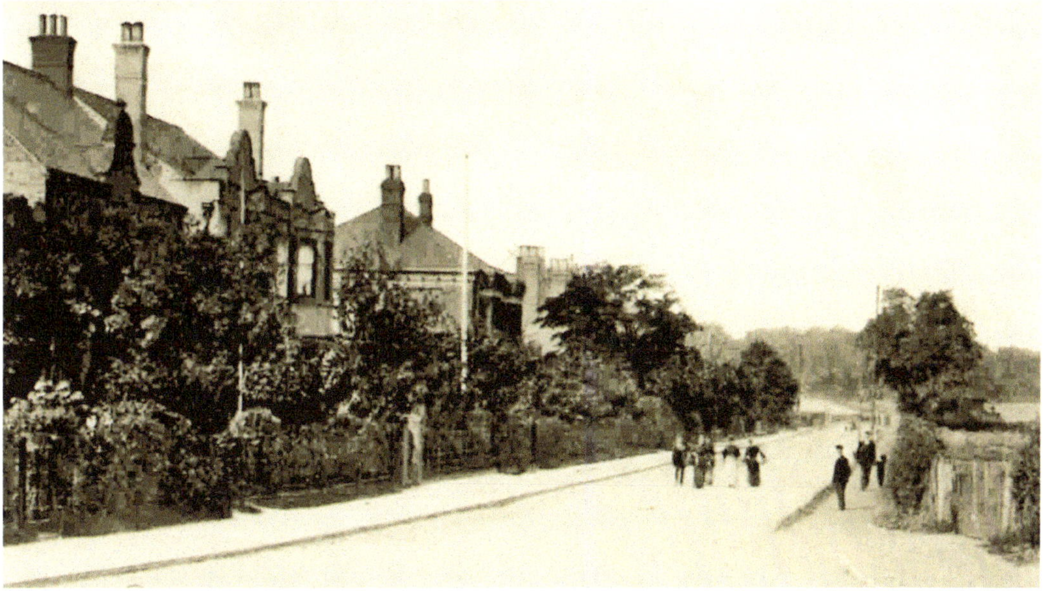

Babworth Road, 1915

Babworth Road is one of the main arteries running into Retford from the A1. Babworth is a parish of considerable extent and has some of the most delightful scenery in the county. In the early twentieth century Babworth maintained its connections with early American heritage when the rector was Frank Wilberforce, the great-grandson of William Wilberforce, who led the campaign to abolish slavery. All along Babworth Road are charming residences, each with their own unique character. On examination, there is an identification with the past as many buildings retain their wonderful historic façade. A great road and a very interesting and beautiful area of Retford.

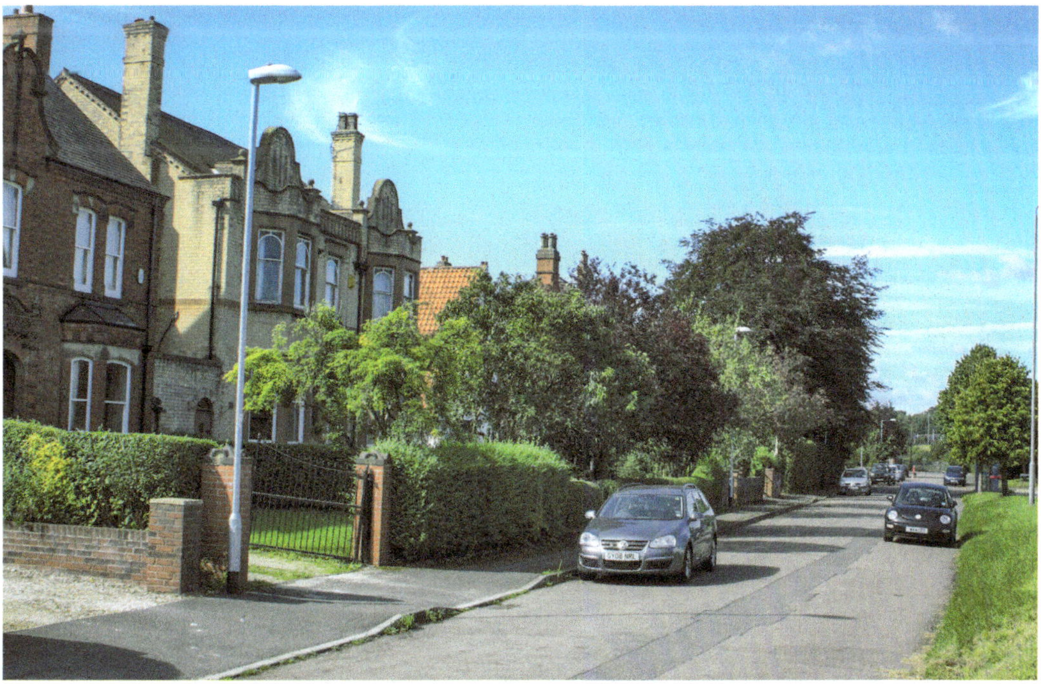

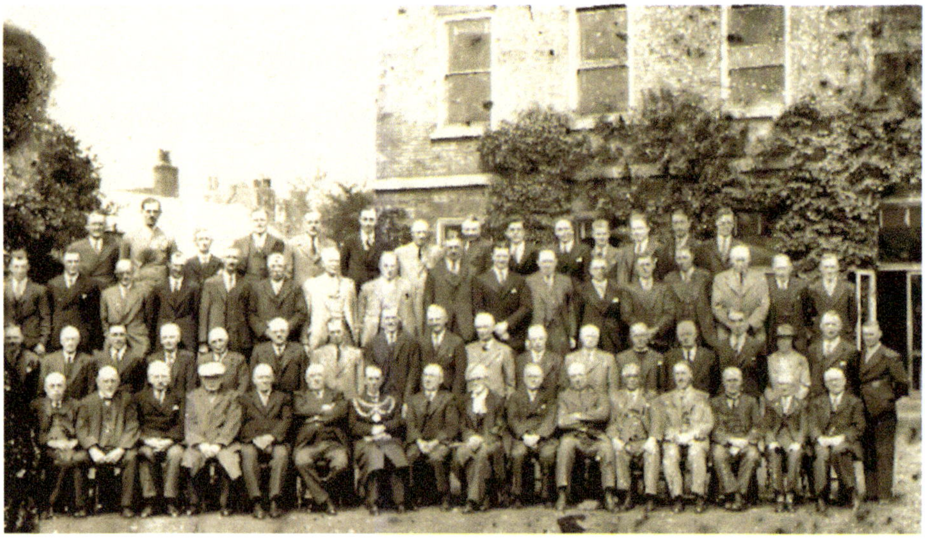

Amcott House, Grove Street, 1938

Sir Wharton Amcotts was the Member of Parliament for East Retford from 1780 to 1790 and 1796 to 1802. The house changed hands several times before being occupied by Alfred Pegler, founder of the Northern Rubber Works in Retford. His son, Stephen Pegler, lived here until 1937. Sam Glasswell is curator of Bassetlaw Museum, based in Amcott House, an eighteenth-century town house. The museum was established in 1983 and charts the history of the whole of Bassetlaw, taking visitors right through from prehistoric times to modern day. Some of the rooms in Amcott House detail the story of the building while others are dedicated to military history. In the summer they hold a farm and country festival exhibiting traditional manufacturing techniques. Currently at Amcott there is an exhibition of paintings by selected artists including Graham Duckmanton, Norman Evans and Richard Combes, which lasted until 6 October 2012.

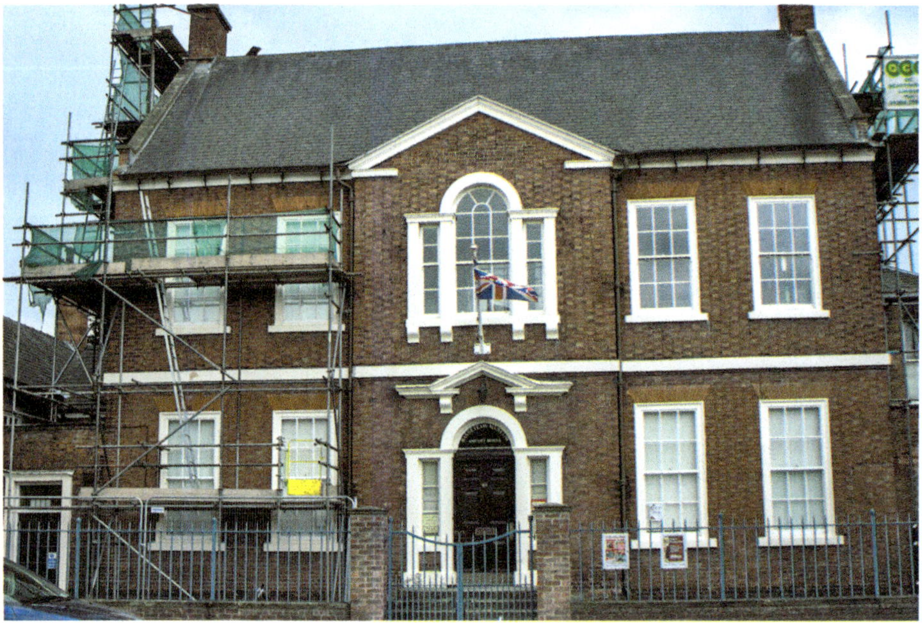

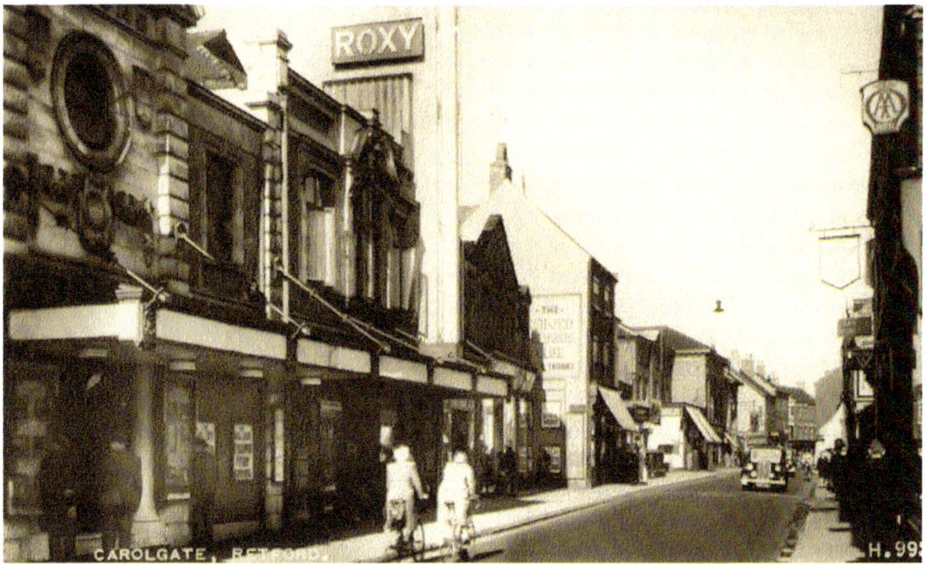

The Roxy Cinema, Carolgate, 1940

There was a time when Retford movie fans had not one but three cinemas to choose from. As seems the case with most wonderful buildings in Retford, two of these, the Ritz and the Roxy, no longer remain, while the Majestic, although it continues to entertain, does so as a theatre. The Roxy Picture House, depicted at the end of its life, was opened in 1917 by local entrepreneur Cyril Getliffe, who also owned and operated the Majestic. Located in the heart of Carolgate, it was an eye-catching building constructed in the Baroque style. The façade was typical of a cinema of that period and had a decorative feature of a swag of fruit and the name Picture House in the stonework over the entrance. In 1936 the name was changed to Roxy Cinema, and at that time it was showing films to packed houses with queues frequently forming along Carolgate. The advent of television sounded the death knell for it, and its doors closed for the last time in the early 1960s. It was demolished to make way for a shopping development now taken by the new Boots chemist shop, which completely changed the look of Carolgate. All that remains are the memories of those who recall some of the thousands of movies that were screened there a lifetime ago.

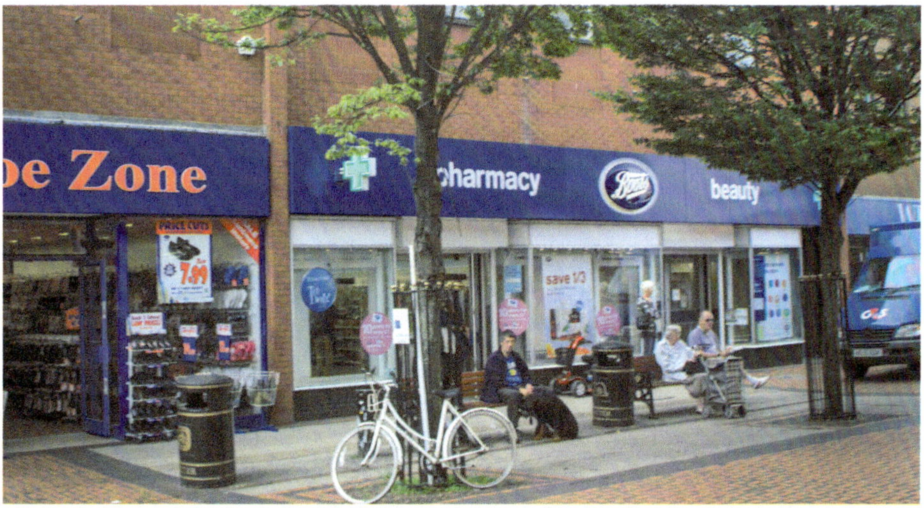

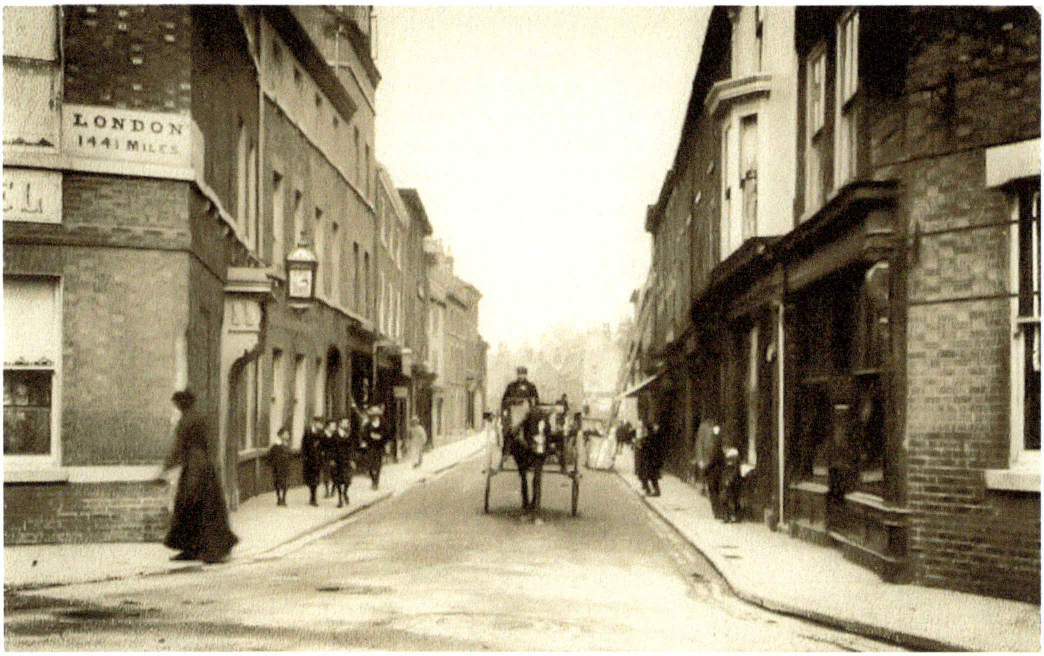

Bridgegate Corner, 1904

The eminent architectural historian Niklaus Pevsner rather unfairly described Retford as 'a singularly unattractive town' in the first edition of his *Buildings of England: Nottinghamshire*, published in 1951. Looking over the Welchman archive to do research for this book I see nothing but a remarkable and beautiful town. However, with this pair of photographs it does sadden me to see how run down the very centre of the town has become, with ugly metal-clad windows on formerly fashionable buildings. Fortunately, the old Posting House has been purchased so maybe this prominent corner will bring some pride and glamour back to the town.

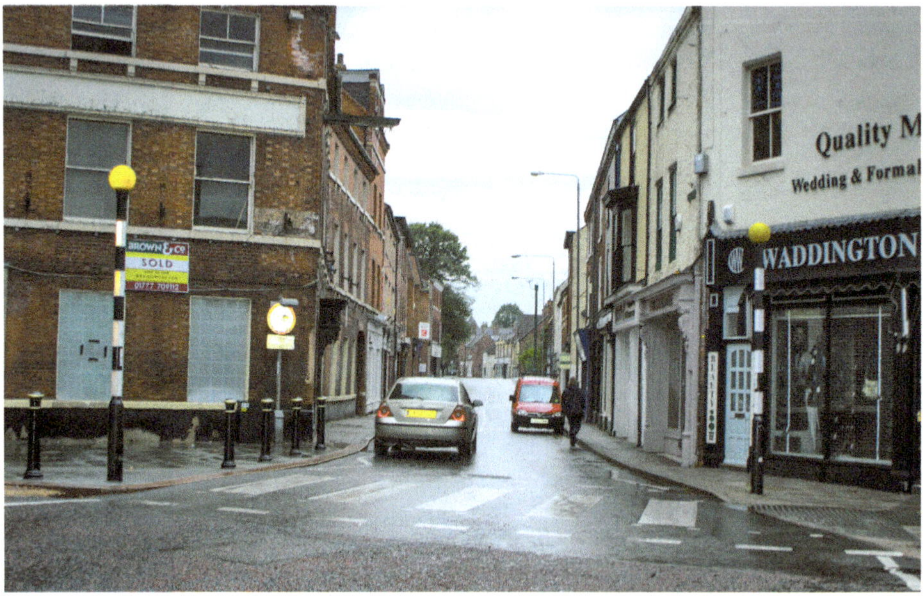

The White Hart Hotel, 1920

The Turnpike Act was passed in 1663, and the roads being made good would enable wheeled carriages to pass rapidly at 10 miles per hour to and from London and York, and so it continued for nearly 100 years. Horses for some of the coaches were changed at the White Hart, Retford, and at Barnby Moor, where stood the Bell Inn, kept in 1835 by Mr William Dennett, grandfather of that old lover of coaches Mr A. C. Dennett, of the White Hart. The White Hart, a Grade II listed building, dates from the eighteenth century and was one of Retford's foremost coaching inns. By 1828 there were nineteen scheduled services a day. In 2012 the White Hart has been rescued from potential ruin and the new owners envisage a return to its former glory and prominence within the town. As a centrepiece in the town the White Hart's reincarnation will be a joy to see.

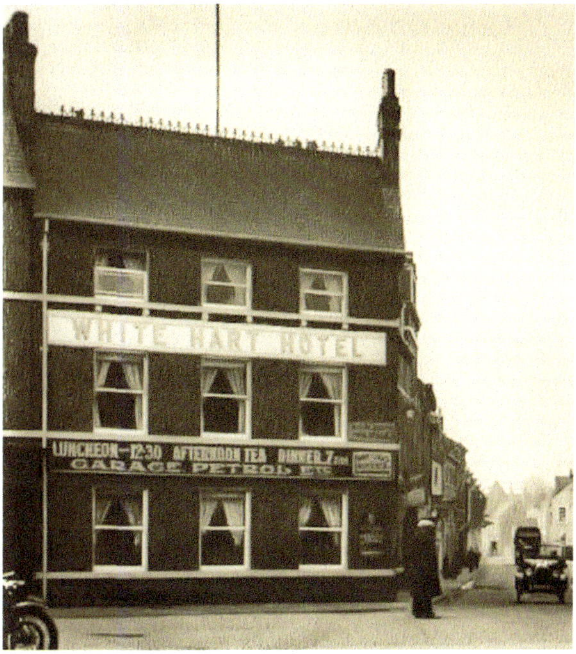

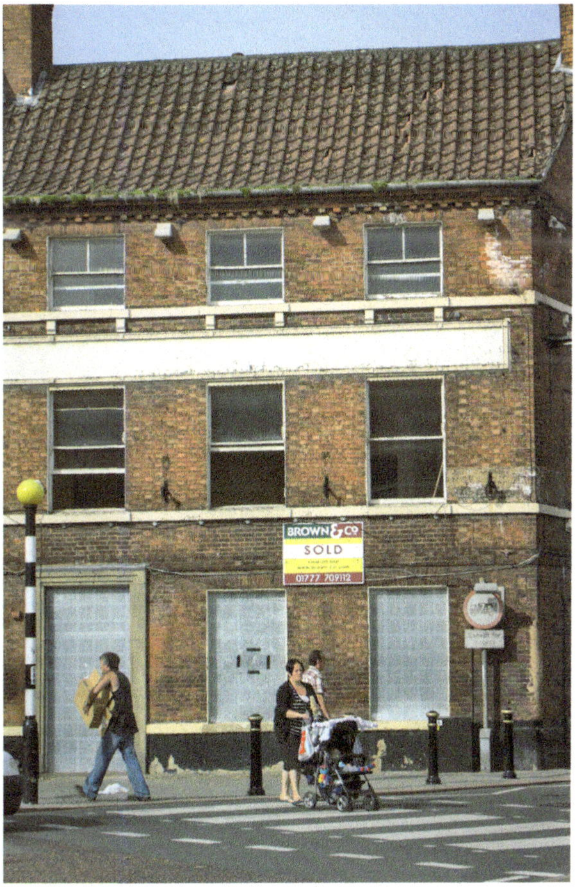

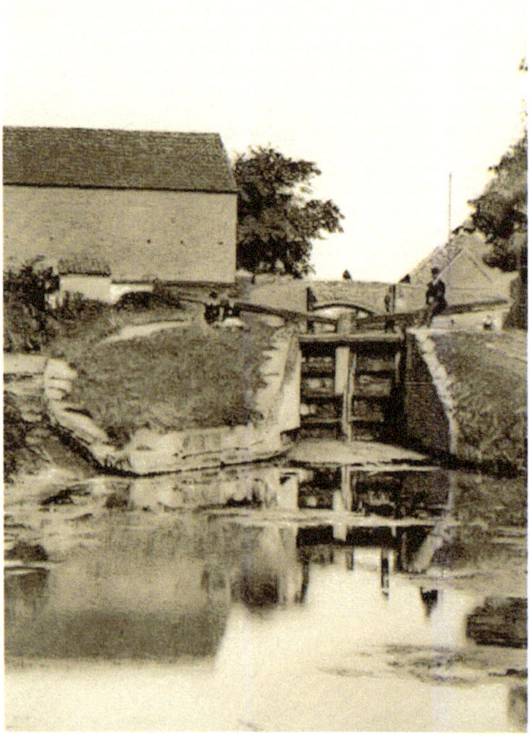

Woodcocks Lock Winding Hole, Chesterfield Canal, 1907

The winding hole is a widened area of the Chesterfield Canal used for turning a canal boat such as a narrow boat. It has been suggested that the word derives from the practice of using the prevailing wind to assist with the turn, but no verifiable reference has been quoted for this suggestion. Because the width of a canal channel (about 30-40 feet) is less than the length of a full-size canal boat, it is not usually possible to turn a boat in the canal. Woodcocks winding hole has typical indentations in the offside (non-towpath side) of the canal, allowing sufficient space to turn the boat. When horses were used to pull the boats, it was not possible for them to assist with the turning, as they were on the wrong side of the canal. Consequently, it was considered favourable to use the wind to assist in turning the boat, to reduce the amount of human power needed.

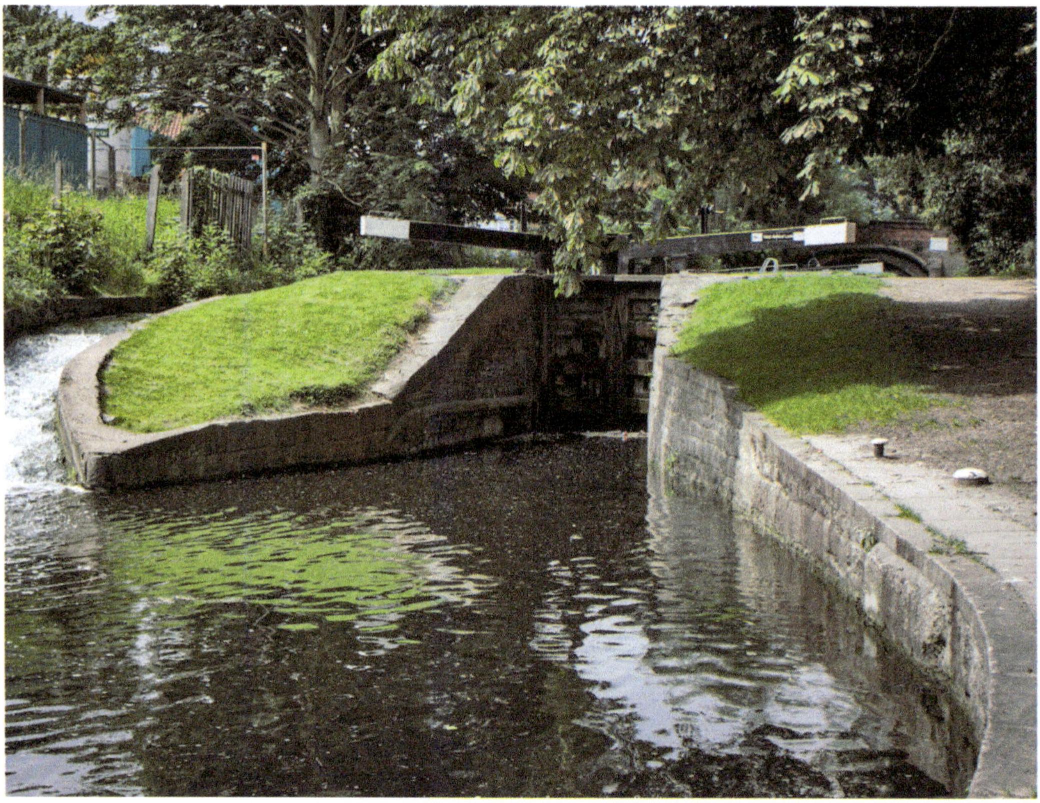

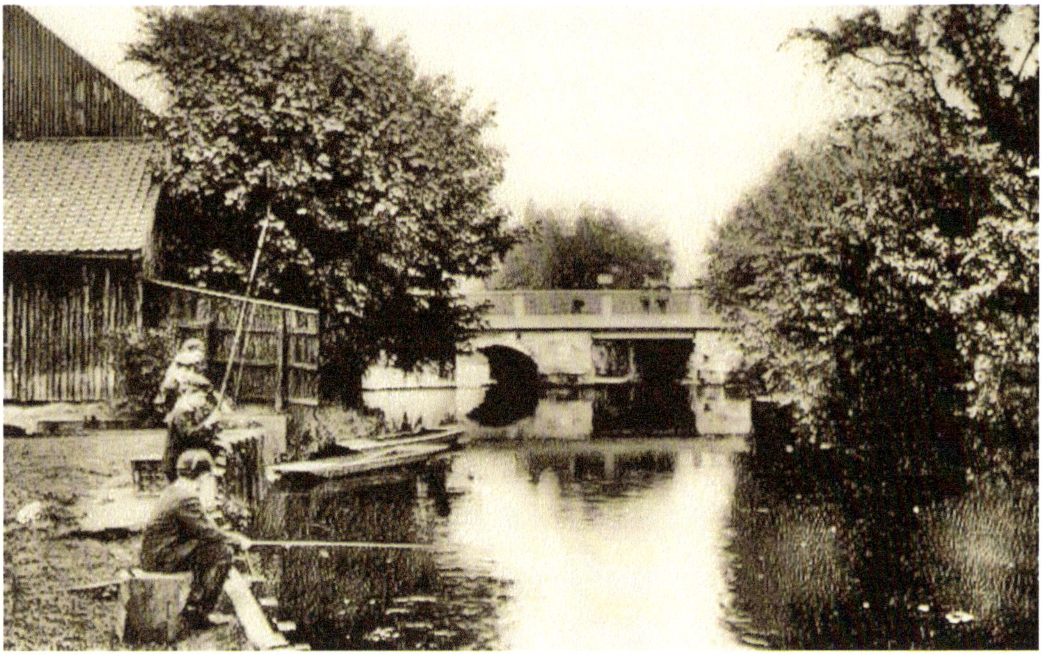

The River Idle at Bridgegate Bridge, 1940

The bankside of the Idle has flourished since the boys sat by it in the first old photograph. On this side of the Bridgegate is the entrance to Kings' Park, the town's jewel in the crown. The source of the Idle is the confluence of the River Maun and River Meden, near Markham Moor. Most of the land surrounding the river is a floodplain. Between Retford and Bawtry, the floodplain is partly occupied by a number of sand and gravel pits. It is also important for conservation, with the Idle Washlands and some of the sand and gravel pits of the Idle Valley being designated Sites of Special Scientific Interest.

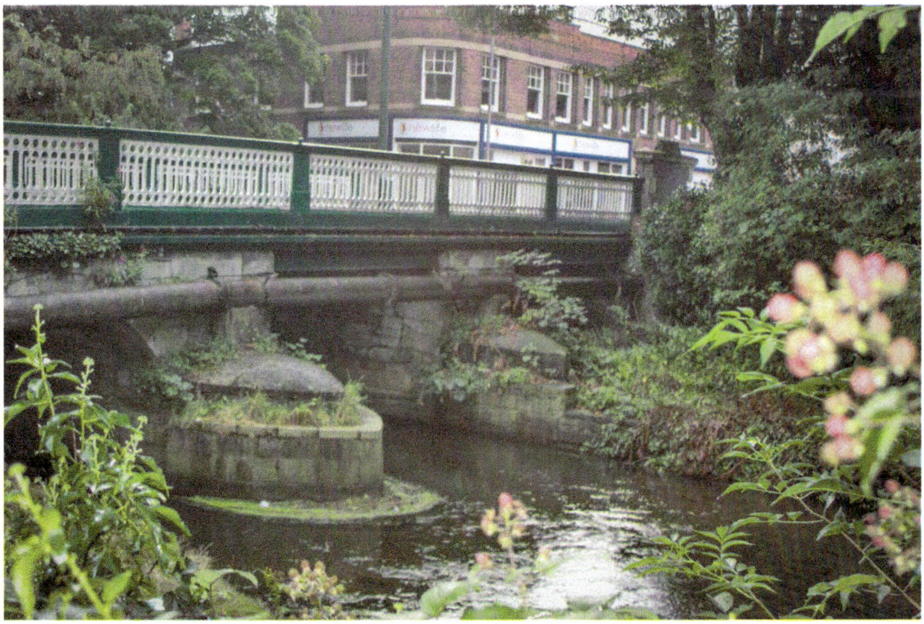

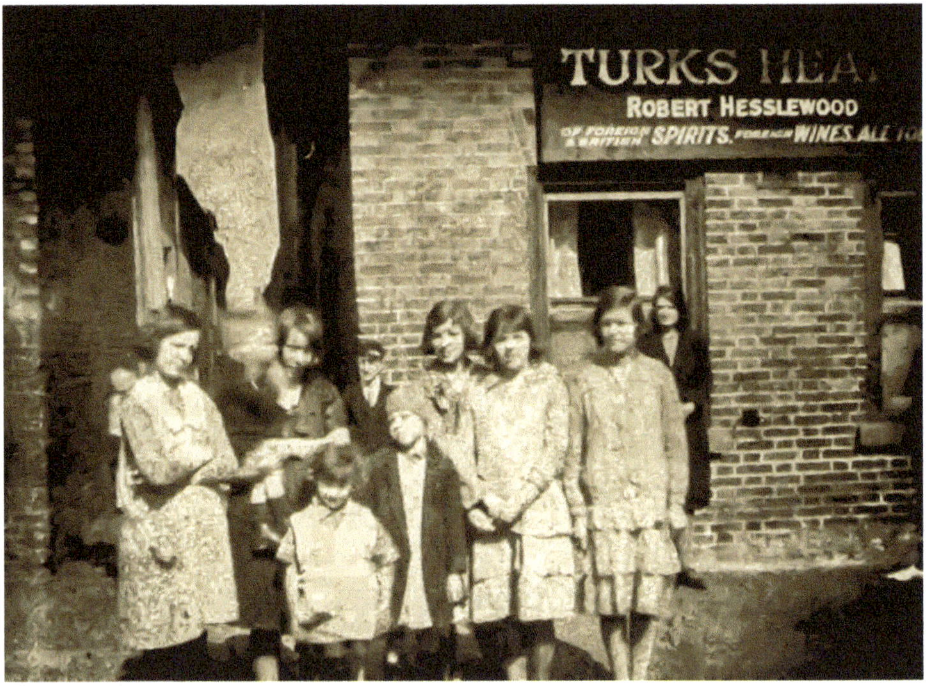

The Turks Head, Grove Street, 1930

In the old photograph we have a group of women and children outside the Turks Head, Grove Street, Retford. The photograph also shows Turks Head Yard. Today this charming public house is renowned for its warm, friendly atmosphere, its real ale and open fire, and even dogs are allowed. Beside the Turks Head is St John Street. Here you will see the remains of another old pub sign – the Fox Inn. This area was the centre of the town and overpopulated, perhaps with two families to a house, leading to slums and open sewers.

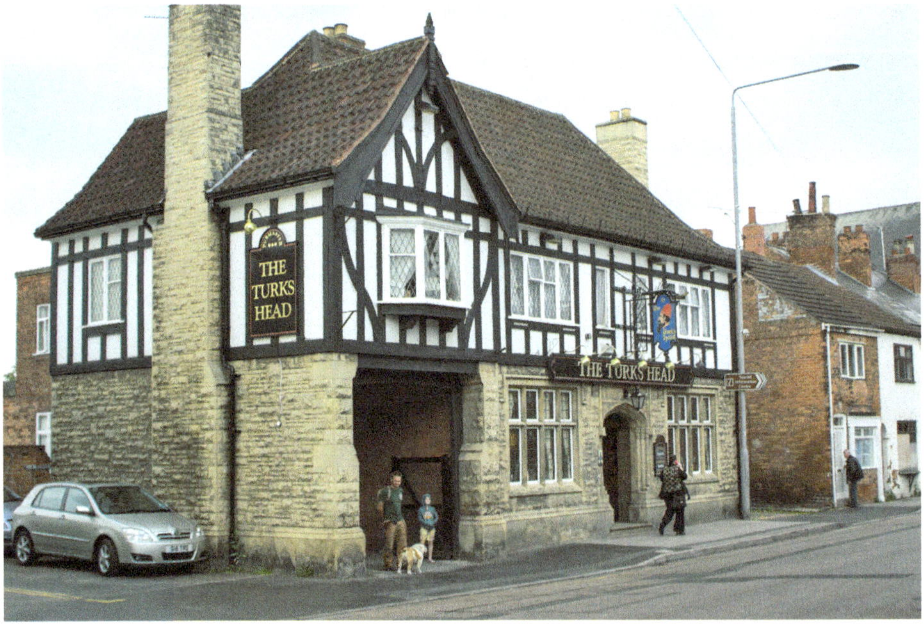

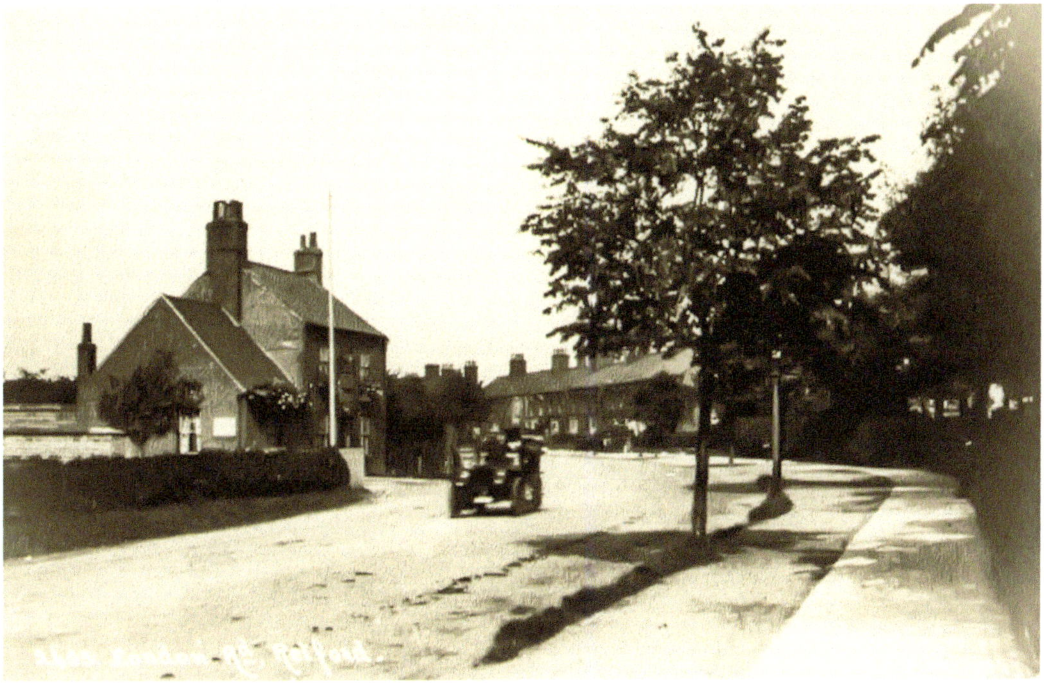

London Road, The Nags Head, 1910

The Retford South Conservation Area is situated to the south-east of Retford town centre along London Road. There are over 100 buildings within the conservation area. The majority of these are private residences, many of which have numerous outbuildings. The Retford South Conservation Area is characterised by the modern-day London Road, which largely still follows the route of the turnpike from the eighteenth century. Here at the Nags Head travellers would enjoy a welcome beverage and possibly some hot food on their arrival into town, with stables at the rear for the horses.

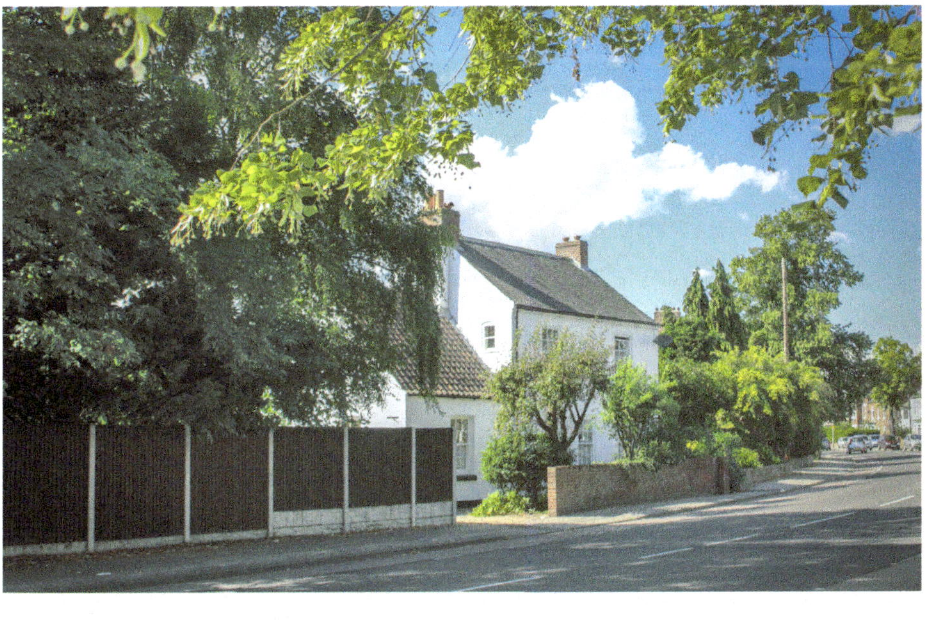

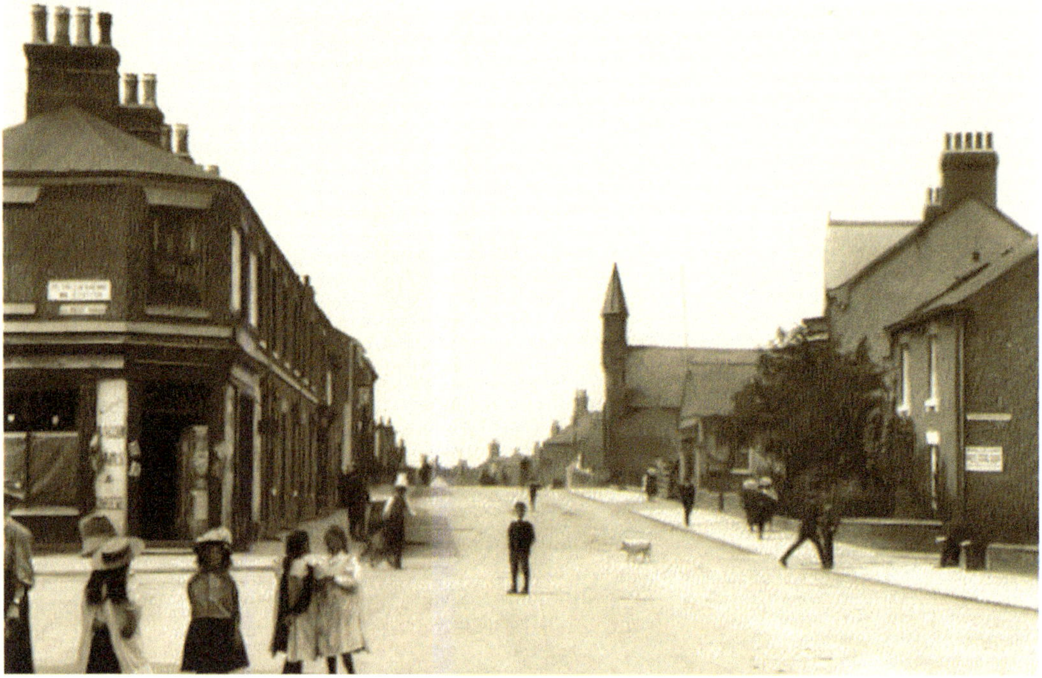

Albert Road Junction, Gladish's Corner, Looking Up Towards Carolgate Bridge, 1900

The modern photograph is taken where Thurman's used to be. Across the road, where the new apartments now stand, was formerly Gladish's Corner grocery shop. Further up there was Darwin's newsagent's. Today there are fresh establishments opening on the gateway to the town from Jojeni bridal shop to Retford's newest eatery, the Bridge Brasserie, which provides innovative dishes from locally sourced seasonal ingredients. On the opposite side of the street is the Masonic hall, a beautiful old building that has been cared for and can be hired for occasions. This busy junction where London Road meets the town has seen many transformations with the building of the ringroad.

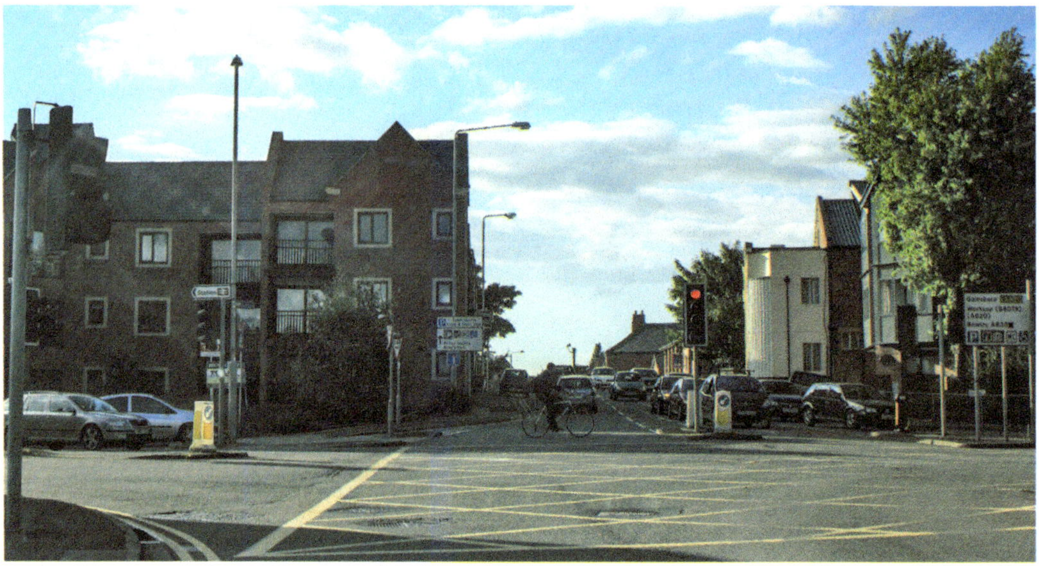

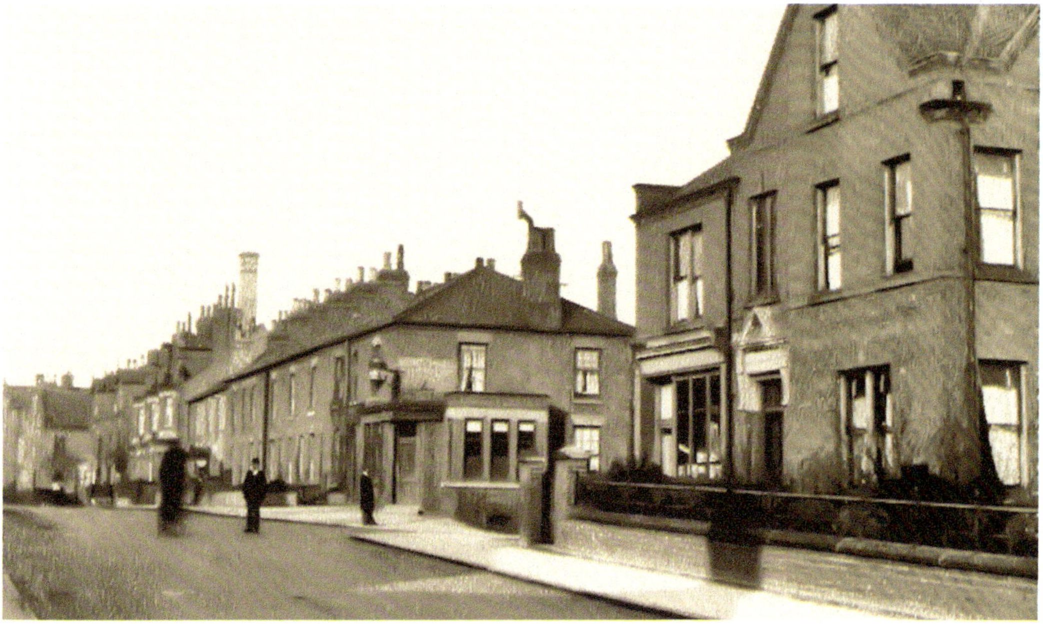

The Northern Inn, Cobwell Road, 1908

A traditional welcoming public house that has somehow managed to stay open through these hard economic times when several other establishments of this type have fallen victim to the larger, more central town breweries. Situated very close to the train station it would have, and still does, offer a haven for a thirsty and hungry commuter. The owners of this pub are also keen on the house's nostalgia and have walls adorned with great black-and-white prints of back in the day. Situated on Cobwell Road, the public house stands among some wonderful Victorian ornate buildings. Obviously the train station introduced some wealth and creativity into the area. The local shop some doors down called 'Busten's' is well worth a visit for its inspiring frontage.

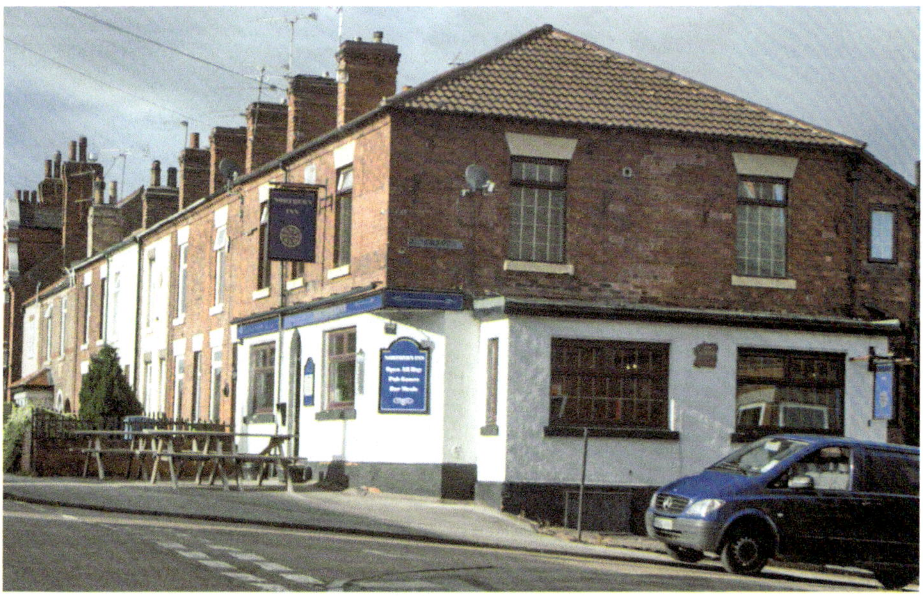

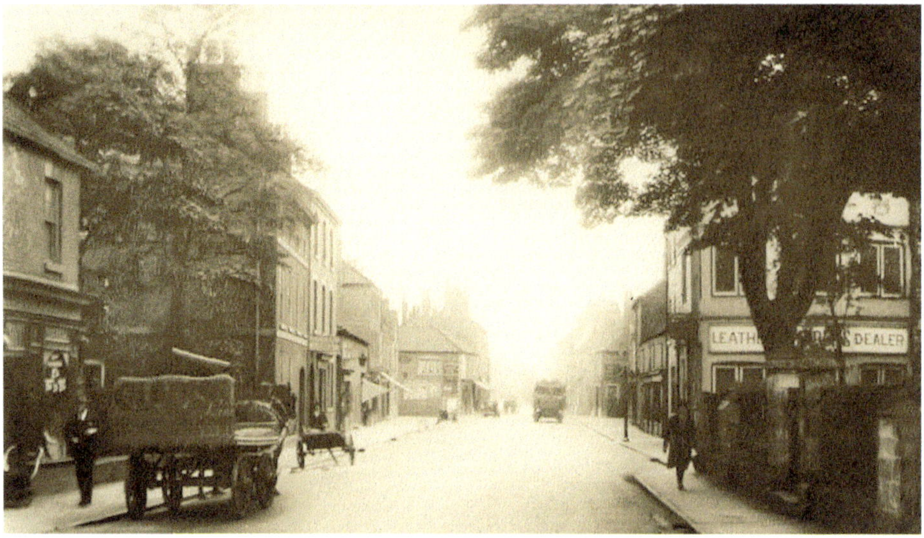

Churchgate, 1920

The market place was the centre of Retford's commercial activity. The open space between the church and the square (known as Cannon Square since the mid-nineteenth century) may have been the original site of the market. The principal streets of Carr Hill Gate (Carolgate), Newgate (Grove Street), Churchgate or Kirkgate, and Bridgegate radiated out from the square. A moot hall (town hall) was built at the north end of the square in 1388, and a triangular plot of land to the north of the building was used as another market area. Today Churchgate is a thriving, bustling square with new shops springing up and old family shops remaining, like Burton butcher's, in the historic buildings that still retain their nineteenth-century features. For example, the chocolate shop on the right of the photographs just after St Swithun's church is a must-visit for its exterior and definitely for what is going on inside!

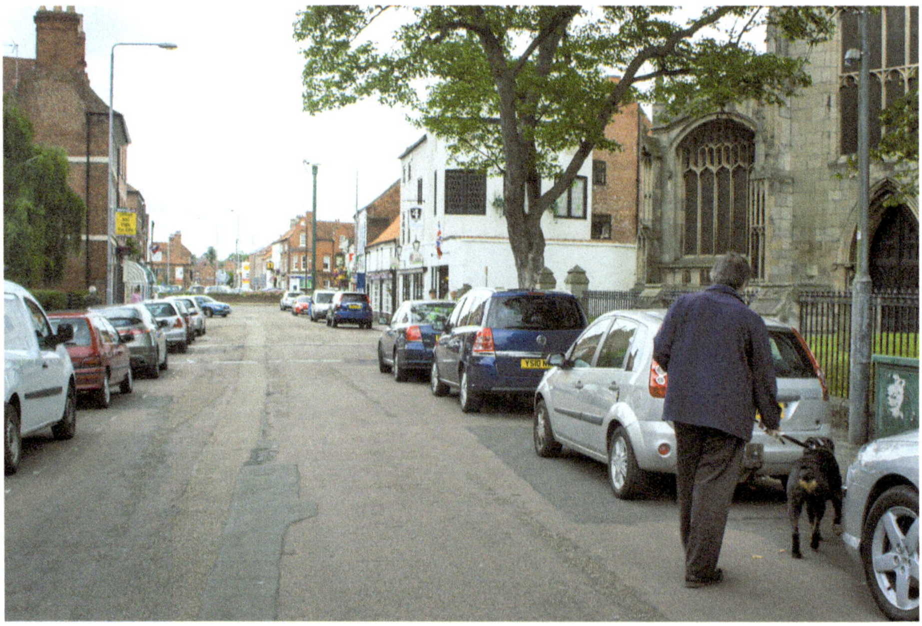

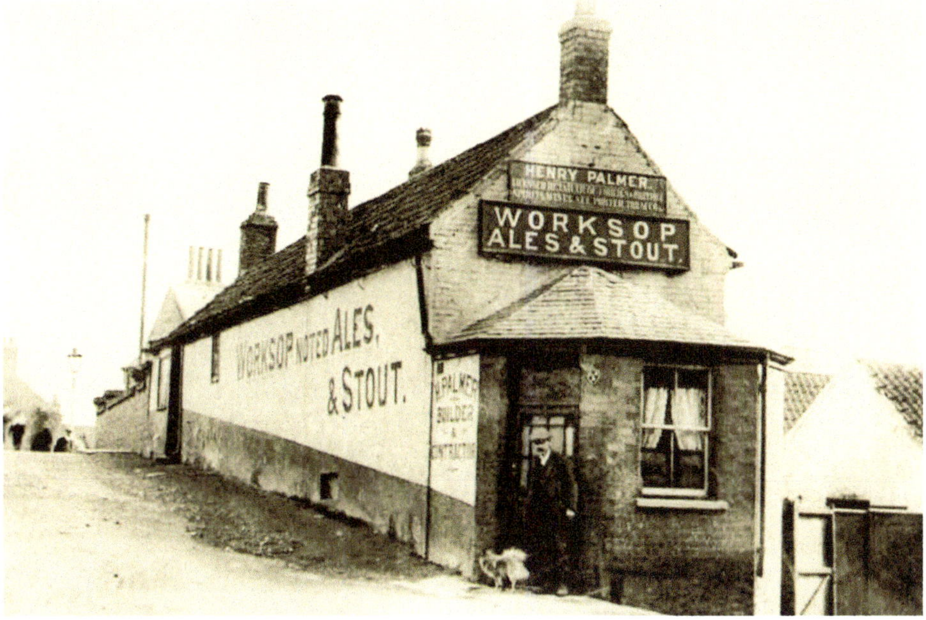

The Packet Inn, Grove Street, 1910

The Packet Inn was a passenger stop at Gas House Bridge along a stretch of canal linking Retford Marina to the Hop Pole. Traditional industries in Retford have declined in recent years. Long-established companies such as Jenkins Newell Dunford (engineering) and Bridon Ropes (wire) both closed in 2004. Like so many other small towns, Retford is now dominated by large supermarkets, charity shops and service industries. The canal sees only boats from the local marina and holiday barges travelling through, as it is a very pretty canal route with many really good, friendly pubs at historic mooring points. Retford has established a new charm of its own.

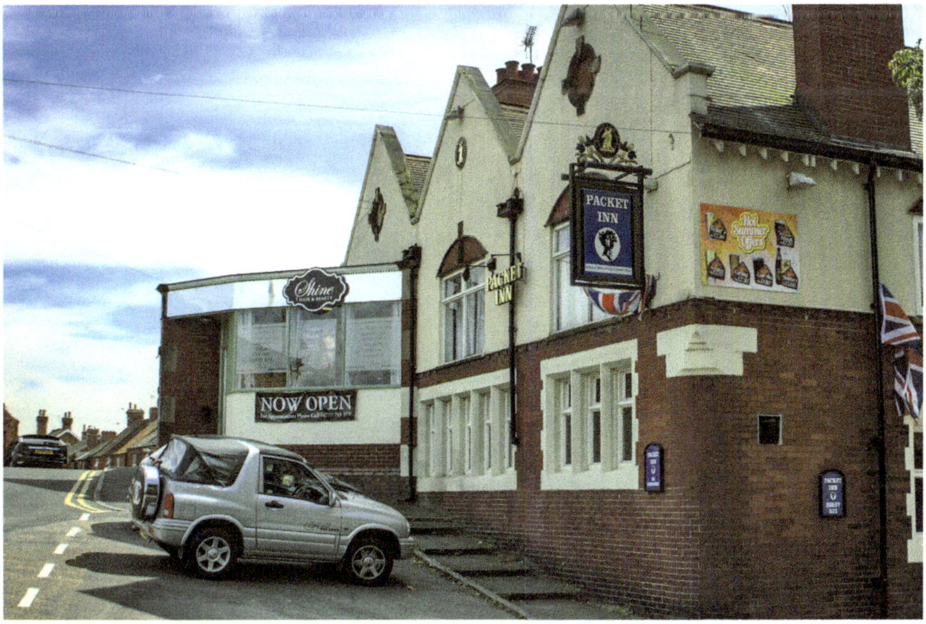

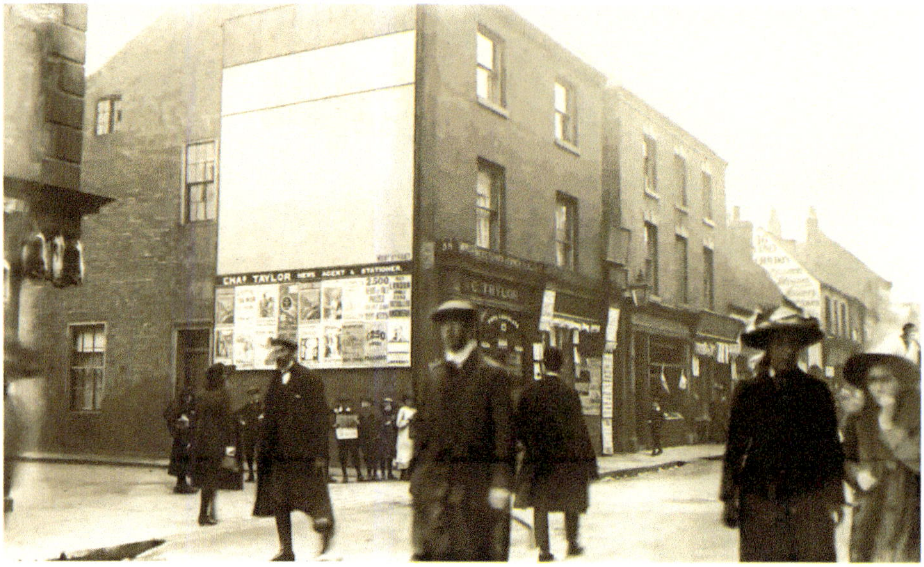

Carolgate, Corner of West Street, 1906

Road congestion in Retford had become an issue as early as the 1920s when calls were made for the construction of a bypass. By the 1950s it was a chronic problem and relief only came when the A1 was opened to the west of the town in the 1960s. A bypass was constructed around the town centre in the 1970s and Carolgate became pedestrianised. On the corner of West Street was a newsagent's for many years. It passed through various different hands but then became a successful hairdresser's called Rouge. The whole appearance of Carolgate has been carved away over the years, supposedly for the better, but looking back at Welchman's old photographs it certainly is not aesthetically for the better. All the wonderful, unique, thriving grocer's, clothes shops, and cafés with their marvellous shopfronts have been sadly lost to a town now, I regret to say, of bargain and charity shops.

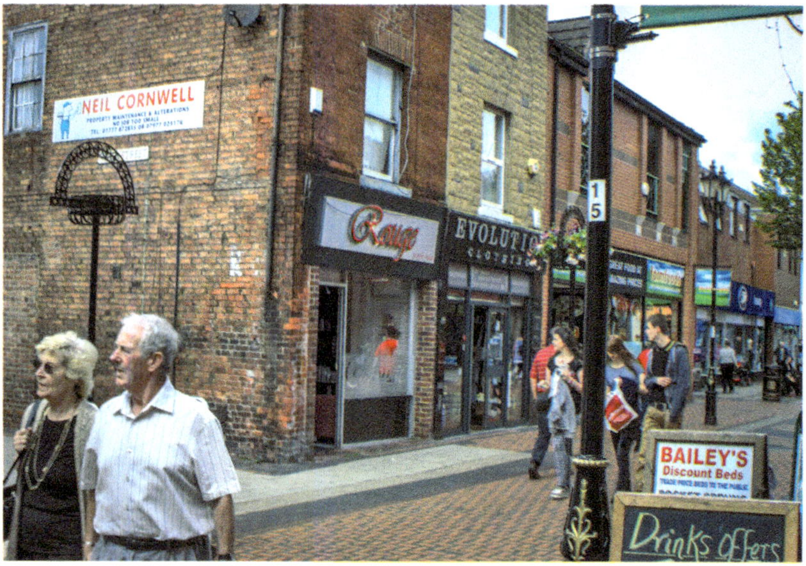

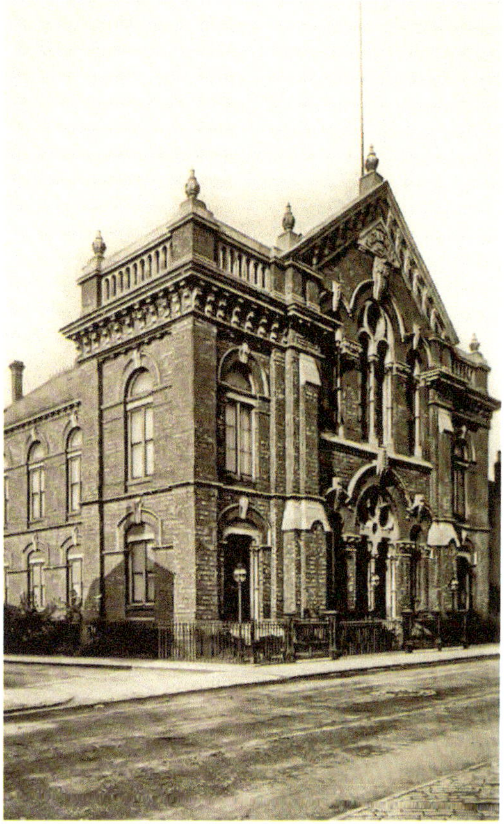

Wesleyan Chapel, Grove Street, 1900

The Wesleyan chapel on Grove Street is a grand structure, built in 1879–80, to accommodate 1,000 Wesleyan Methodists. At the end of Grove Street we have, on the left, the residential neighbourhood of Alma Road and, on the right, Spa Common, where in 1837 pumping apparatus was erected in the hope of its proving a benefit to humanity and a profit to the town. The optimistic expectations were not realised, and all evidence of the spa is now long gone. The same architects that were used to build Retford town hall built this chapel.

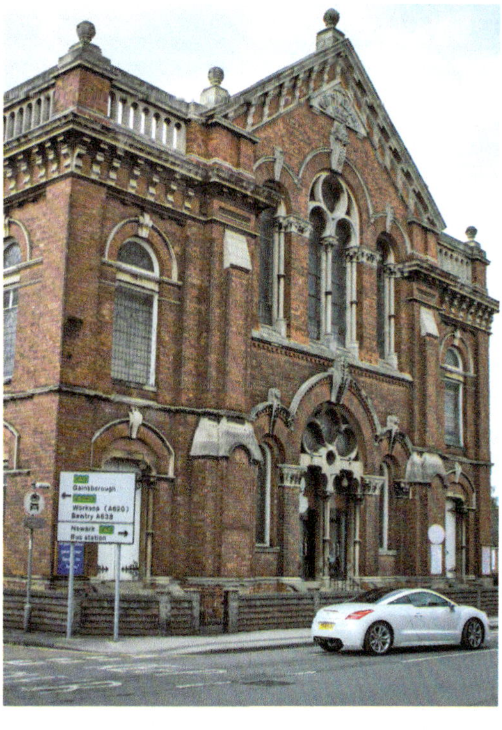

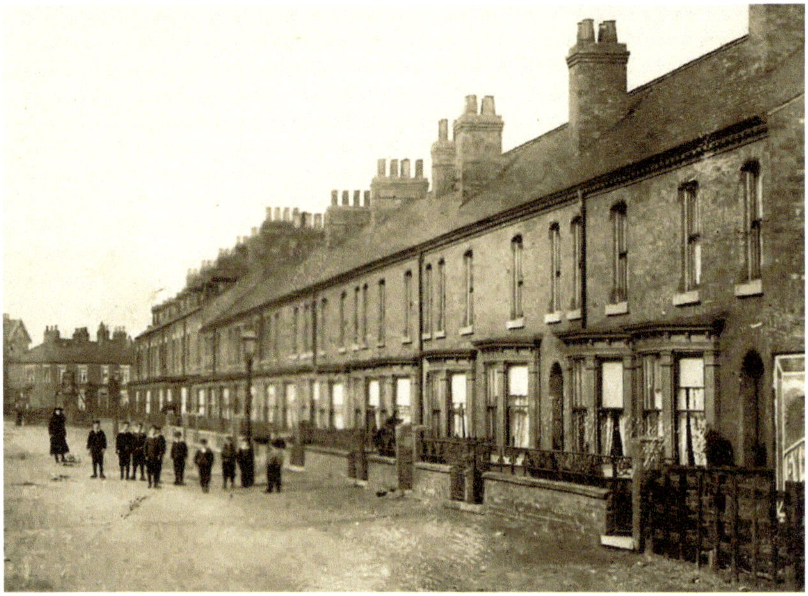

Station Road, 1910

Railway refreshment staff, workers and mechanics would have lived on Station Road, which is a stone's throw from the railway. The average price for a two-bedroom property on this street today is £83,000. As in the old photograph of the street, Station Road is very much filled with families, and in the summer you can see residents sitting outside having neighbourly chats while the children play on the wide street. This area of Retford is surrounded by ornate Victorian buildings full of charm and character, probably because they would be the first view for visitors to the market town. The former residents of Station Road were probably involved in the railway accident that occurred on 13 February 1923 when the driver and fireman of the express were killed and seventeen passengers and five railwaymen travelling as passengers suffered injuries.

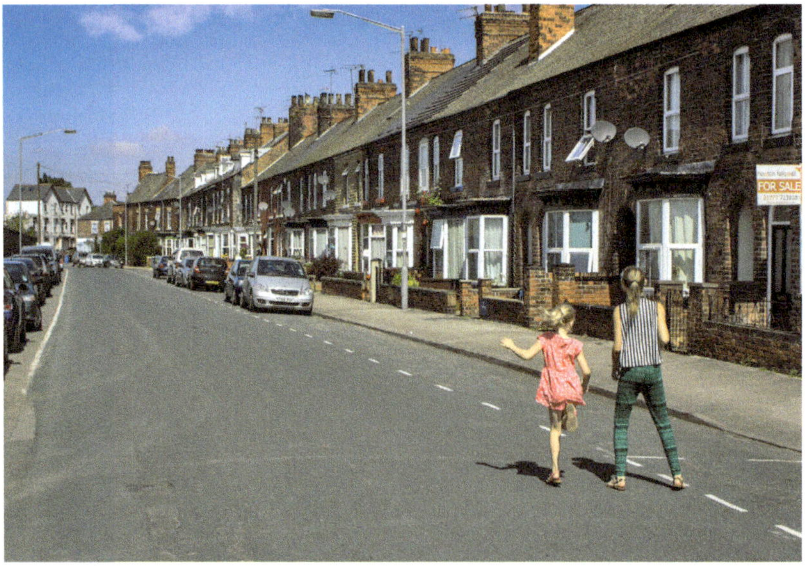

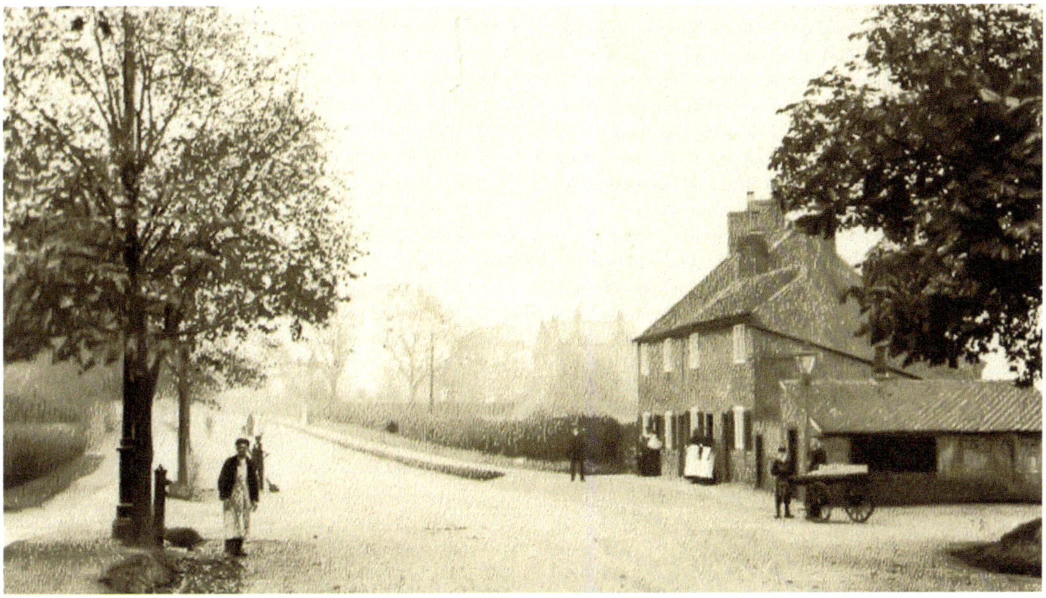

Whinney Moor Lane, Crossing with London Road, 1905

The entrance to Retford hosts several excellent examples of eighteenth- and nineteenth-century vernacular architecture. The setting remains the dominant feature of the area. The late nineteenth- and twentieth-century development pattern has been characterised by large houses in large plots, often partially obscured behind attractive green boundaries of hedges and trees. The two roads leading in and out of the town, London Road and North Road, are essentially full of more ostentatious housing. Here, in the old picture, the house is seen to have wooden shutters, apparently to discourage drunken revellers on the route home from the nearby Nags Head. This junction today is an extremely busy thoroughfare and also serves two primary schools. Another parent and I campaigned successfully to get a safer crossing, and here is a brand-new pedestrian crossing to keep this generation and the next a bit safer.

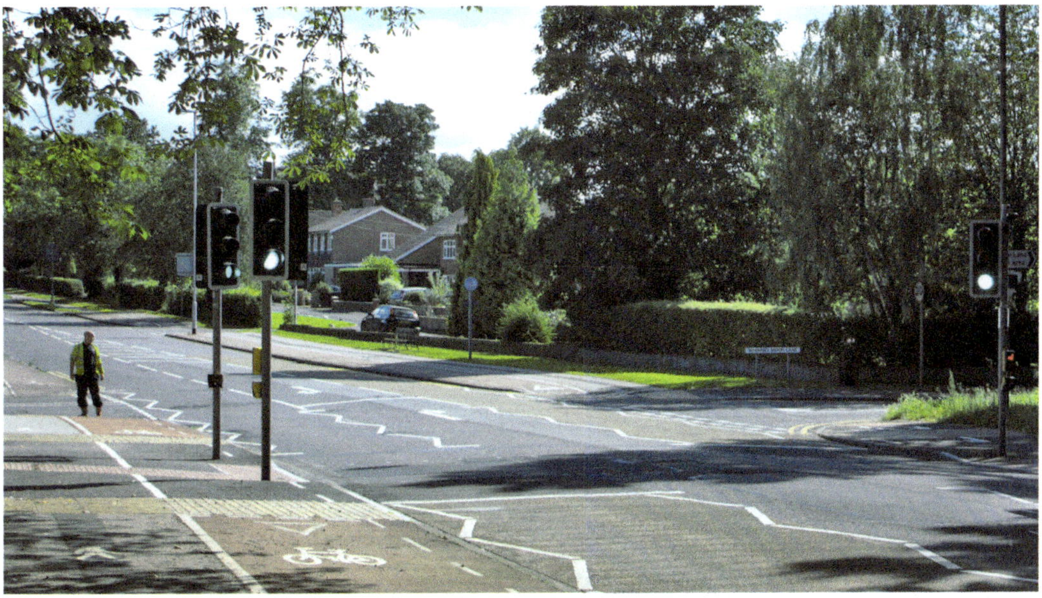

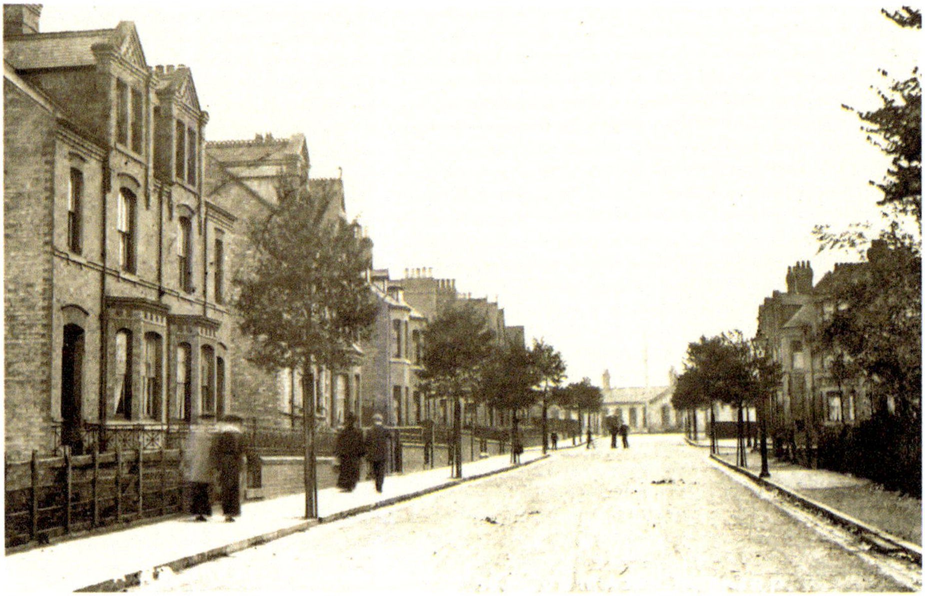

Victoria Road, Looking Towards the Railway Station, 1908

Retford is served by two railway lines, the East Coast Mainline, which runs between London and Scotland, with trains taking from 1 hour 20 minutes to London King's Cross, and the Sheffield to Lincoln line, which has links to Sheffield, Lincoln, Gainsborough, Worksop, Grimsby and Cleethorpes. These two lines meet at Retford, which acts as an important interchange in the British rail network. If you enter Retford from the railway station then Victoria Road is the road you will take, and it is a grand one. By 1901 Retford's population had doubled from 5,999 in 1801 to 12,340, and the hamlet of Thrumpton off the end of Victoria Road developed as a new 'railway town' to accommodate the growing railway workforce. Today, Victoria Road retains its ornate nineteenth-century charm with many Victorian dwellings with original ornate features.

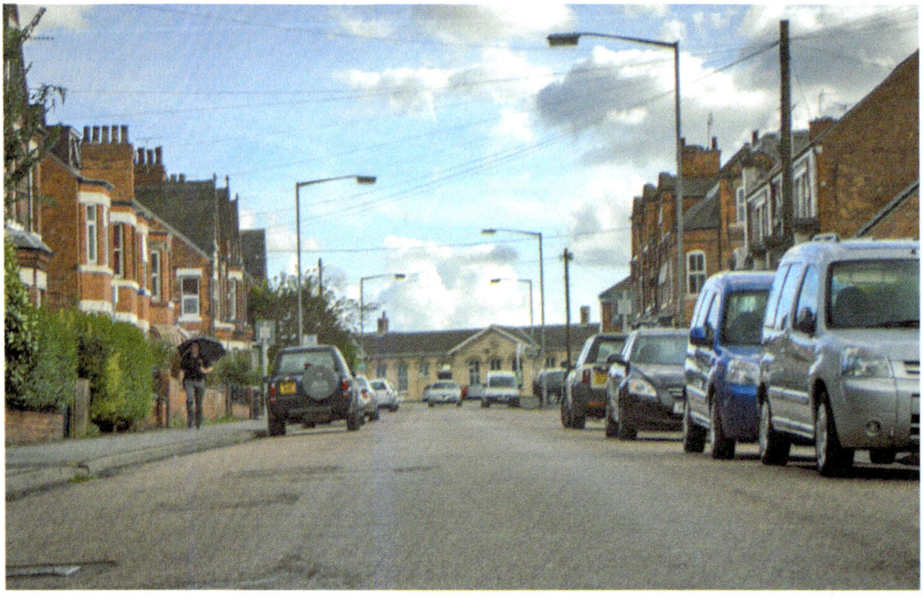

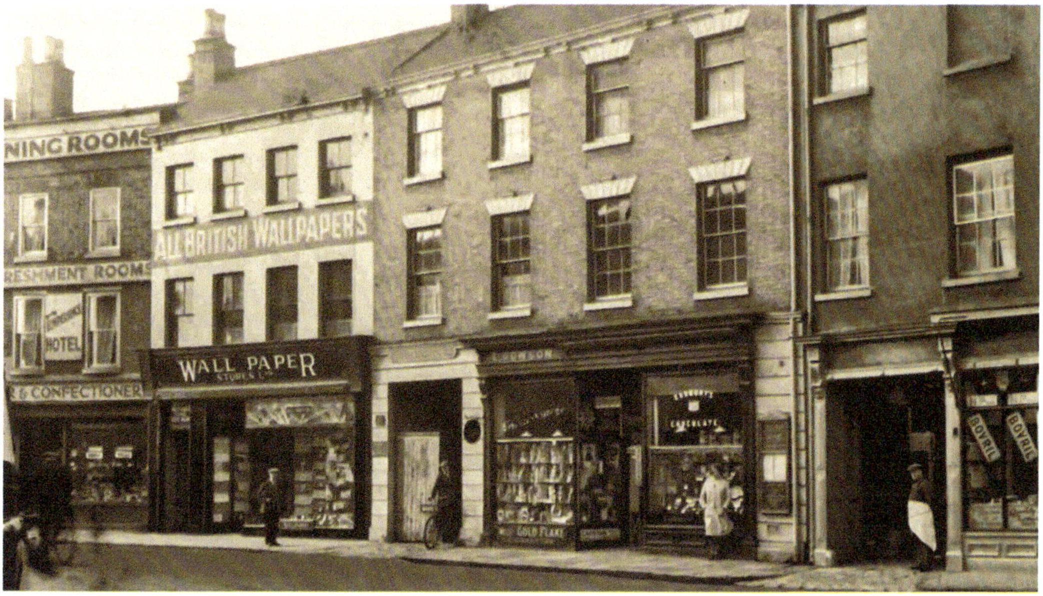

Market Square, Approaching Cannon Square, 1931

Retford has a strong economy, mainly consisting of services with some light industry. The town itself is an important commercial centre for the local area, with large supermarkets, many independent shops and a market every Thursday, Friday and Saturday. Retford's town centre has an empty shop rate of only 5 per cent, which is impressive considering the national average of 14.6 per cent. Here, in the old Welchman photograph, we see the town centre dressed with a row of interesting and varied shops including wallpaper stores. The same is true today, although the charity shops and the pawnbroker shops seem to be springing up more and more.

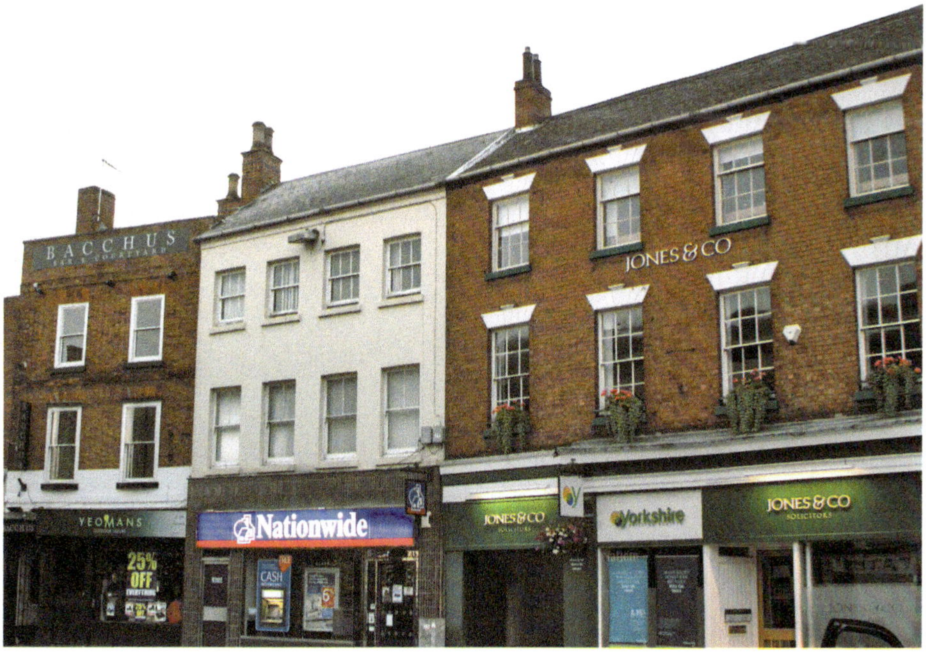

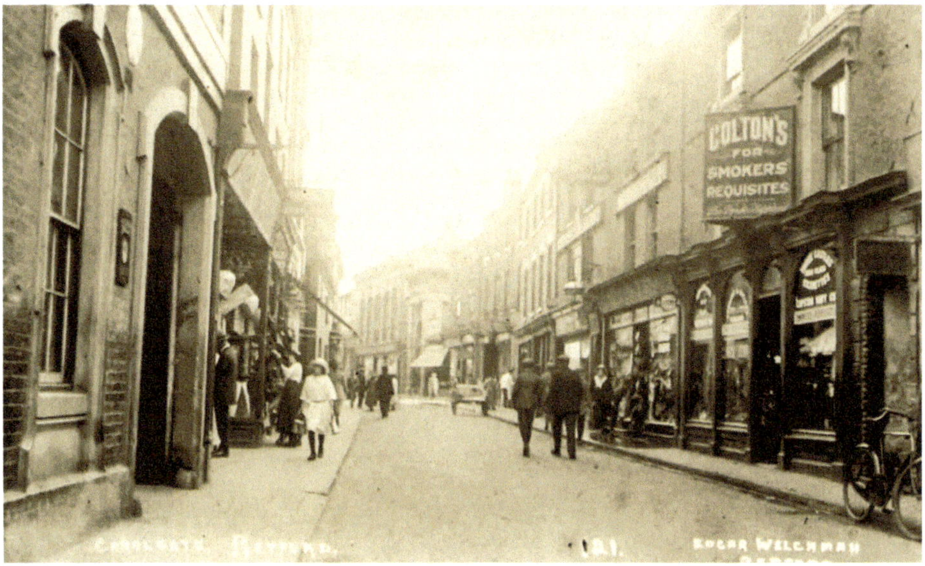

The Granby Hotel on Carolgate, 1920

East Retford continued to thrive but no more so than after 1776 when the Great North Road was diverted to run through the town. As a result, Carolgate and Bridgegate formed the main route through the borough, and many of the inns that still stand today owe their presence to this event. Retford became a 'natural point' for travellers to break their journey. The prosperity Retford found during this Georgian period is reflected in the town's fine Georgian buildings and spacious market square. If you are looking for a Retford bed & breakfast, for maybe an overnight stay or long-term accommodation, Retford hosts many, although sadly the beautiful Granby Hotel is now a shop.

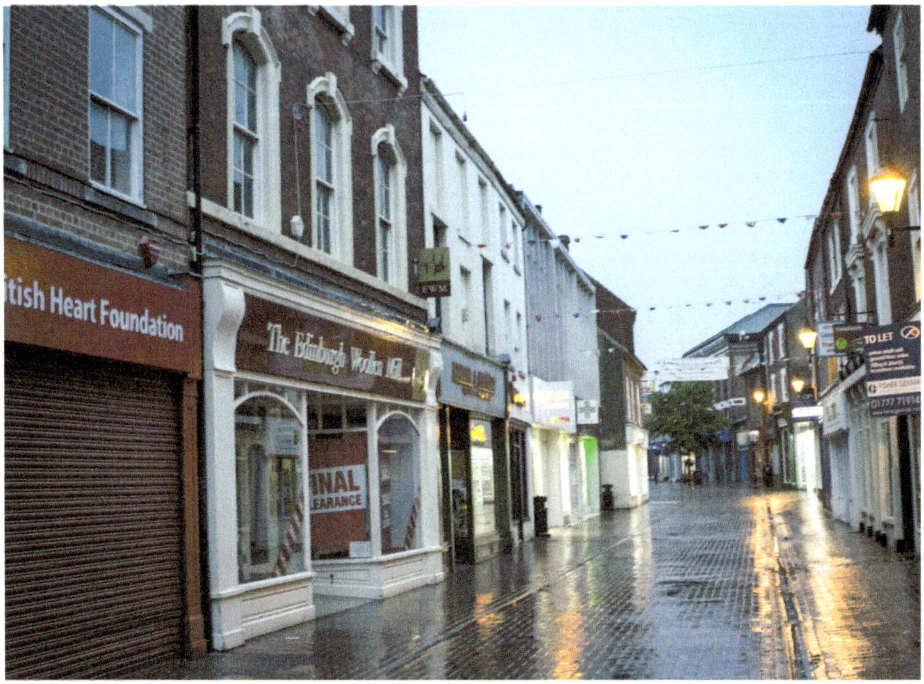

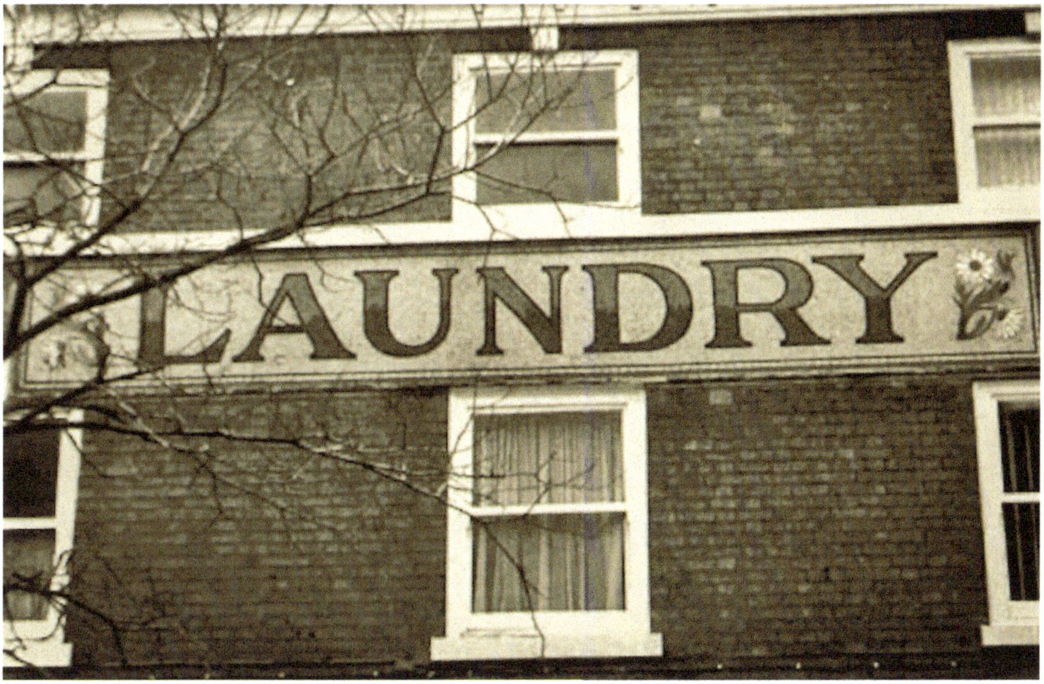

Clark's Dyeworks Offices on Grove Street, 1970

There is a long line of Clarks whose ancestors established an early dyeing business in Retford in 1798. Dry-cleaning and laundering developed in to what became Hallcroft Works in Retford. The laundry office shown here was one link in a chain of over 100 laundry and dry-cleaning shops that were part of the Clark industry. The Clarks were responsible for developing the early stages of dyeing non-natural fabrics like rayon. Underneath the sign is an archway where there is another reference to the Clark industry in the street name 'Dyers Court'. A recent scheme by Retford's Civic Society conservation team has seen the splendid restoration of the flower 'laundry' mosaic.

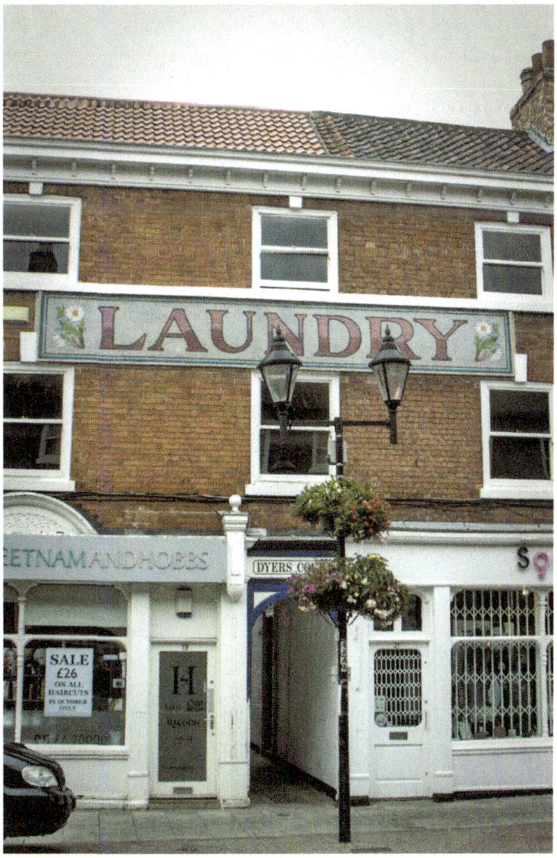

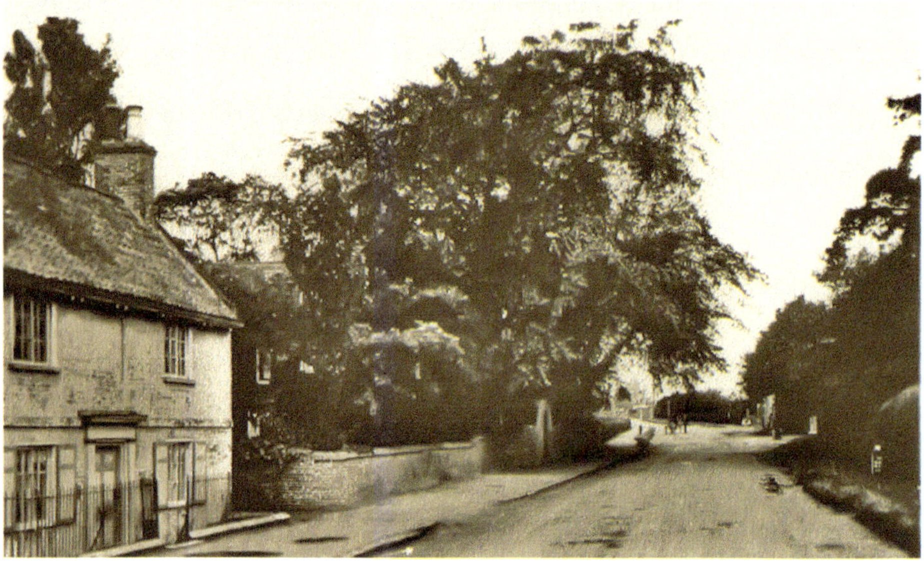

White House Cottage, 1917

One of the oldest buildings in the area, the White House Cottage, was an eighteenth-century development in conjunction with the emergence of the coaching road. The building is more vernacular than architecturally outstanding. The Retford historian John S. Piercy remarked, 'White houses, which takes its name from two very ancient white cottages which time is rapidly devouring, is situated on the North Road, one mile south of Retford, and contains besides an inn, two or three Tolerably good houses.' As a group, these three buildings provide a strong focus for the street scene, possessing well-proportioned frontages directly sited on to the pavement. The open spaces around the white houses on the entry to the town contribute positively to the plan, the historic layout and the ambiance of the area.

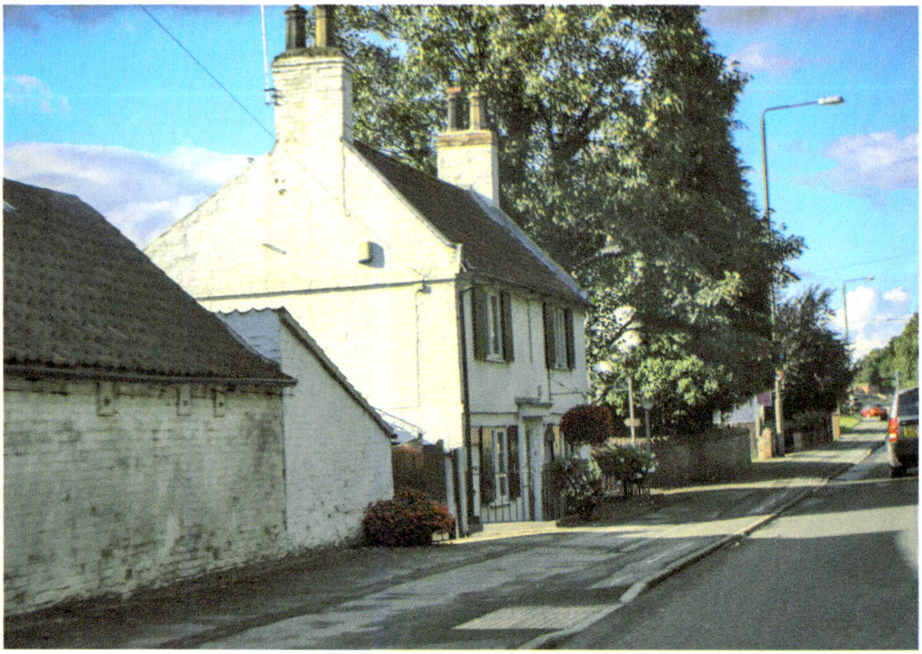

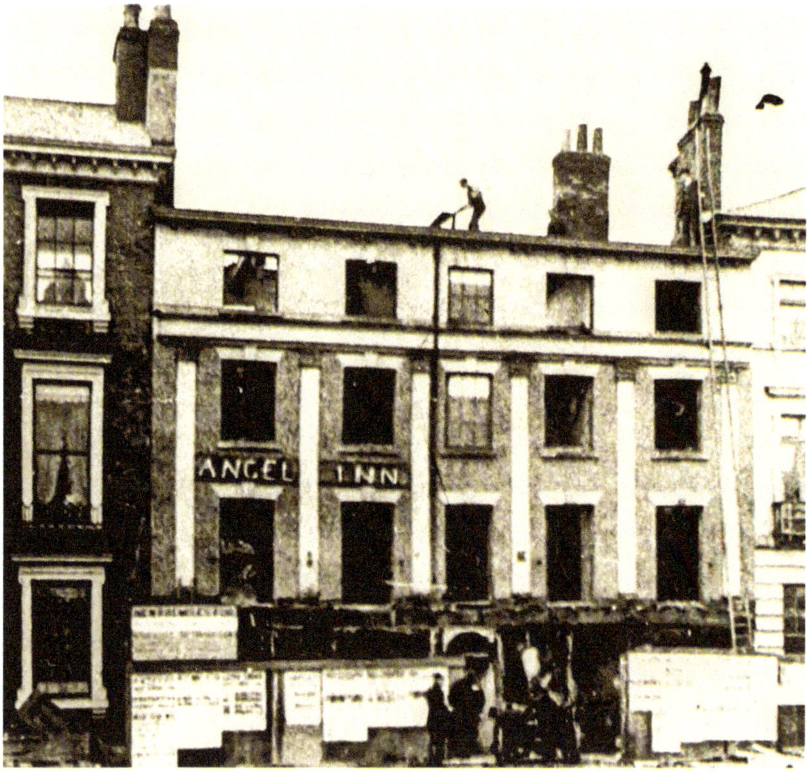

The Angel & Exchange Inn, Market Square, 1900

Here we see in the old photograph alterations being made to the old Angel & Exchange Inn, which was to become Henry Spencer's auction room. Today the building has been returned to its former use as a public house and is the Broadstone, named after the stone that, tradition has it, was used as a boundary marker during the plague of 1665. People put money in it for food left nearby, to avoid infection.

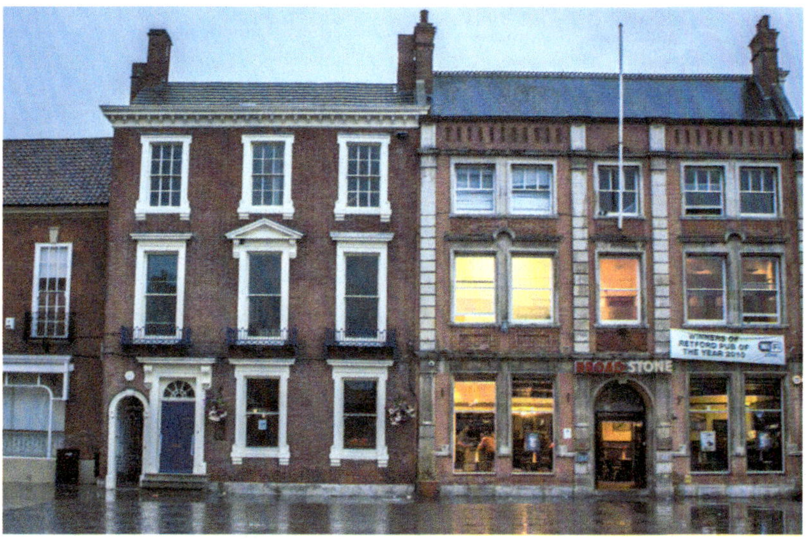

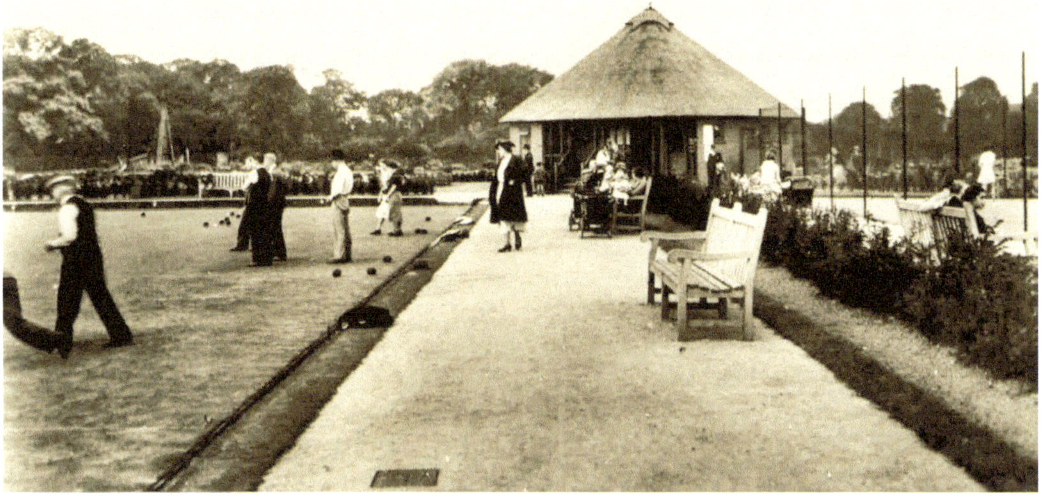

Kings' Park Bowling Green

The pavilion at the award-winning Kings' Park is open during the summer months, from May to September. The pavilion provides access to the bowling green, tennis courts and toilet facilities and offers refreshments and confectionery. Kings' Park bowling club plays bowls in local leagues and on a friendly basis. Surrounded by well-cared-for wonderful gardens, it really is the best way to bowl! Very little has changed here over time. Perhaps just the relocation for health and safety reasons of the children's play park, which in today's terms would be considered a 'retro' park (remember the oily swing?). The tennis courts to the right – now behind a grown hedgerow – and the quaint pavilion remain. The toilets are pretty much as they were and are quite charming. During the summer months this is a very popular and relaxing place for all ages, which makes for a very successful park.

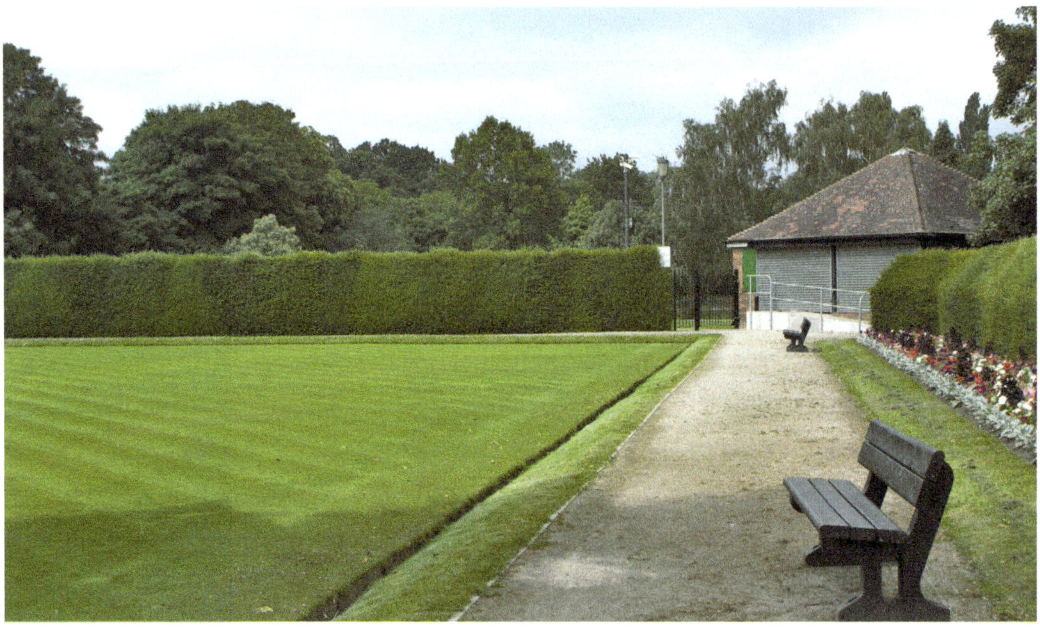

Clark's Dyeworks, Market Square, 1948

Clark's Dyeworks Ltd, Hallcroft, Retford. Clark's shop in the Square, Retford has 'Clark's' 150th Year' in large letters on the roof. Hezekiah Clark came from Derby in the 1780s to work at the Revolution Mill as a dyer. He failed to find work so he established his own dyeing business in Retford in 1798. Dry-cleaning and laundering developed, necessitating a move to what became Hallcroft Works in Retford. Retford Civic Society commissioned a wonderful wall mural in town commemorating the Clark Laundry. The premises are now occupied by KFC.

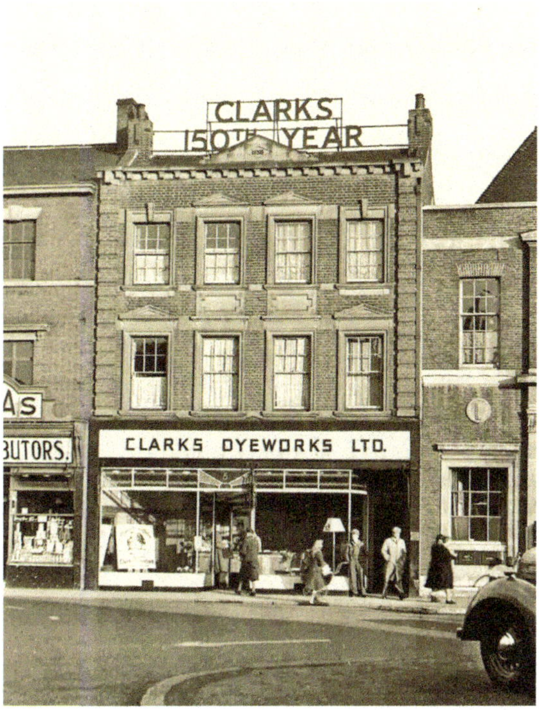

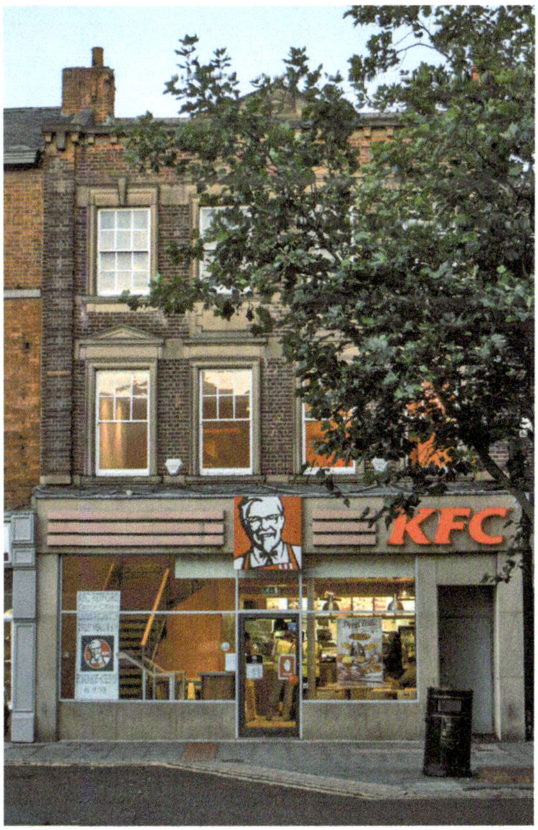

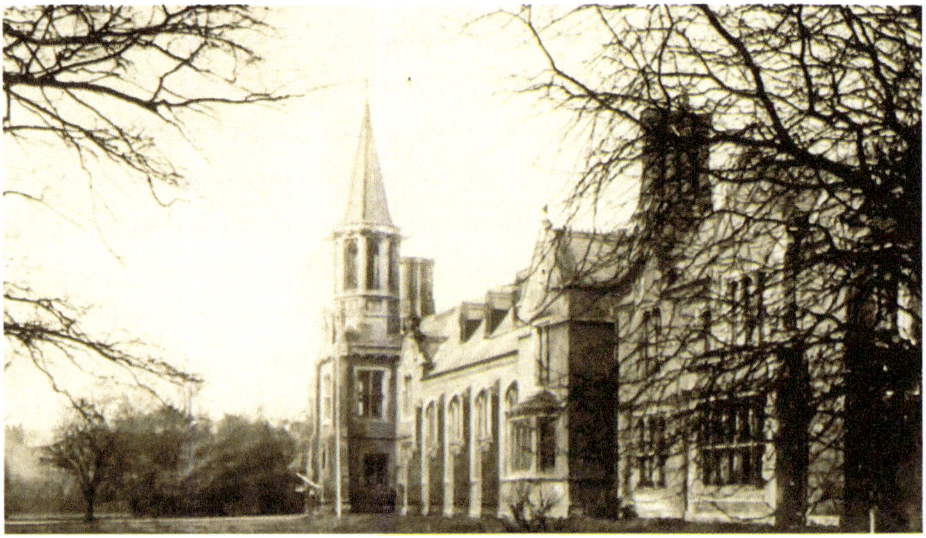

King Edward VI Grammar School, 1905

The origins of King Edward VI School go back almost as far as the town itself. Thomas Gunthorpe, 'parson of Babworth', made a handsome gift of money to the town of East Retford for the building of a new school in 1518. The school was of a timber construction. It may have perished in the great Retford fire of 1528. The present buildings on London Road were opened in August 1857, but it is now history itself as it has been sold off to developers. After 450 years there will no longer be a King Edward VI School in Retford. It was around 1941 that half of the railings round the grammar school frontage were taken down as part of Retford's patriotic donation to the war effort, as was the case with most of the low stone walls all over the town and particularly around East Retford church. If you walk around town you will notice the stumps of railings.

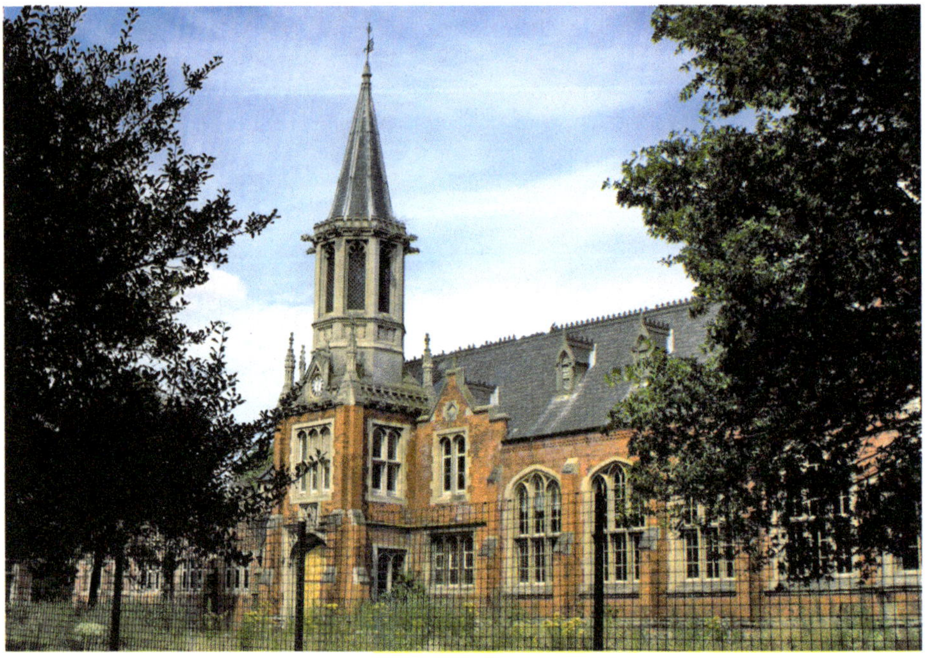

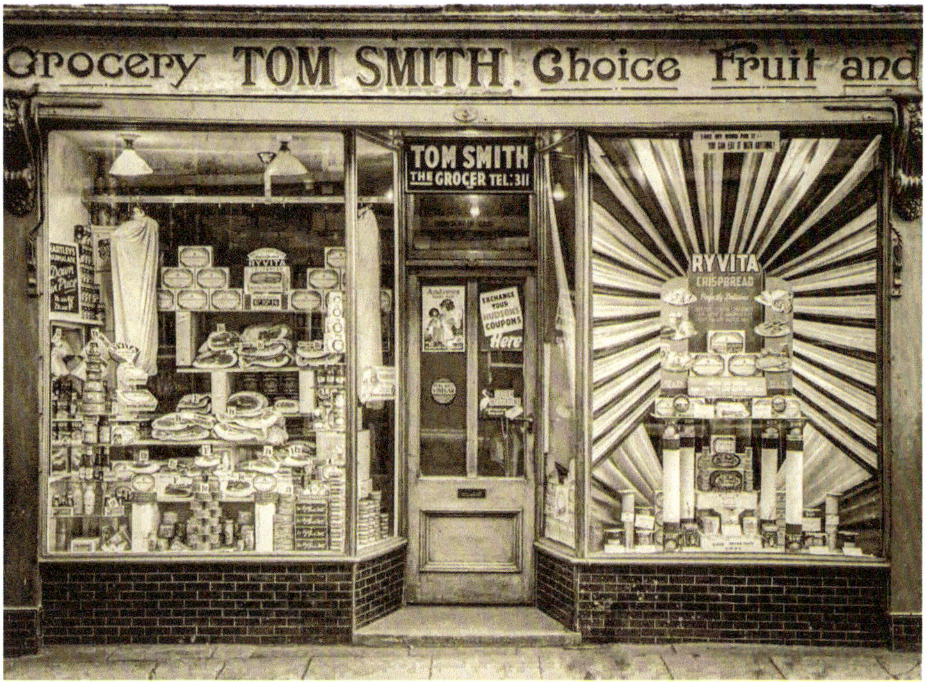

Tom Smith's Grocer's Shop, Bridgegate, 1937

Retford has a relatively strong economy with pockets of poverty. The town mainly consists of services with some light industry. Small independent retailers bravely shoulder the rental prices and work hard to give the town choice and quality. However, we cannot turn back the hand of time to yesteryear when the town flourished with independent grocer's, butcher's, saddler's and baker's.

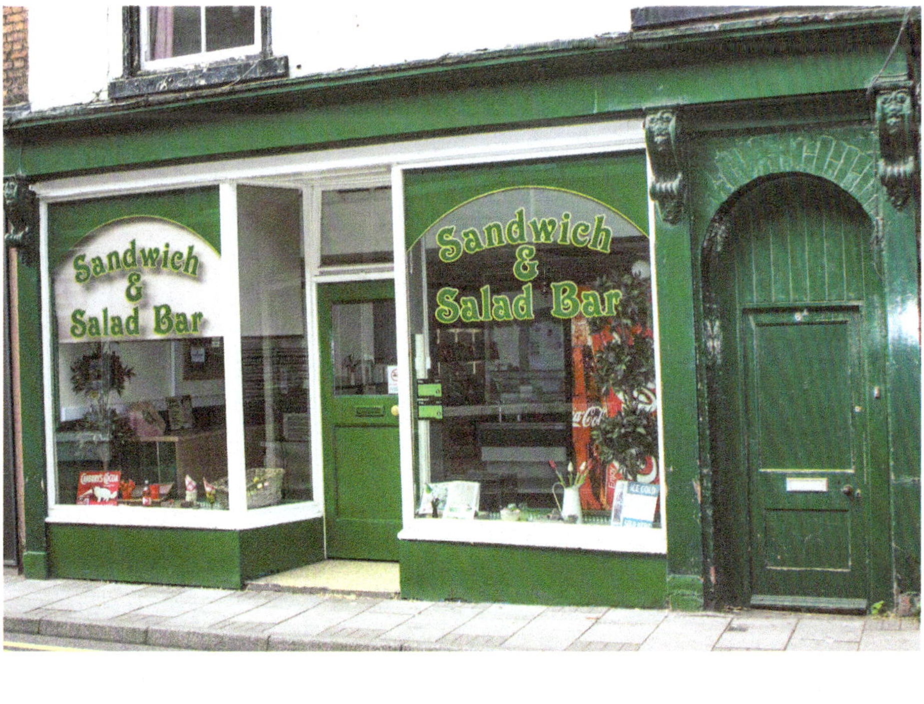

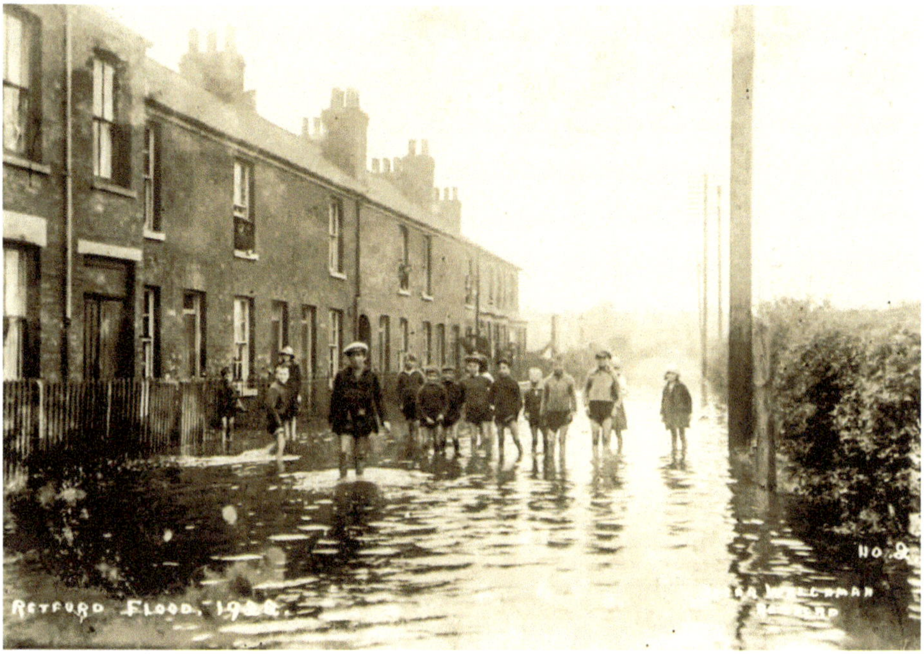

Floods, 1922

Retford is no stranger to flooding. Any local resident will tell you that they have lived through a couple or more serious floods in the town. Flooding in this pair of images on West Street is because the housing is located near to the south end of Kings' Park towards the River Idle. It is no great surprise, with Retford being situated in a valley with the Idle and the Chesterfield Canal running through the centre, that the town watches and waits carefully for the Bassetlaw Environment Agency to inform the townsfolk of what perils may lie ahead, like the serious flooding on the morning of Wednesday 27 June 2007 in Kings' Park.

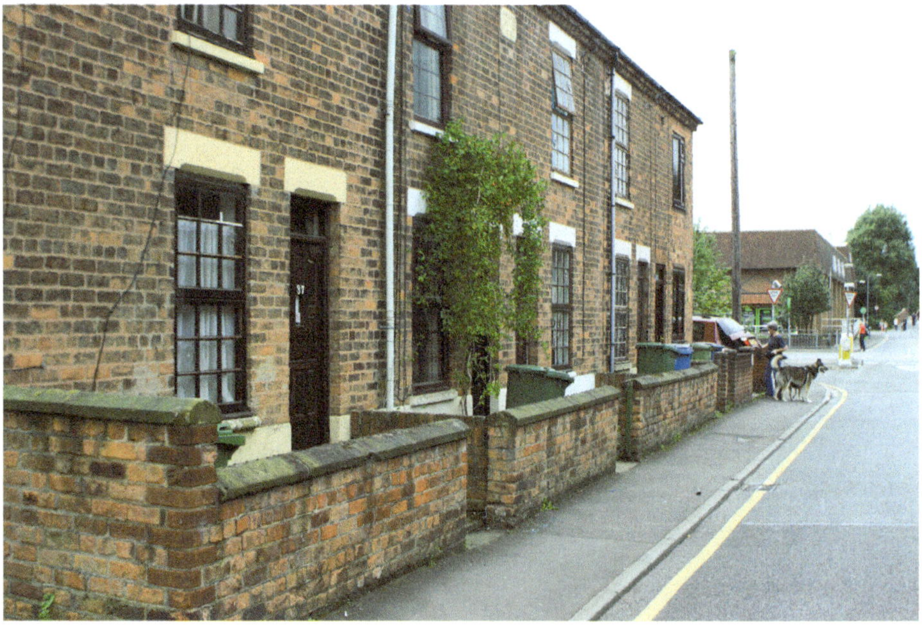

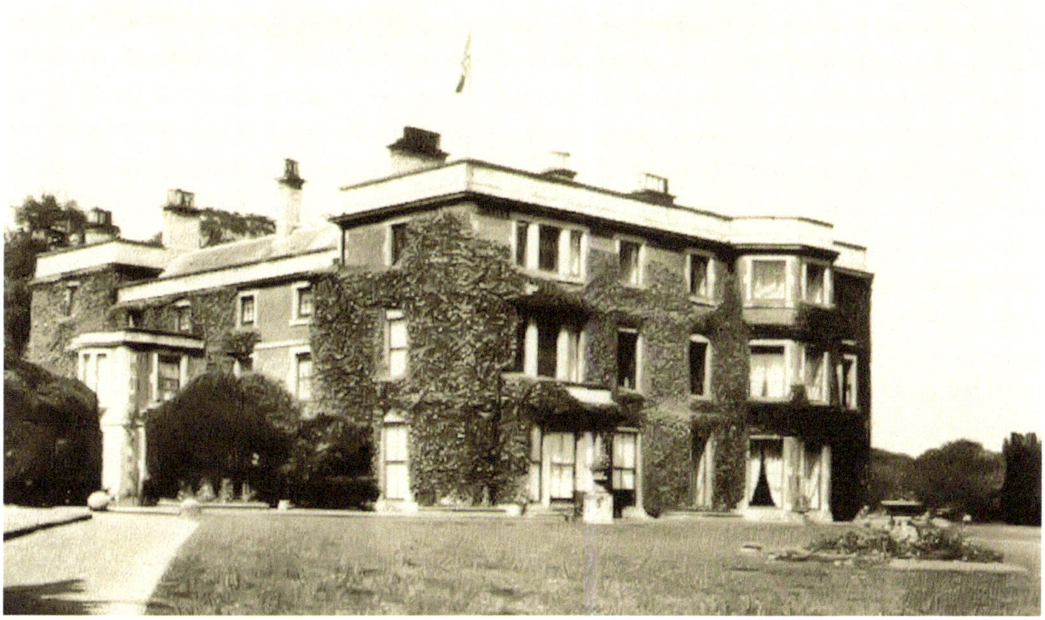

Babworth Hall, 1910

After the Norman Conquest, Roger de Busli bought the whole of Babworth. Later it became the property of the Earl of Shrewsbury and Lord Cavendish, and in the eighteenth century it was purchased by Sir Gervas Elwes, and lastly by John Simpson. Babworth, just on the edge of Retford, is well known for its connection with the Pilgrim Fathers. William Wilberforce led the campaign to abolish slavery, and in the early twentieth century his great-grandson was rector of Babworth. The lake that used to cast shimmers on the house was later drained and is now a stand of trees. However, the faint indentation in the landscape can still be made out today.

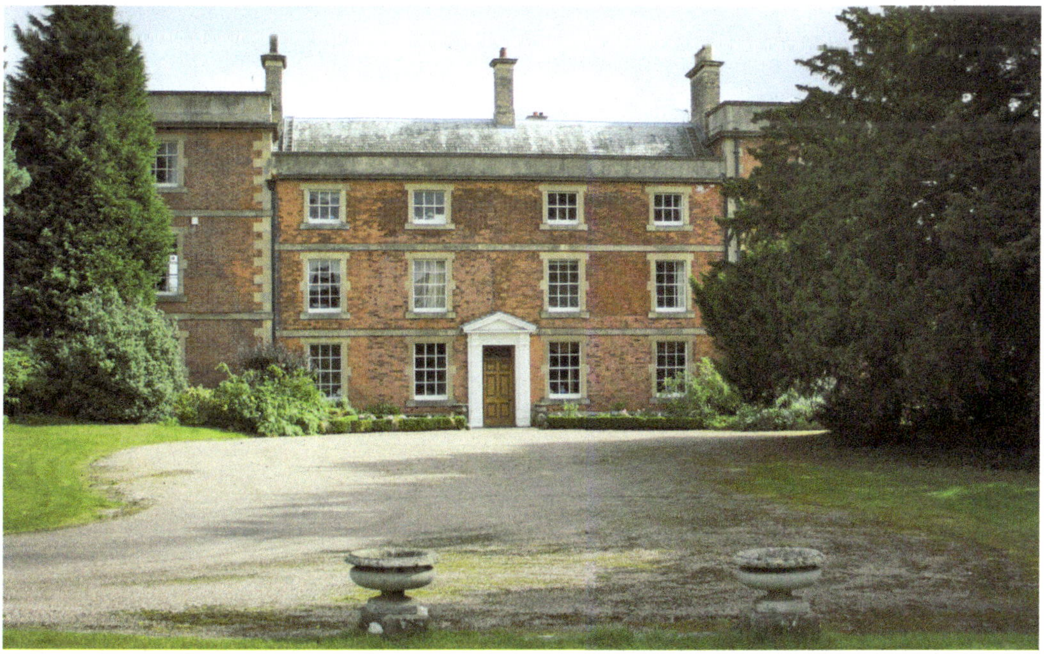

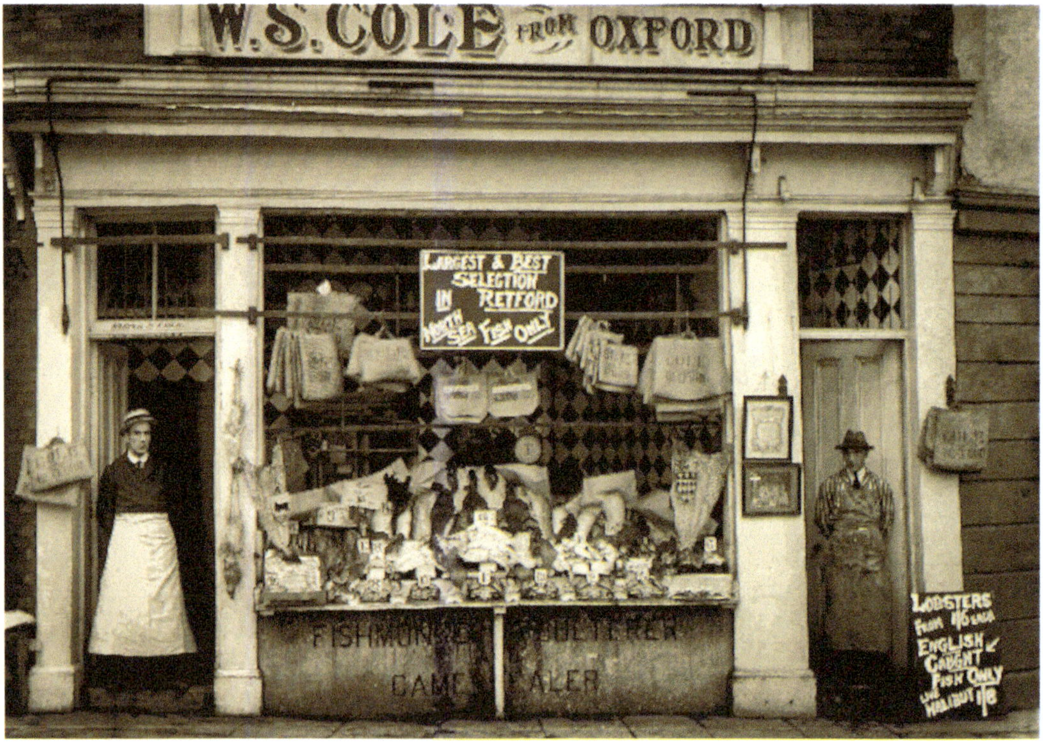

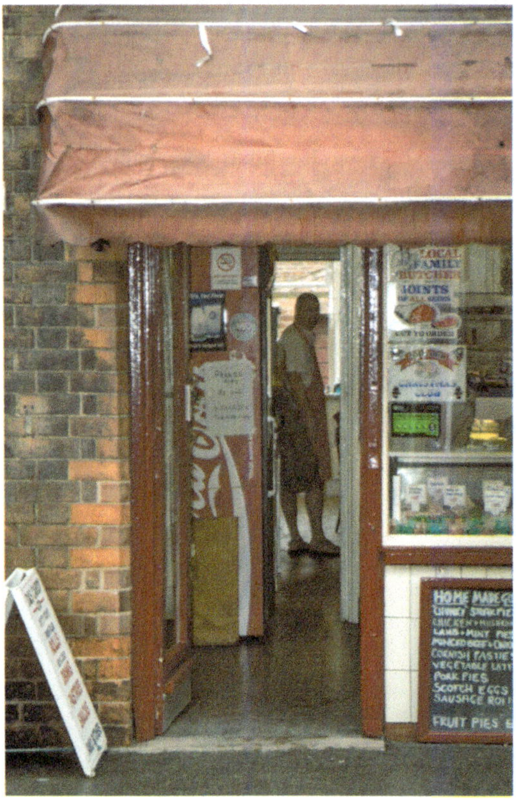

Butchers & Game Dealers, 1927

W. S. Cole was a fishmonger, poulterer and game dealer in the square. There were many butchers in Retford in the early 1900s, and each shop beautifully displayed its wares. I really wish I could have included every photograph. Today in Retford, sadly that number of independent butchers has declined. The wonderful D. & S. Cardy Ltd is seen here on Bridgegate; George Burton on Churchgate is a great family butcher and Bacon's and Crawshaw's are on Carolgate. The oldest family butchers, like Burton's, keep the tradition strong and their meat is delicious!

Storcroft Mill, 1900

Storcroft sadly is no longer to be seen and its former location originally proved tricky to locate. Not many local people knew of the old mills of Retford. This particular mill was built in 1866 but was burnt to the ground in 1904 so there is no converted mill, just a space where it stood in the triangle between Caledonian Road, Strawberry Road and Storcroft Road. Storcroft Mill, 65 feet of brickwork, 26 feet wide at the base, cost £1,000 to build. The mill's six 33-foot sails and four pairs of stones would labour to grind 6½ stone of grain per hour.

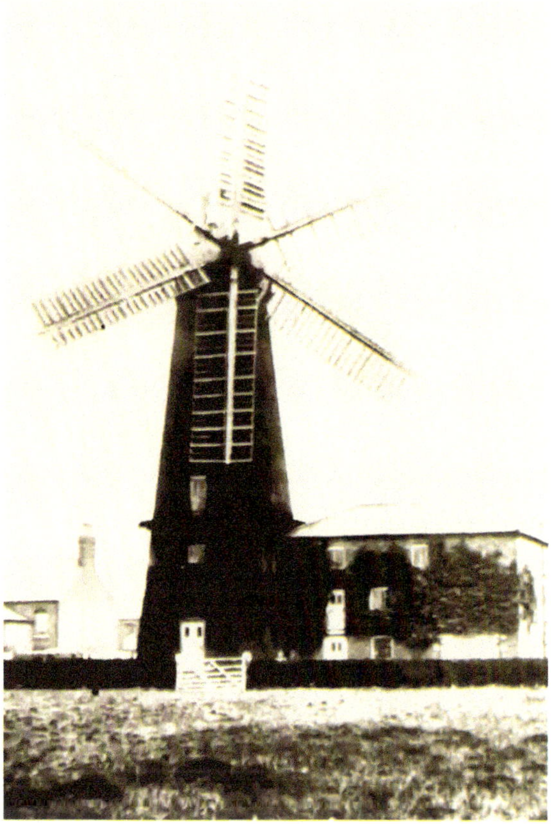

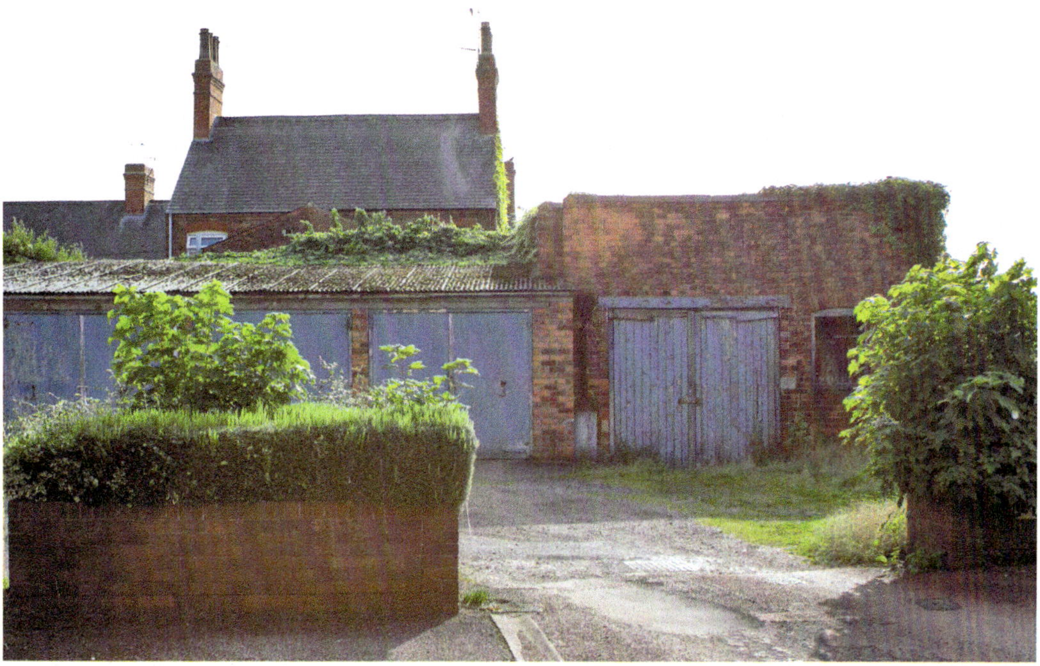

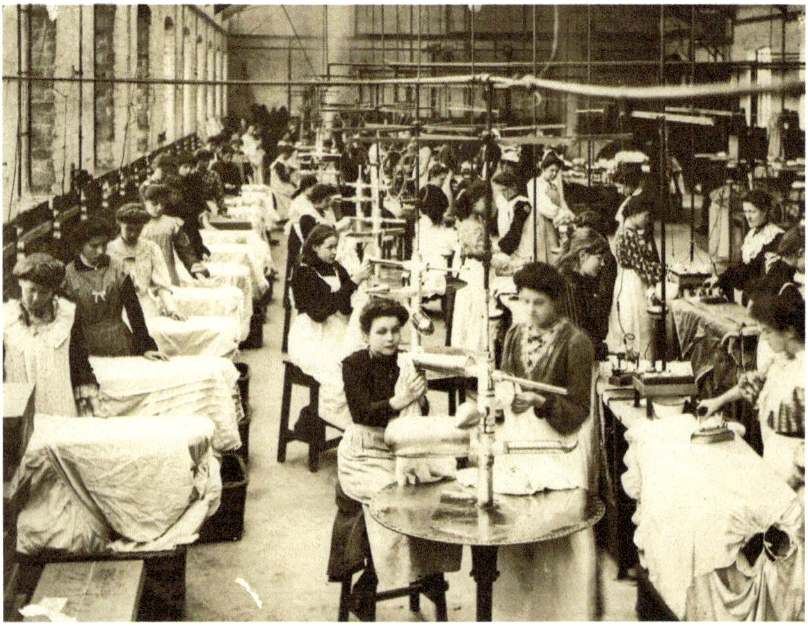

The Clark's Factory, Hallcroft Road, 1900

In Hallcroft there was a large steel-framed/corrugated-iron-sheet building on the main road frontage of Hallcroft Works, adjacent to the Clark's post office, which was built by the Air Ministry. This was where all the incoming forces laundry and dry-cleaning was sorted prior to processing in the main works, after which it was dispatched from the same building to various parts of the North East of England. The building was eventually demolished in the early 1950s. This view shows the finishing room at the Hallcroft works in 1908. The hand irons used here were all electrically heated. The machine in the foreground is a steam-heated cylinder for finishing bedspreads, blinds and other flat articles after dyeing or dry-cleaning. Where Clark's once stood is a new housing estate, so I thought it would be fitting to show this mural in Dyers Court commissioned by the Civic Society.

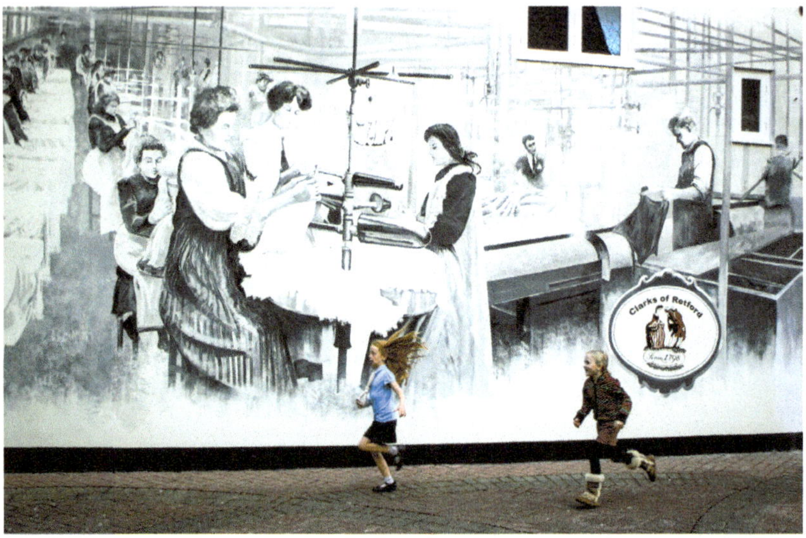

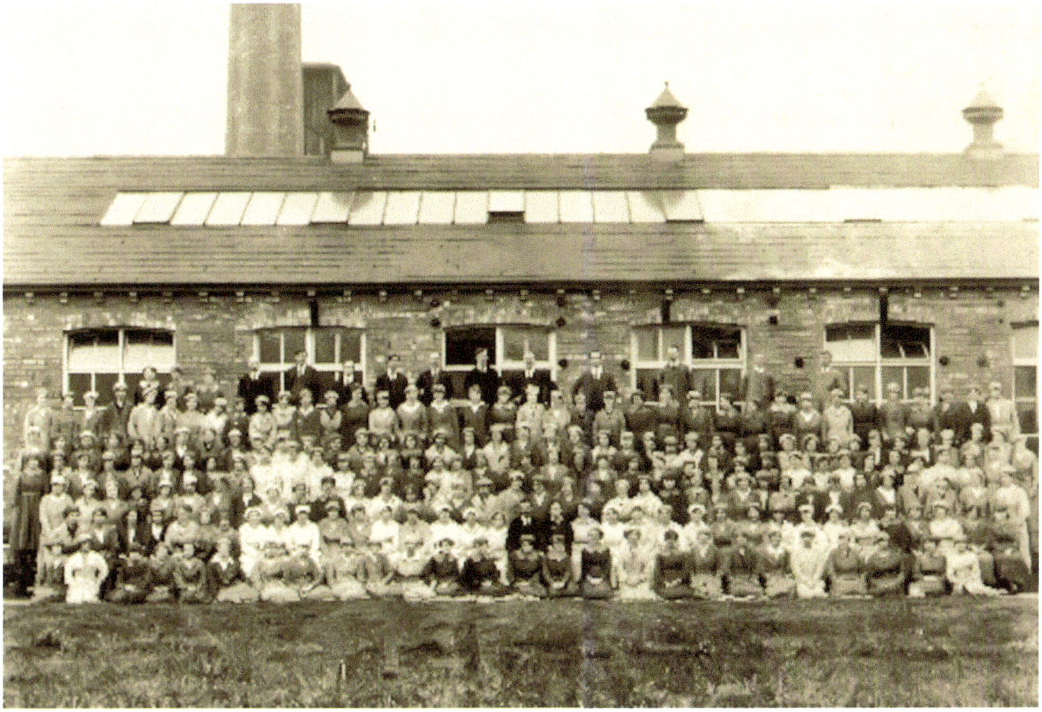

Ordsall Wireworks, Bridon Wire, 1918

The staff of Ordsall Wireworks with factory buildings behind. Women began to be employed there during the First World War. Among them was Ivy Bradley, who was an instructor at the mill. Today there is a new housing development but luckily the cricket pitch has managed to hang on in there and is still used by Ordsall Bridon Cricket Club. Long-established companies such as Jenkins Newell Dunford (engineering) and Bridon Ropes (wire) both closed in 2004 and with that, sadly, the popular social clubs saw their demise also.

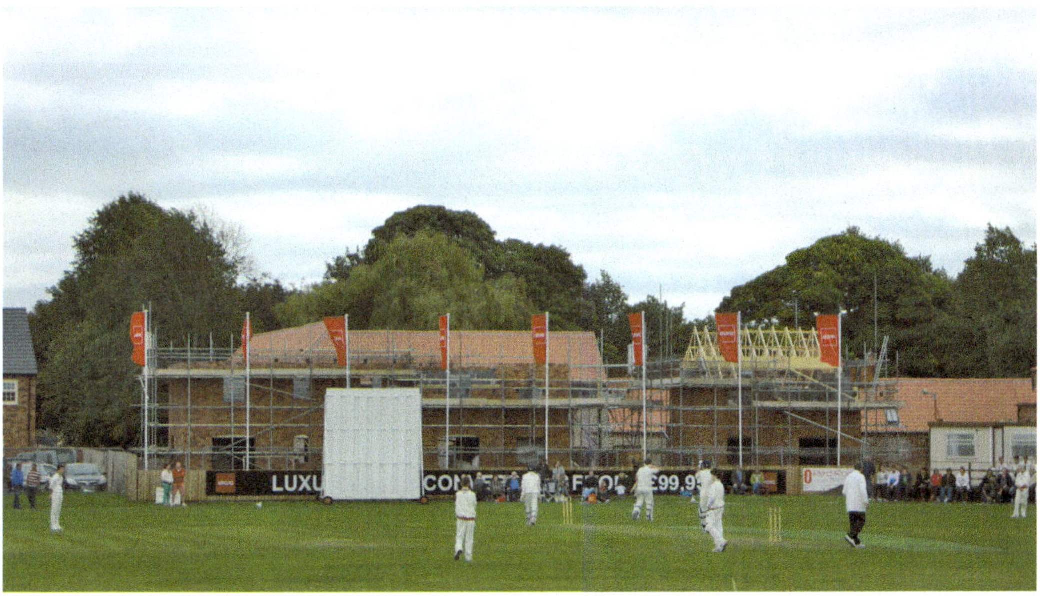

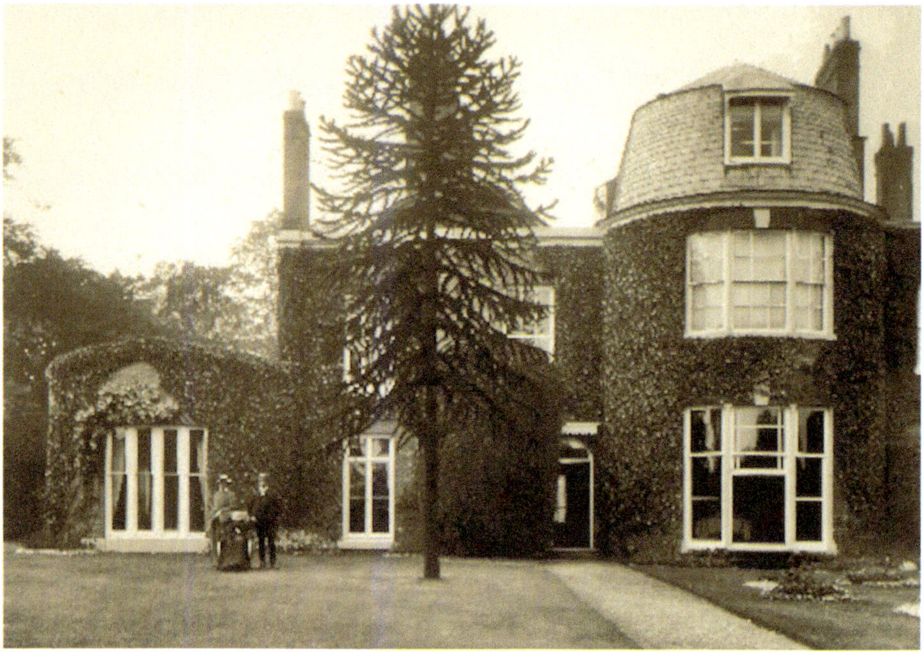

The West, Retford, 1896

The main part of the beautiful hotel was built in 1762. It was purchased in April 2005 by businessman Tony Lavin, who restored the hotel to its former glory by renovating the bedrooms and landscaping the grounds (one of his passions). Mr Lavin sadly passed away in 2011 but the hotel remains in the family, who are continuing to invest and grow the business. The many fine trees in the stunning grounds matured and today include three cedars, several tall beeches, many chestnuts and elms, and the almost legendary tulip tree. Most of these trees are as old as the house. Local books suggest that King George IV stopped and admired the house on a journey from Scotland. This is commemorated by one of the rooms being named 'The Prince Regent Room', now known as the 'Dukeries Suite'.

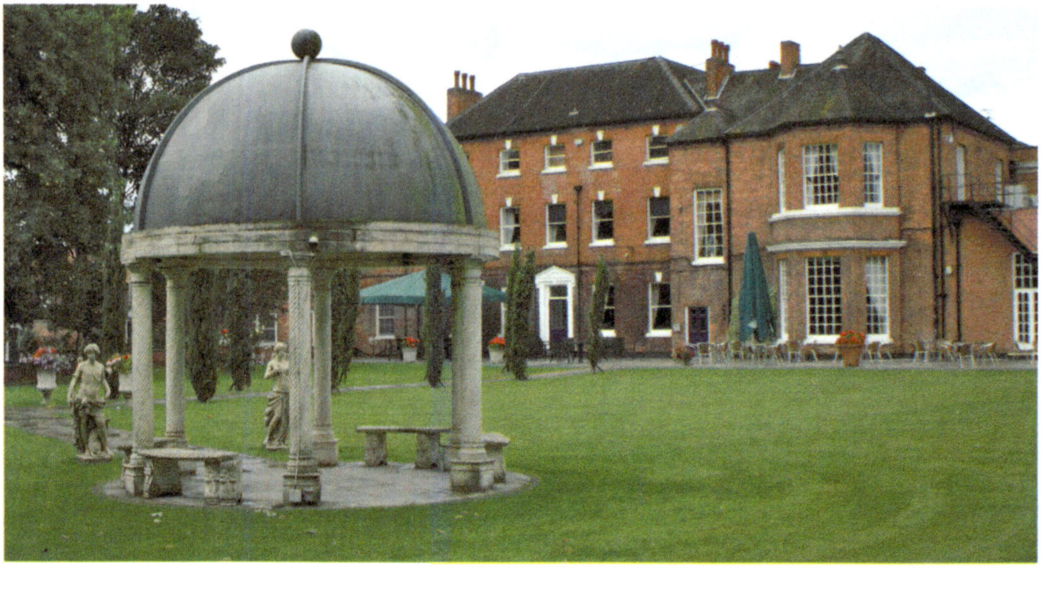

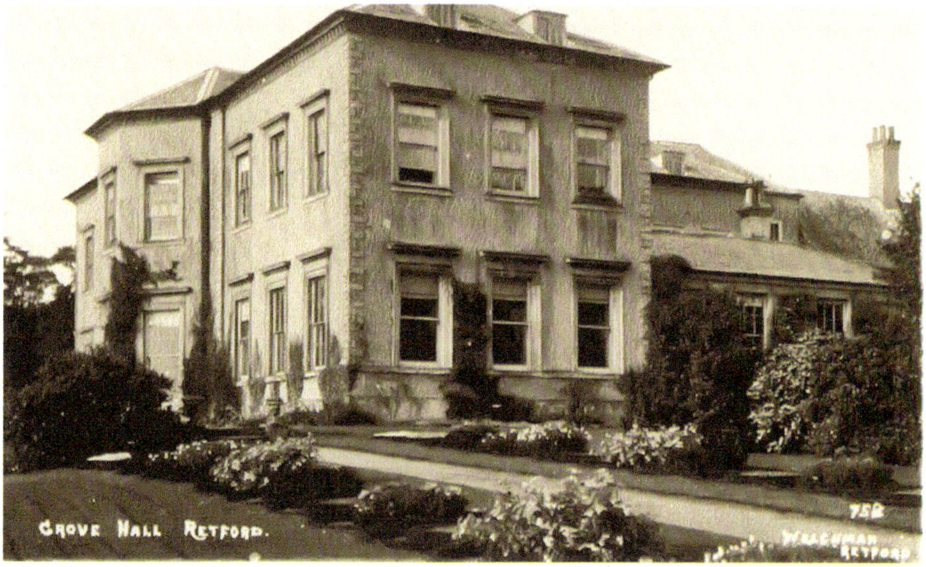

Grove Hall, Grove, 1910

Grove, on the edge of Retford, is steeped in history. Within the precincts of the lovely parish is a wood, generally designated 'Castle Hill Wood', where a castle on a mound formerly stood. The Eyre family came over from Normandy with William the Conqueror. Charles, the third son of Anthony Eyre, was brought up in the church, and became rector of Headon-cum-Upton, and of Grove, and died unmarried. Mr Eyre, after he purchased Grove Hall, entirely altered the character of it, removing the whole of the ancient roof. In making this alteration he took down a stone tower, which must have been built in the time of Queen Elizabeth I, and under it were found a considerable number of coins of that queen's reign. Later, the house came into the possession of the Vernons. Grove Hall was reputed to be one of the best houses in the north of the county and its demolition in 1951 now seems unthinkable.

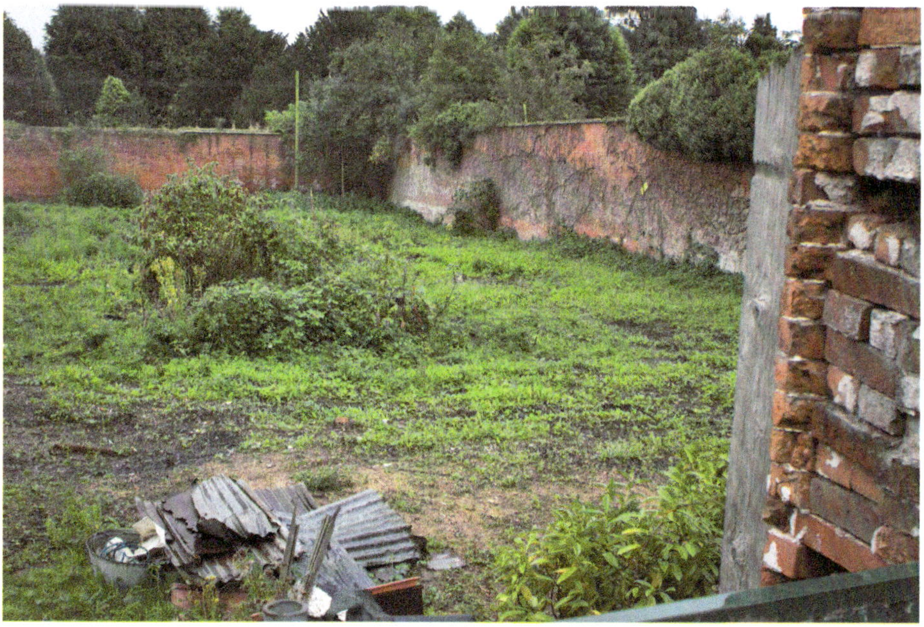

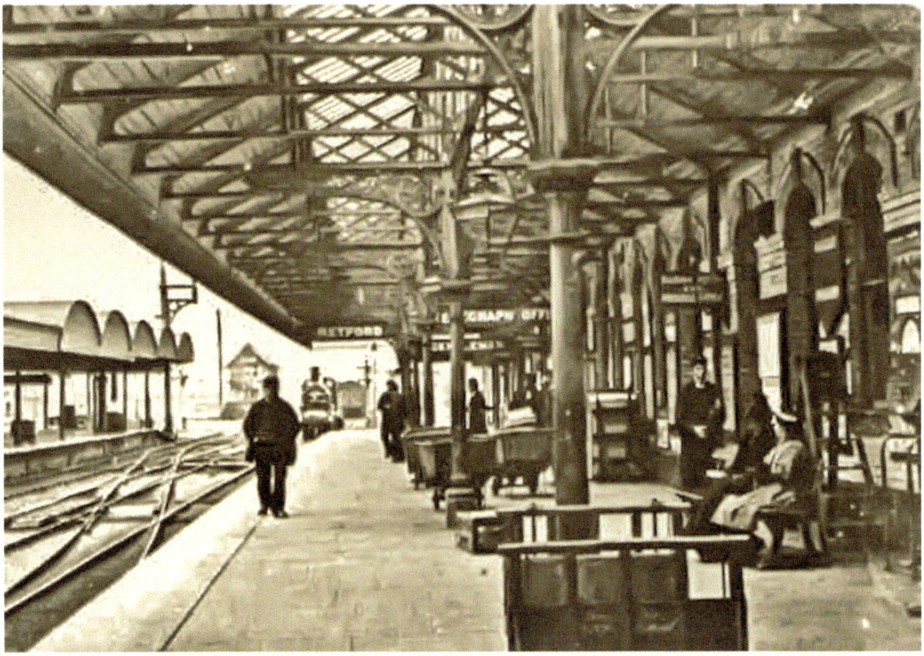

Retford Railway Station, 1894

Retford train station was built in 1849 but the northbound platform was rebuilt in the 1970s. A small part of the Manchester, Sheffield & Lincolnshire Railway station buildings, also dating from 1849, survives in Thrumpton. Retford is served by two railway lines: the East Coast Main Line, which runs between London and Scotland, and the Sheffield to Lincoln Line. Retford station is another jewel in the crown for the town. The former buffet and first class dining room on Platform 1 are currently used as clubrooms by the North Nottinghamshire Railway Society, which has installed a wonderful display of local railway images.

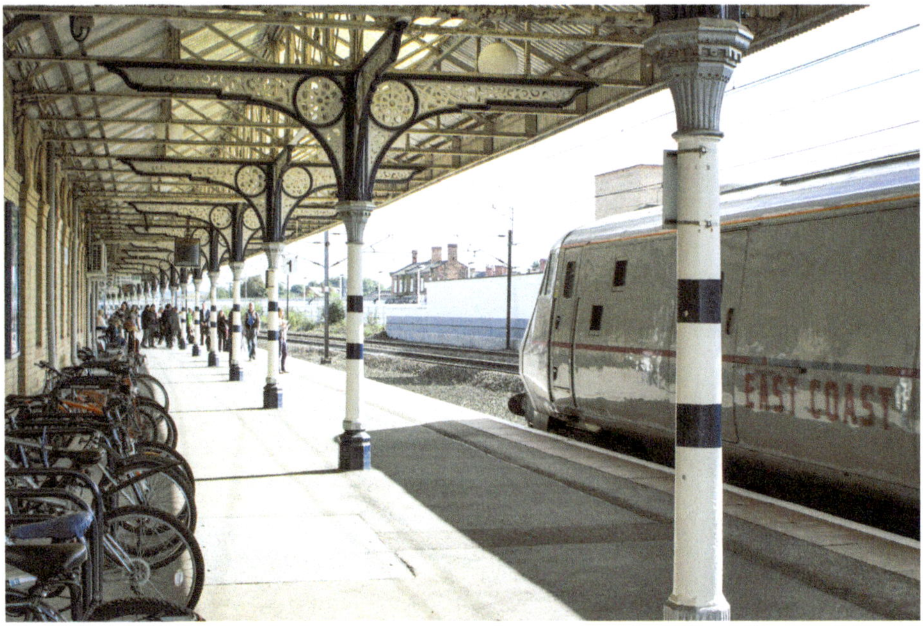

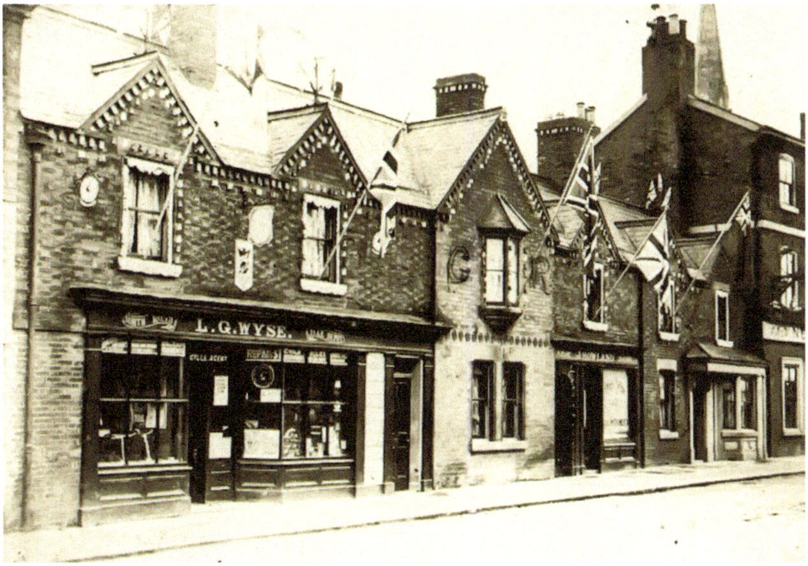

Bridgegate Near West Retford Church, 1911

West Retford is seated on the Great North Road and separated from East Retford by the River Idle. Many of the houses bear the stamp of antiquity. In the old photograph Bridgegate is celebrating the Coronation of George V. The church at West Retford, the spire of which is visible in the photographs, is dedicated to St Michael and was originally a rectory of medieties, founded in the thirteenth century. From early times there was a manor of West Retford belonging to the Hercy family. With the manor went the advowson of the parish church of West Retford. The family resided at the Old Hall, West Retford, which stood on the site of the present Trinity Hospital. The parish church of St Michael the Archangel in West Retford reflects the history of the people of the town from its dedication in 1227 to the present day.

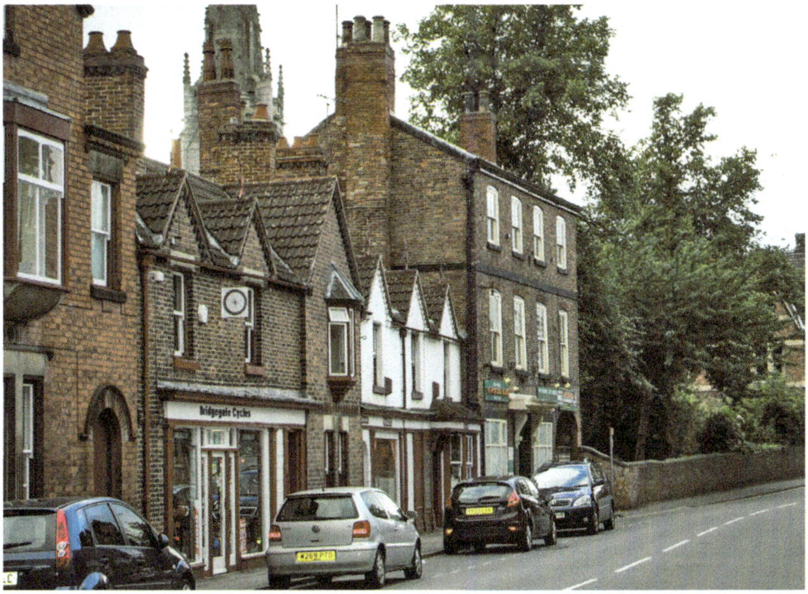

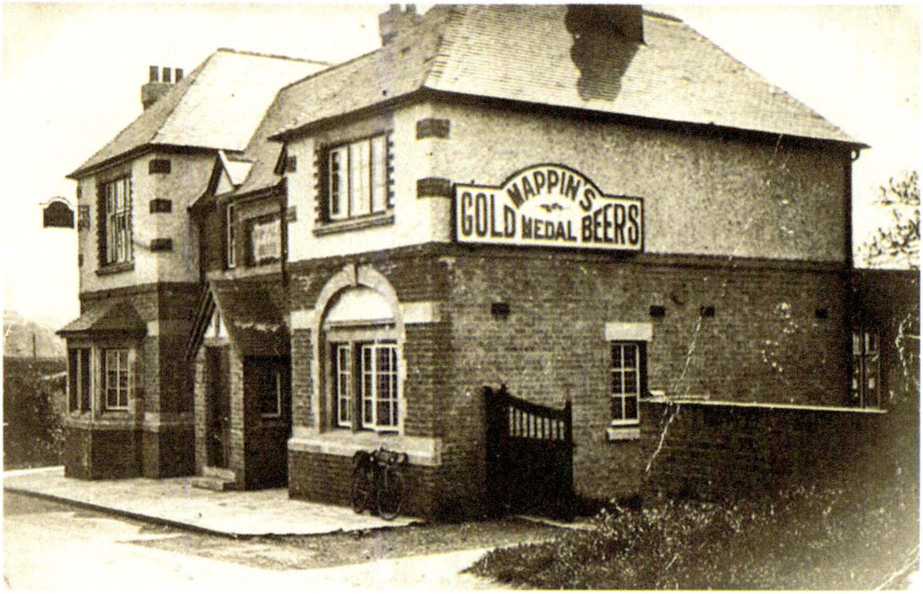

The Hop Pole, 1938

The hop fields have now gone but their influence remains, with the Hop Pole Inn, another fine towpath inn providing great food with tasty homemade chunky chips and drinks for adults and children travelling through or living in Retford. The Hop Pole has seen numerous changes over the years and is now in its best times ever with impressive décor and canal and countryside views – a very relaxing and calming place to sit after a walk down the towpath or a moor of the barge with attentive friendly staff. A hop pole is a tall pole to support the wires on which the hop plant is trained. The hop plant – grown in the fields around the pub – is a vigorous, climbing herbaceous perennial used for particular styles of beer.

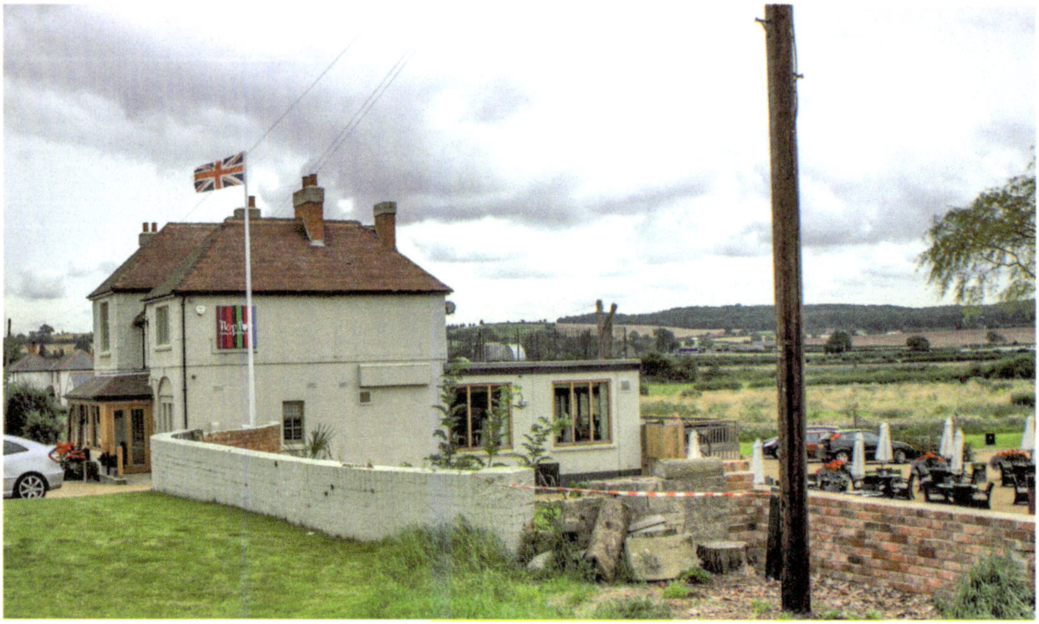

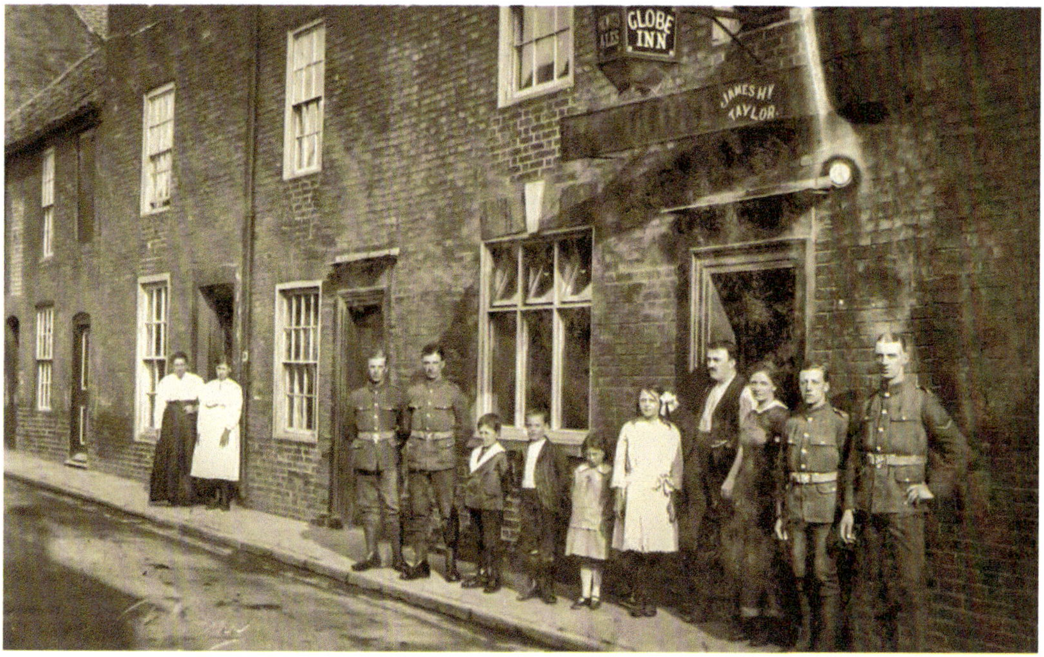

The Globe Inn, 1914

One of the greatest things about doing this book was meeting the local people of Retford who were more than willing to share their knowledge of Retford over time. At the butter market in the town hall I met a lady whose relatives owned the Globe Inn on New Street and she remembers the blue globe ornament from the pub that her family still owns. Retford had a pub on nearly every corner back in the day. Today, the beer pumps have gone and most of New Street has changed into a popular café-style street.

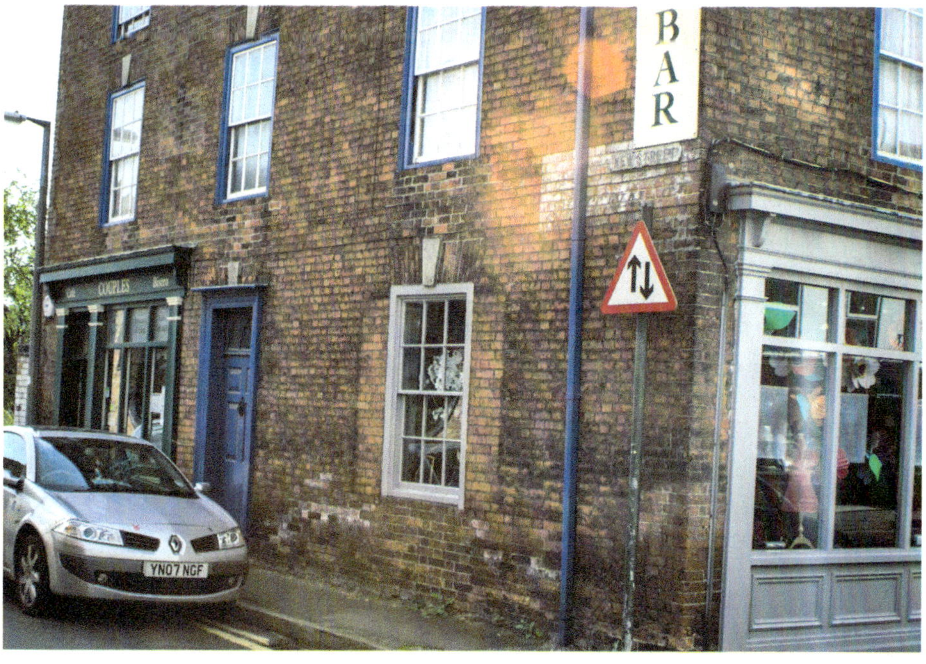

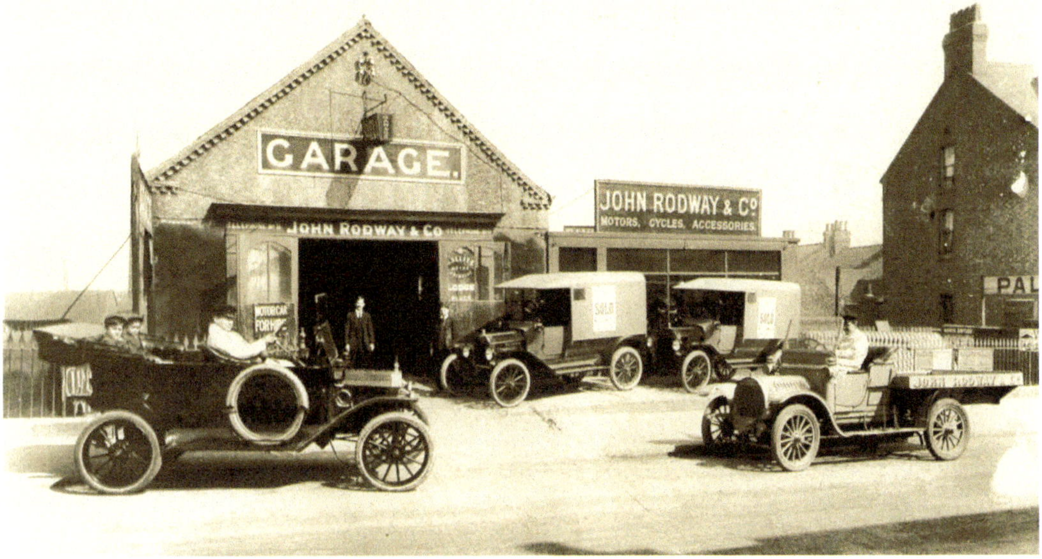

Carolgate Bridge, J. Rodway & Co. Garage, 1910

The Masonic hall of Retford is a beautiful building on a site that has seen many transformations. The Masonic hall is housed in a former cinema originally called the Regent, which was later renamed the Ritz. At that time Retford had four places where moving pictures could be seen. As television tightened its grip, the popularity of the nation's picture houses diminished, and the Ritz closed in 1957. In 1962 the building was offered for sale and was purchased by the Vernon Masonic Lodge for £2,300 and internal alterations were made. To the left stood Retford and Worksop Brewery on Brewery Lane, now part of Aldi's supermarket car park.

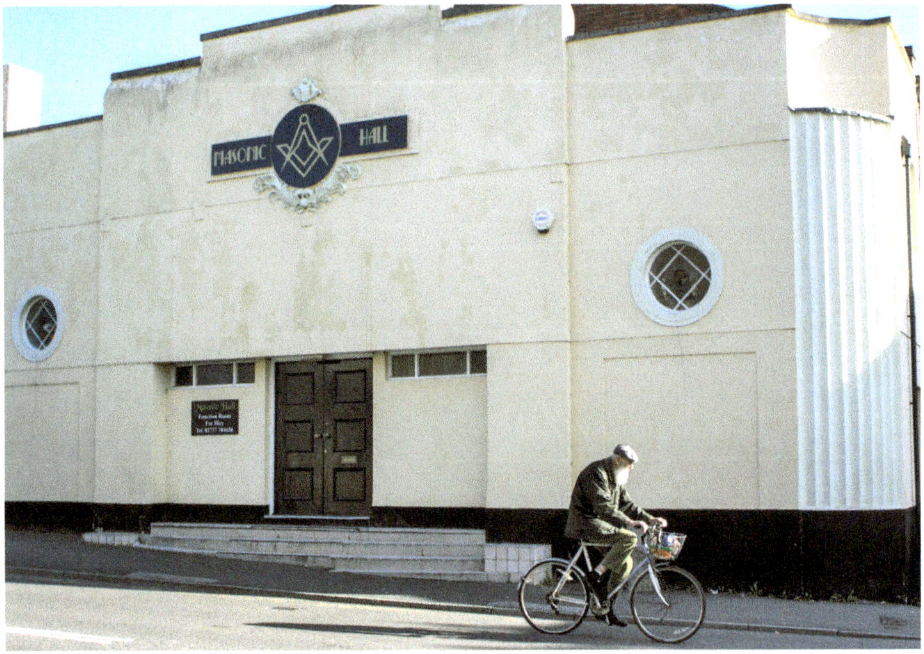

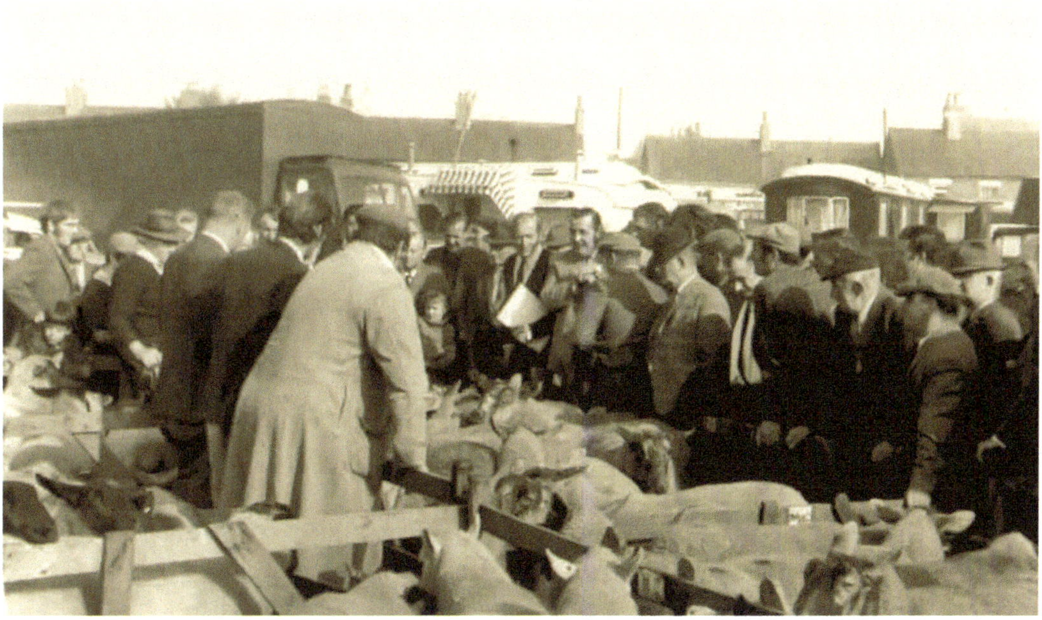

Spa Common Sheep Fair, 1960

It is hard for anyone walking down the pretty towpath of Chesterfield Canal to believe that this green and empty space of Spa Common was once the site of a very popular sheep fair, one in October for four days and another in March for eight days. The fairground visits Retford twice every year, again once in March and once in October, used to be located on the common for a time before re-establishing itself to where itis located this day near Cannon Square. Spa Common is a very popular spot now for dog walkers and is a very attractive, well-kept green space used to access town or to sit and relax.

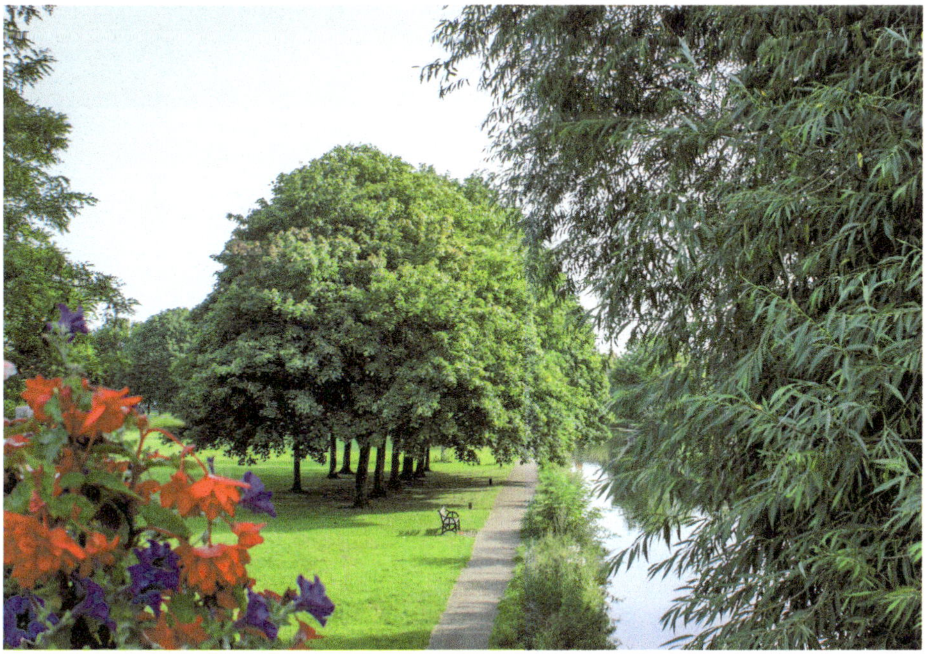

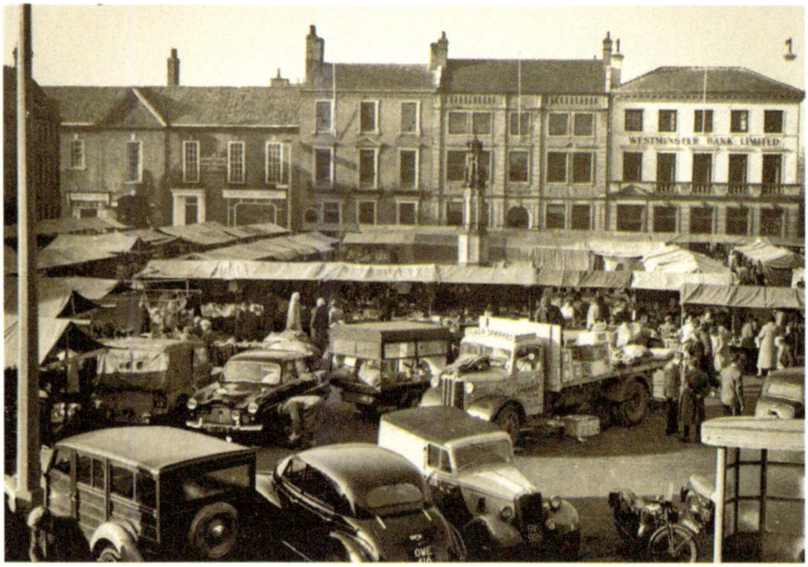

Retford Market Square, 1958

Retford was granted its first charter (the right to hold a fair) by King Henry III in 1246, and this was extended in 1275 by King Edward I to allow a Saturday Market. Retford became an important market town and administrative centre, the market being held in and around the Cannon Square. Fairs were held twice a year and were used to distribute cattle, horses, cheese and hops. Today, the tradition continues. The very popular open-air market is held in the market square each Thursday and Saturday against the backdrop of fine Georgian buildings. On Fridays, browsers can seek out bargains at the Antique and Collectors Market. On the third Saturday of every month, Retford plays host to a popular Farmers' Market where a variety of locally grown produce including fruit and vegetables, jams, meat, honey, ice creams, dairy produce and freshly prepared food and drink is on sale.

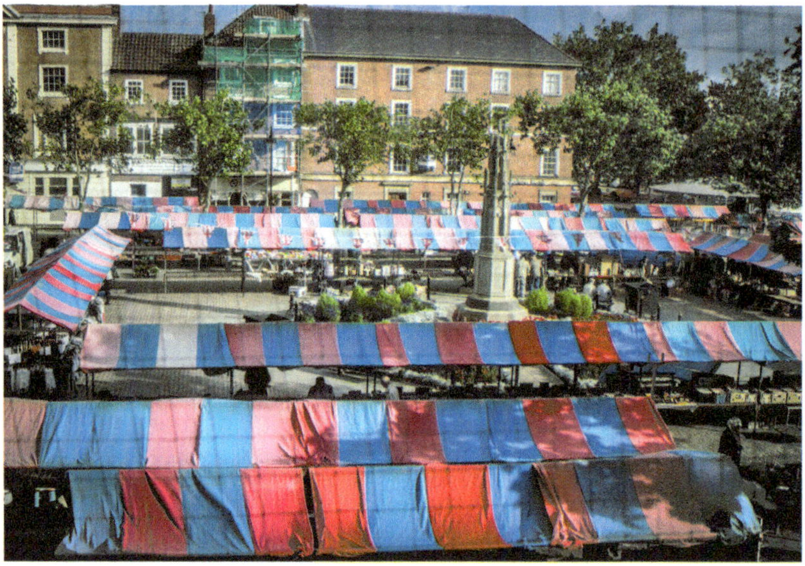

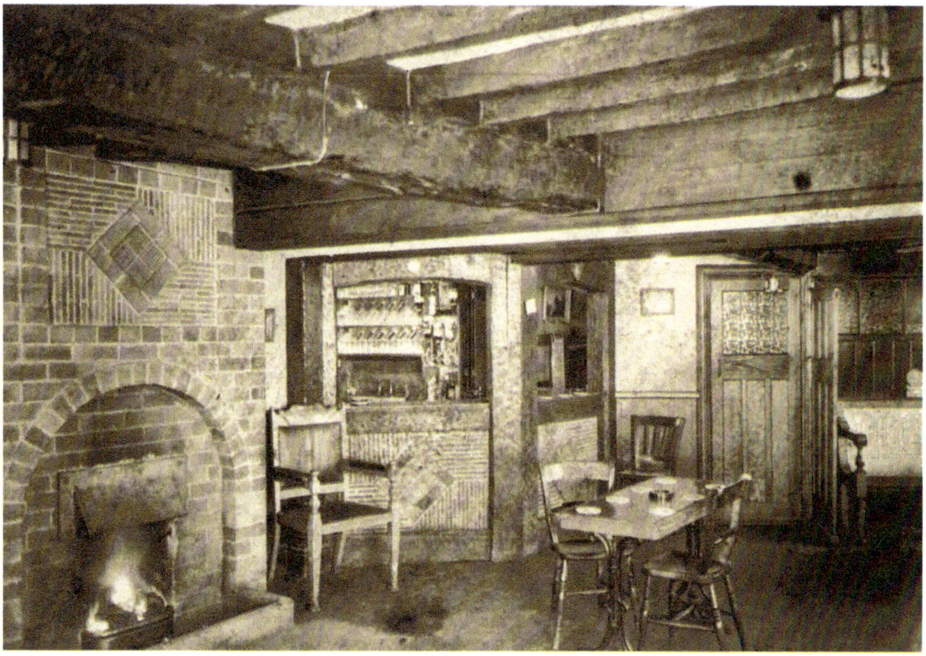

Ye Olde Sun (Interior), 1933

There still remains a great historic charm in the Olde Sun. The timber-framed establishment creates a welcoming atmosphere and once inside you can take a seat by the window and enjoy the equally unspoilt and charming St Swithun's church. The landlord has been in residence for some years and he makes sure to welcome all and offers fine real ales. You can easily imagine a traveller *en route* to London back in the day resting at the bar and feeling just as welcome.

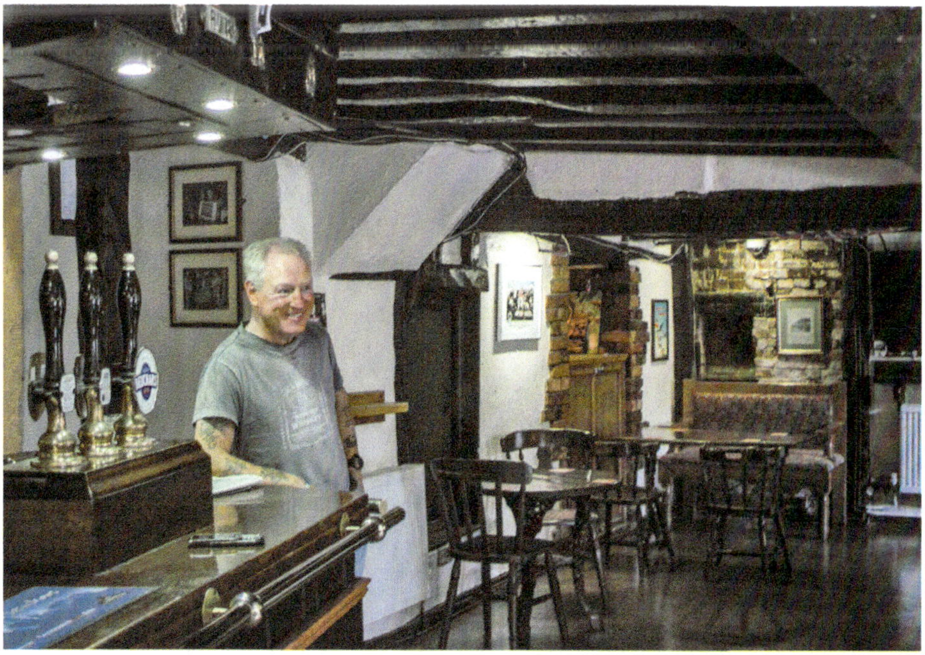

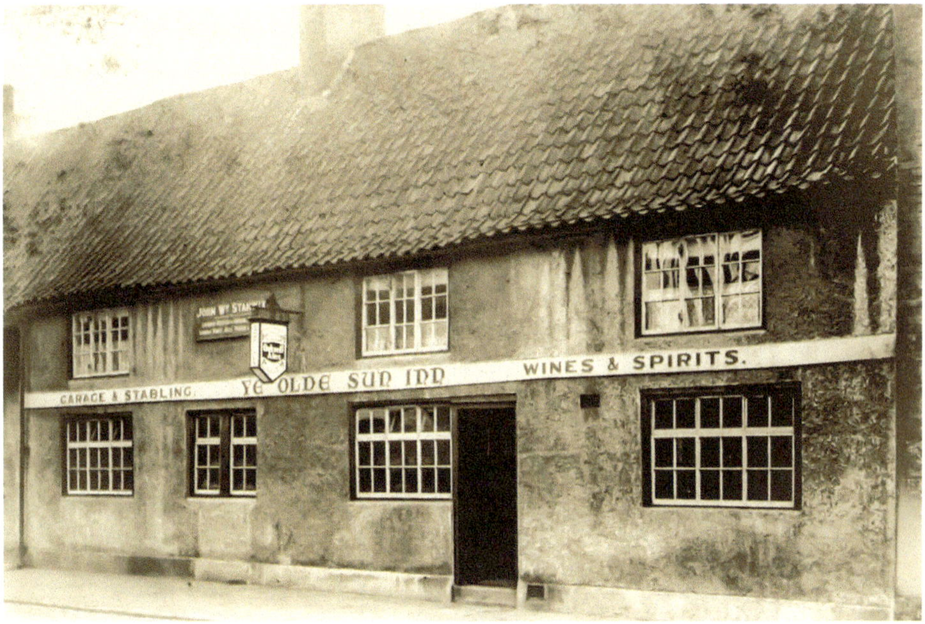

Ye Olde Sun Inn (Exterior), 1933

On Chapelgate is a timber-framed building that dates back to the sixteenth century. The inn sits nearby what was once the principal inn called the Crown, which was used for a wide range of business administrative purposes. It is now a modern bar called Yates's. The Great North Road was routed through Retford in 1777, which brought travellers and merchants to the market town. They needed somewhere to stay so coaching inns were built near the market square beside banks and shops. Ye Olde Sun remains a very popular Retford public house and a definite stop-off on any night out.

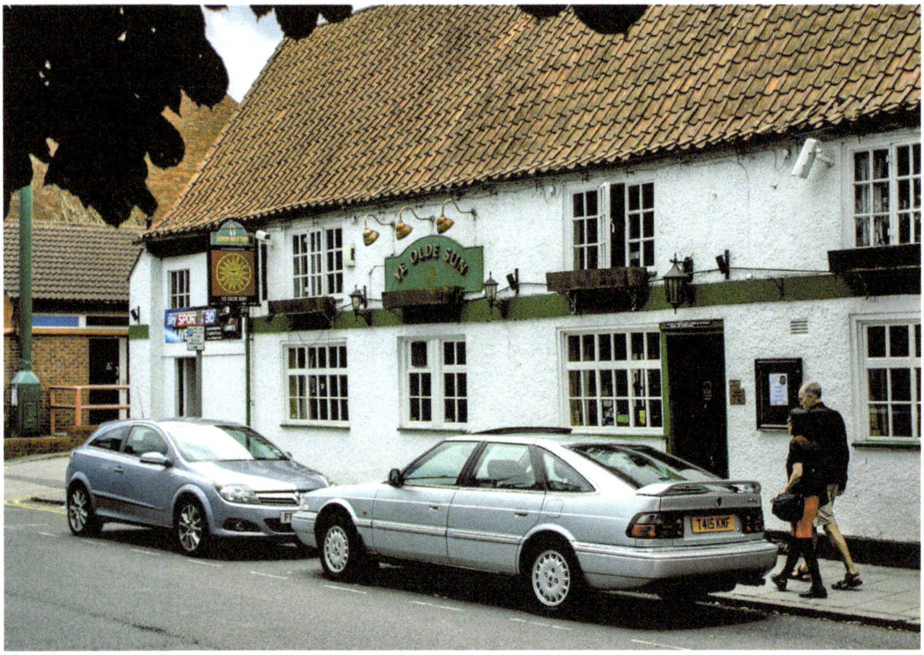

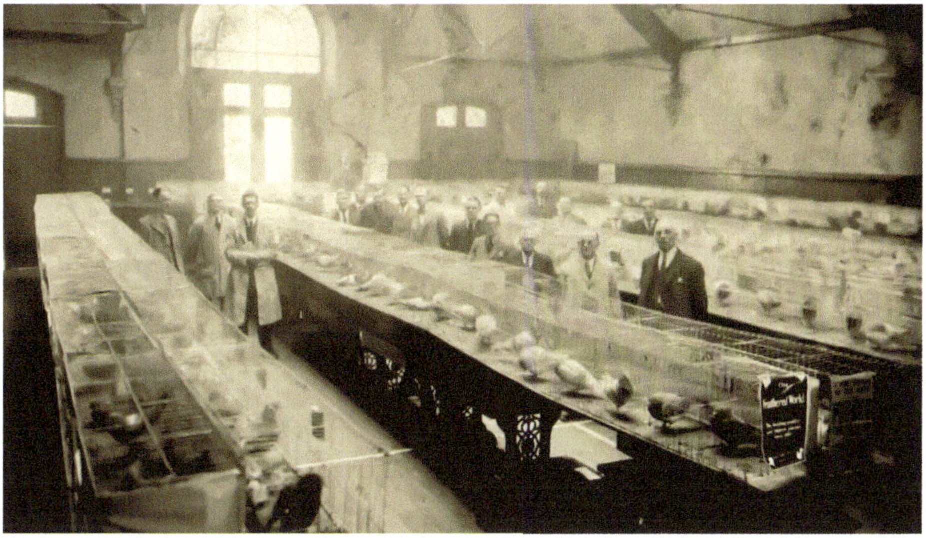

The Corn Exchange, 1932 Pigeon Show

In 1868 the municipal buildings of Retford were erected, namely the town hall, court house, corn exchange and butter market, at a cost of about £11,000. During the process of putting this book together I relied on the help and the knowledge of the elders of the town, who meet up on a Thursday at the butter market, and they educated me about the good old days of the corn exchange. In 1887, John Bartholomew's *Gazetteer of the British Isles* described East Retford like this: 'East Retford is a well-built town with a spacious market place in the centre, an handsome town hall, a corn exchange, and a grammar school. It carries on a considerable trade in horses, cattle, cheese, and hops. The industrial establishments include iron foundries and paper mills.' Sadly, the corn exchange is no more, hence the modern photograph I have paired with the old image is the rear view of what would have been the adjacent building – the old courthouse. One can see the history in this beautiful architecture. The building itself is no longer used but I hope they do not knock this one down too. For this photograph, I am standing where the corn exchange once stood, now the backyard of local small businesses and Costa coffee. Among Welchman's photographs this one of the pigeon show is one of my favourites.

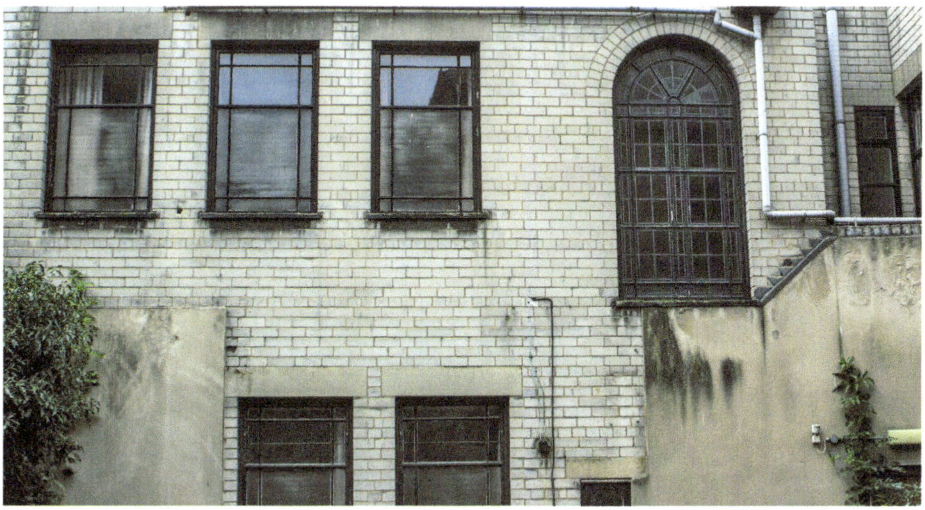

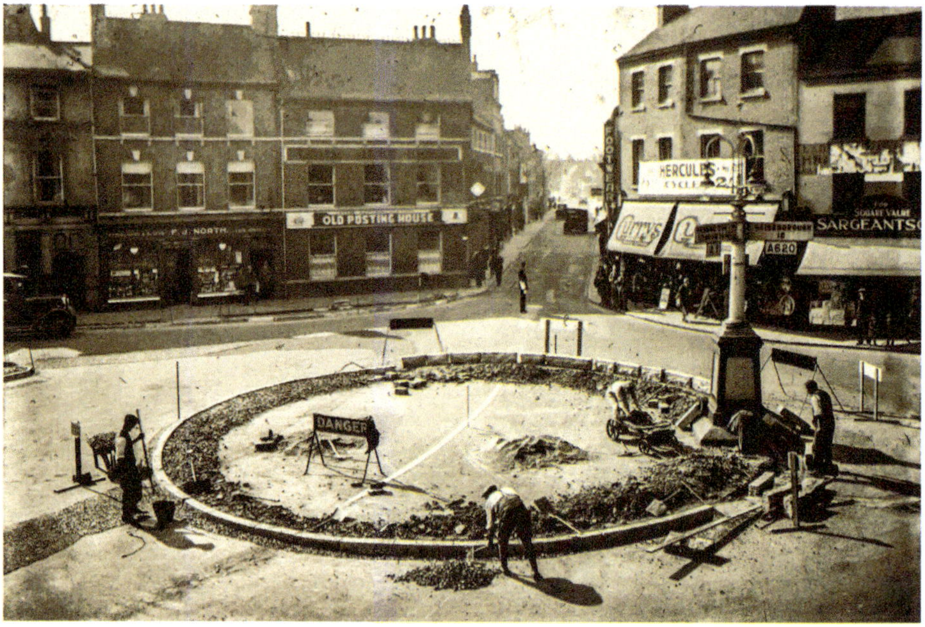

A New Roundabout for Retford, 1934

The main road to Scotland ran through Retford along Bridgegate, past the posting house at the White Hart Hotel and along Carolgate to London Road. The hotel is seen here boarded up and is currently in new hands, due to reopen in December 2012, which is great news for the town. The new roundabout, although taking away some of the charm of the open roads, was imperative to control the increase in traffic volume coming through the market town, although eventually Carolgate would be pedestrianised altogether and the Great North Road would end here with traffic diverted around the edge of the town.

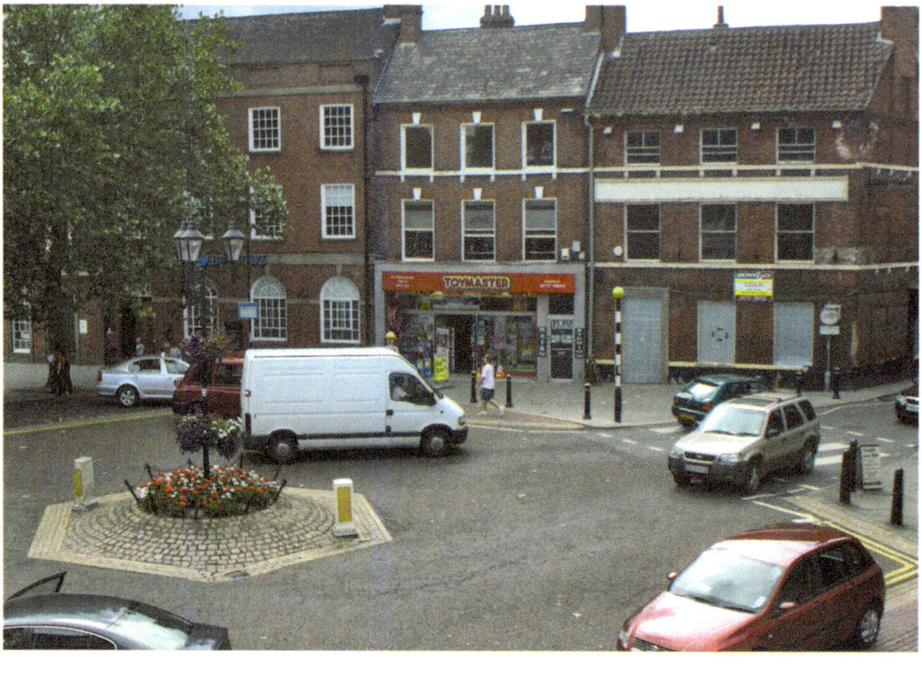

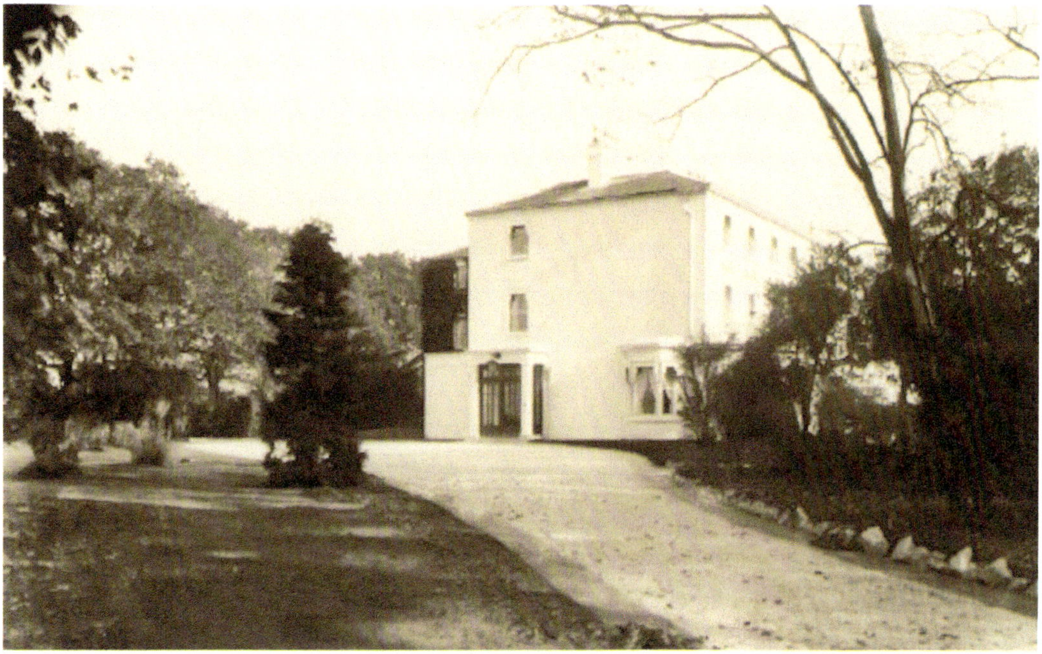

Eaton Hall College, Jamia Al-Karam, 1900

This was a Georgian country house which was later extended and used as a teacher training college, then a private school. Today the hall is called Jamia Al-Karam and it is a Muslim boarding school and Islamic Studies College, which was established in 1985 by Muhammad Imdad Hussain Pirzada to cater for the education of British Muslims. It is affiliated to the University of Al-Azhar in Cairo, Egypt. Graduates of Jamia Al-Karam are offered admission into the third year of the university's BA degree courses. In 1995, Pirzada launched a new project, the Al-Karam secondary school, a boarding school providing education up to GSCE level in an Islamic atmosphere. The school achieves very high results.

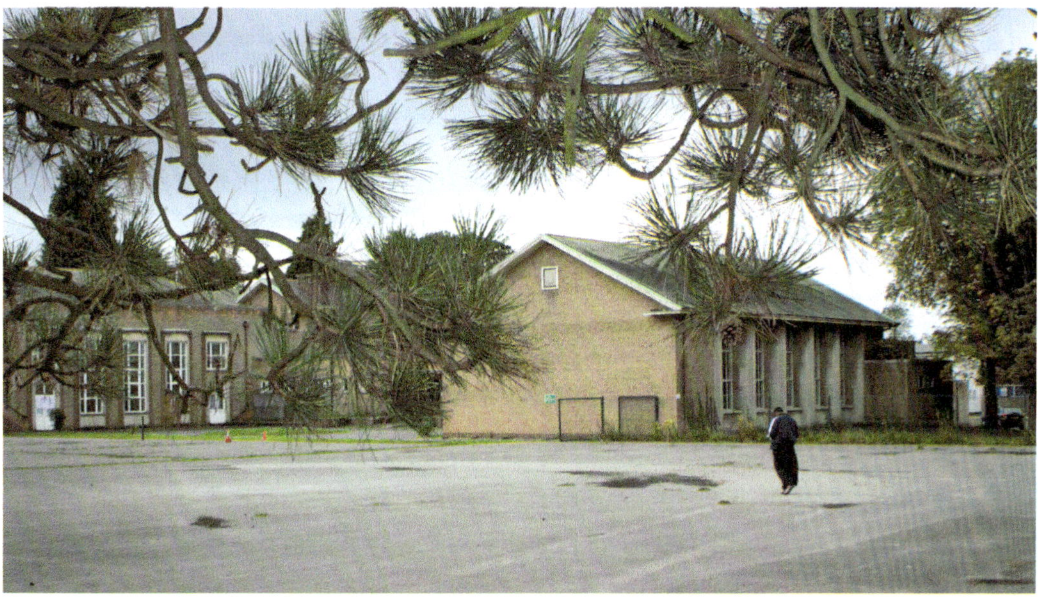

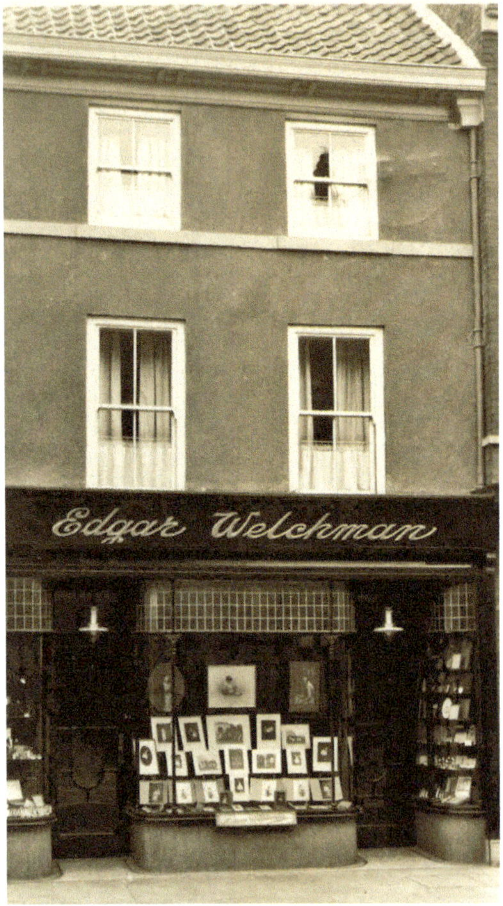

Edgar Welchman's Photography Shop, Grove Street, 1921

Many people had their portraits taken here. Bassetlaw Museum further up the street, formerly Amcott House, purchased and digitised 20,000 negatives taken by professional photographers Edgar Welchman & Son of Grove Street, Retford, between 1910 and 1960. All of the old photographs in this book have been taken by this wonderful photographer. The Trade Directory of 1864 details nine commercial photographers in Retford; Edgar, who set up his studio in town in 1904, and Percy Laws, who opened his studio in 1923, among them. Their diligent and extensive photography and knowing when they were in business help when trying to date the old photographs. Today Edgar's huge shop is a second-hand clearance furniture shop, although one day I shall return it to a photography studio.

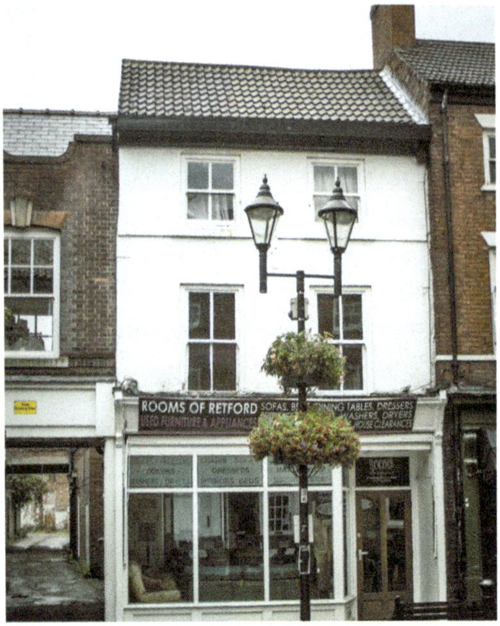

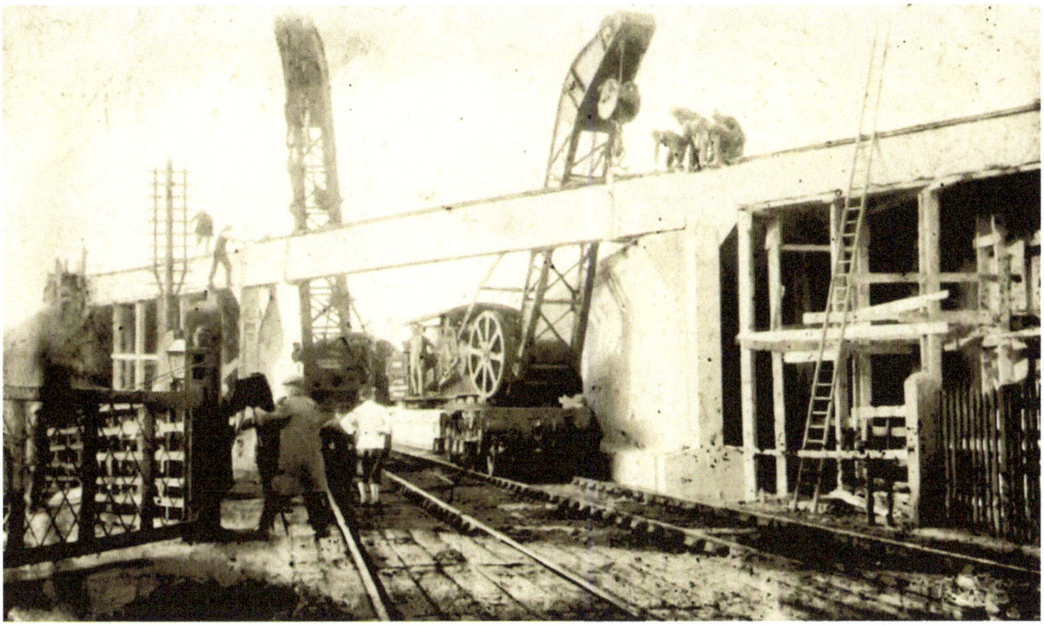

The Building of Babworth Railway Bridge, 1928

You enter Retford over Babworth Road rail bridge. Babworth signal box was situated on the LNER and, before Babworth bridge was built, the box controlled the mechanical gates on the main road between Babworth and Retford. The bridge was built on 11 February 1937. This would then divert the main road away from the railway and eventually see Babworth crossing closed and the closure of the signal box. In 1923 a rail crash occurred 340 yards south of the signal box.

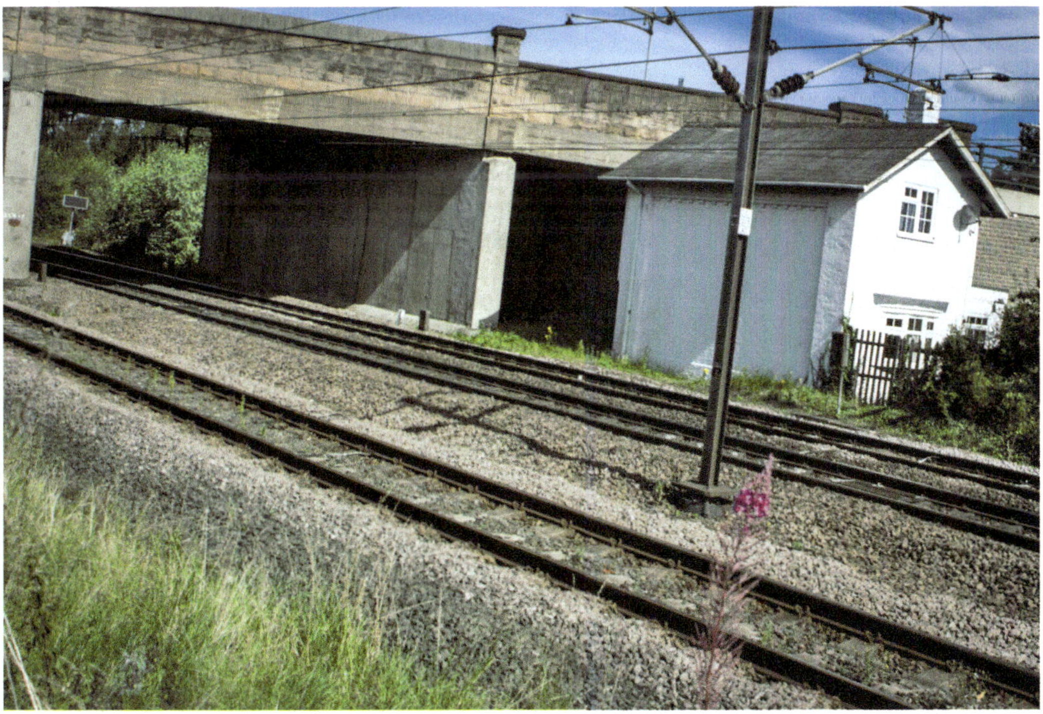

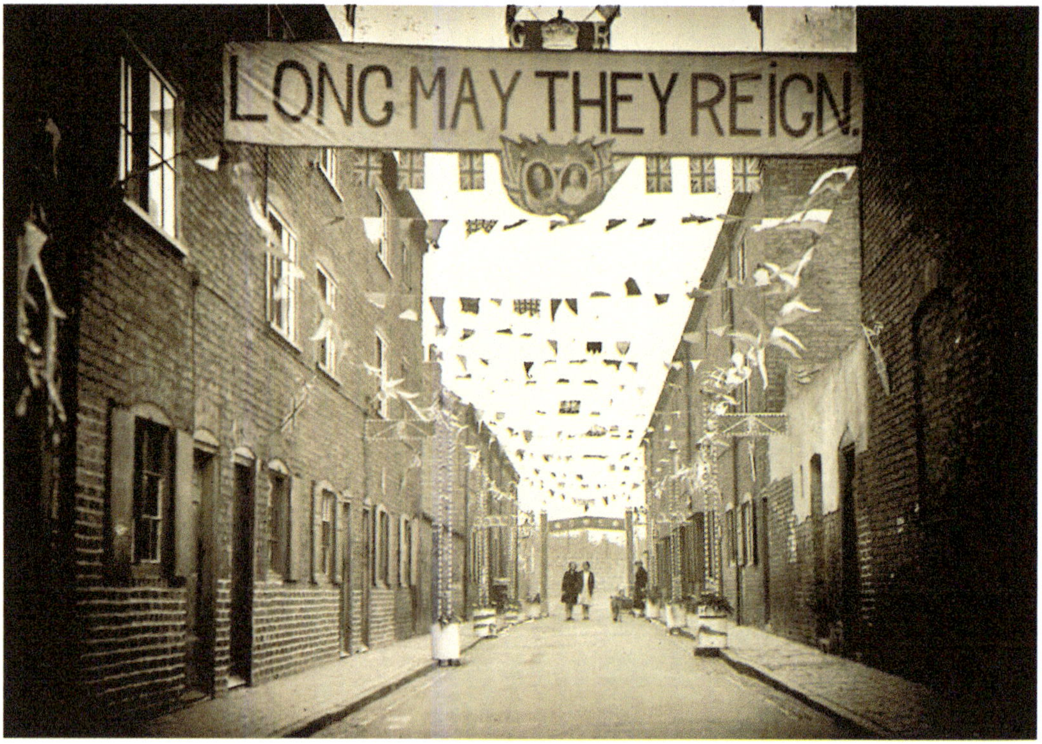

Wellington Street, 1937

This pair of images is of Wellington Street on Spital Hill. The two images differ as there have been significant changes to the town planning of this area of Retford. As you will see, both sides of Terrace Street have been knocked down. One side is a block of new urban flats and to the left is a garage. The old image displays beautifully Wellington Street decorated to celebrate the coronation of George VI.

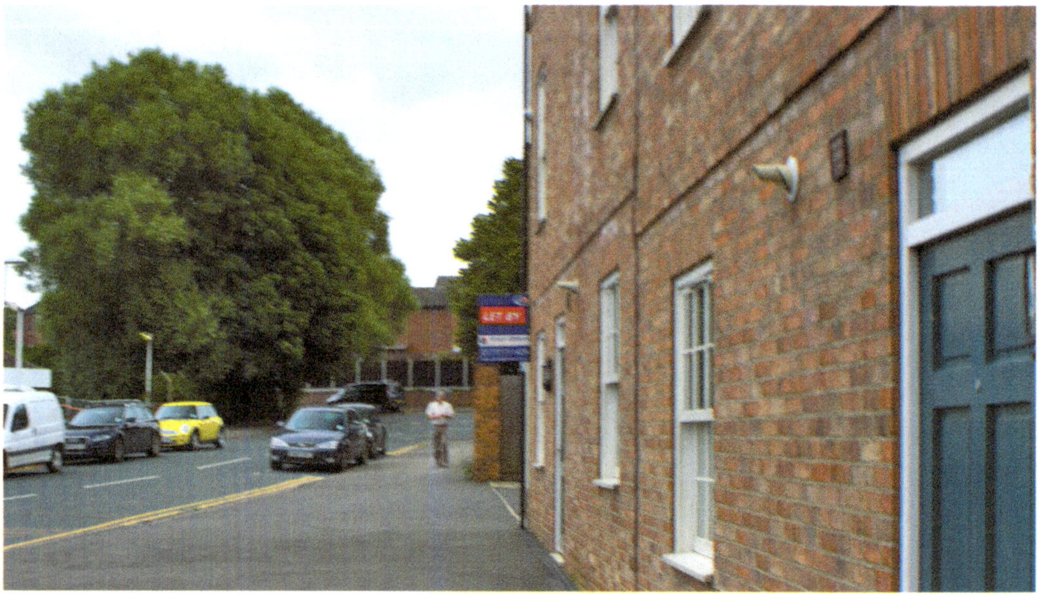

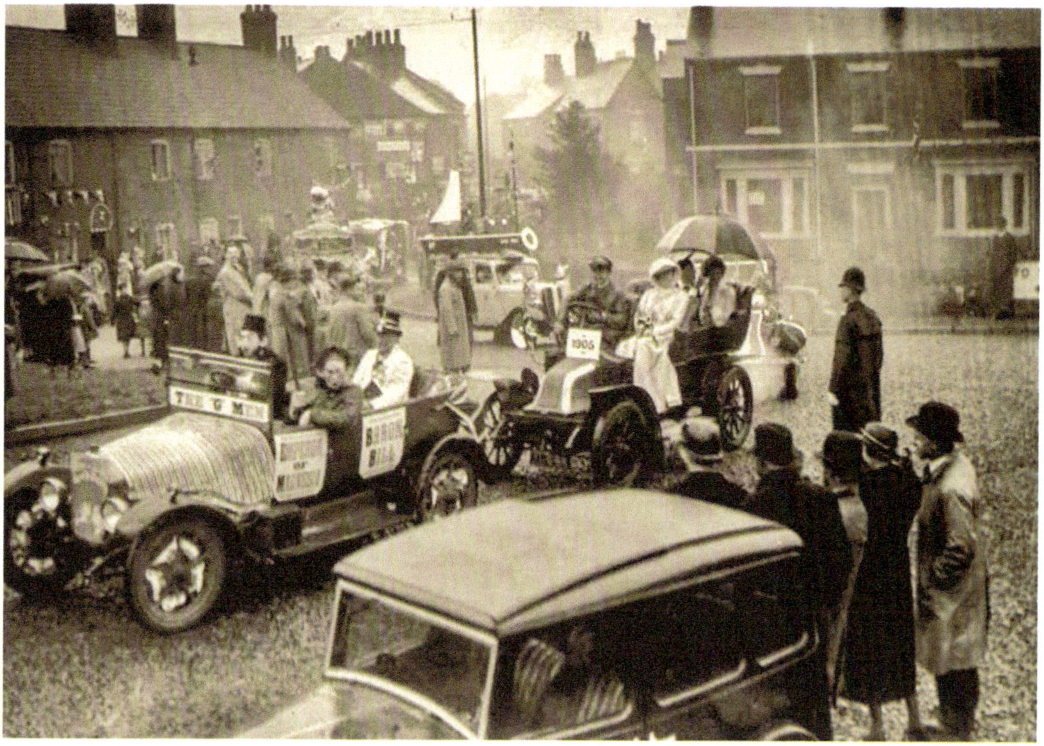

Queen Street and Babworth Road, 1937

Retford people celebrate the Coronation of King George VI. Retford really 'went to town' during this time of festivities with parties and gardens, canals and churches lit up with candles and fireworks, and even naming the town's park Kings' park in 1938. Queen Street is the road leading from the A620 Babworth Road to Retford railway station in the area known as West Field close to the East Coast Main Line. I cannot pass this road now without imagining this wonderful scene – what a great day they must have all had.

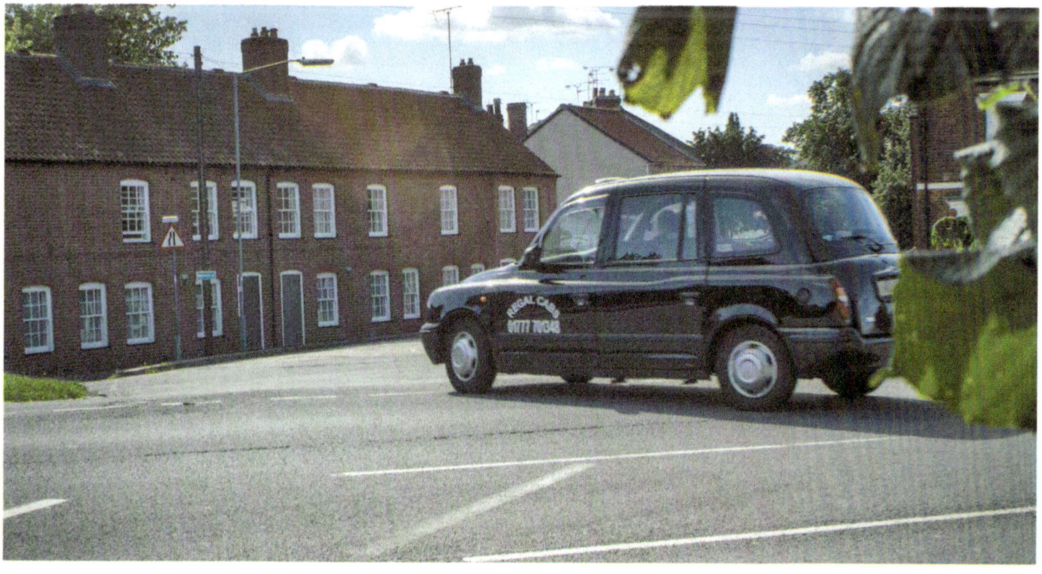

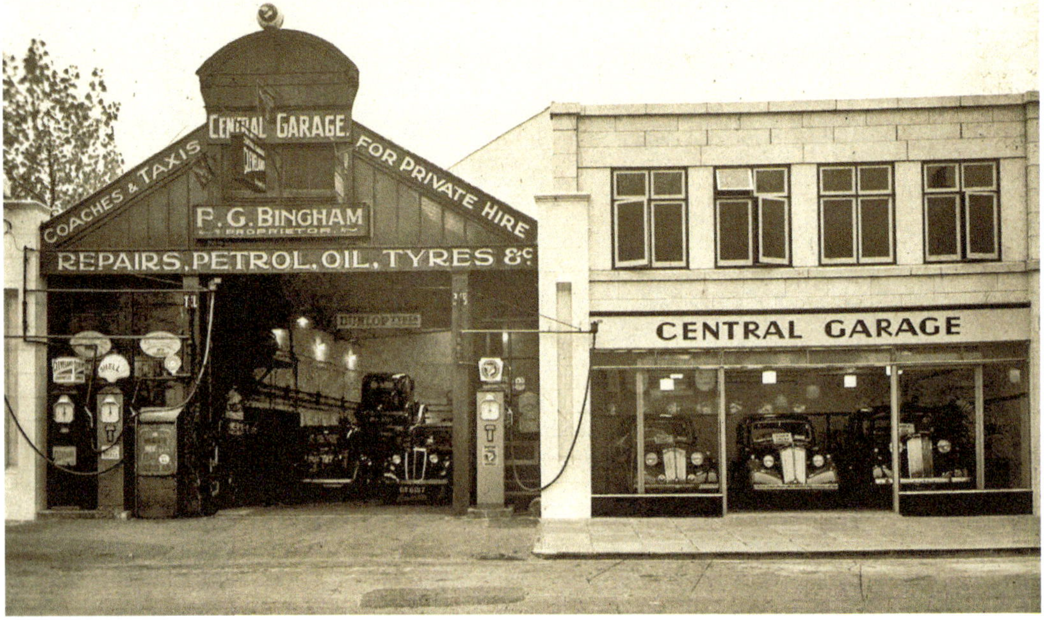

Central Garage, Grove Street, 1937

Owned by P. G. Bingham, this garage hired out taxis and coaches. Grove Street was a very busy thriving area of Retford with hotels, coaching inns, a sawmill, cafés and shops. It was the gateway to the market and on market day Grove Street would have been full of coaches, carriages and horses. Indeed today on market day it is very busy with people and traffic. What used to be the Central Garage has seen many changes over the years from a supermarket to a popular public house today. Indeed it is these larger, cheaper public houses that have challenged the smaller 'corner of the street' privately owned pubs. The big breweries win every time sadly to the detriment of the community.

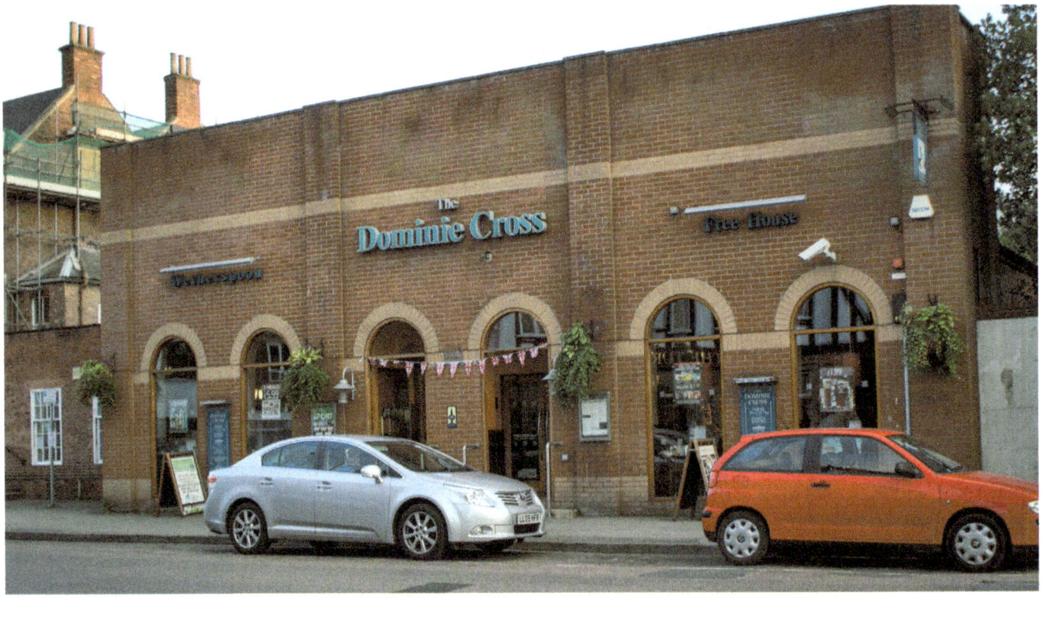

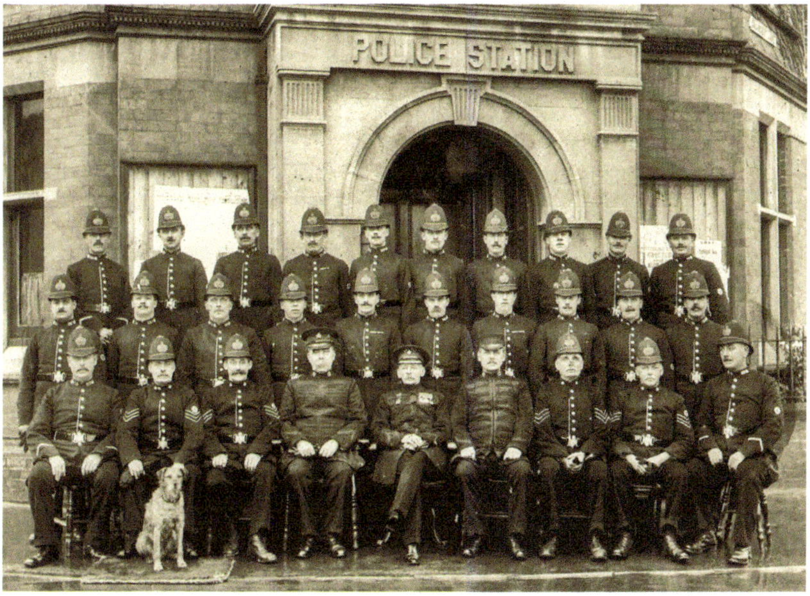

Retford Police Station, Exchange Street, 1920

Policing in Nottinghamshire started in 1840, although separate town-based forces in Nottingham, Newark-on-Trent and Retford had existed since 1836. The following year, in 1841, Nottinghamshire absorbed Retford Borough Police. By the turn of the century the county force had 200 officers, including nine inspectors and twenty-seven sergeants. In 1914, with the outbreak of the First World War imminent, the first Nottinghamshire special constables were appointed. Five years later the force in Nottingham, which was now a city, recruited its first woman constable, although the first women to serve in the county police were not appointed until 1946. In 1932 the city force was the first in the country to introduce walkie-talkie radios, and another innovation came the following year with the opening of the first forensic science laboratory in a provincial police force. Retford townspeople have seen the local police station pass through many transitions over the decades and, excuse the pun, witnessed a more truncated service. As it stands the station operates, 10 a.m. to 6 p.m., Monday to Friday.

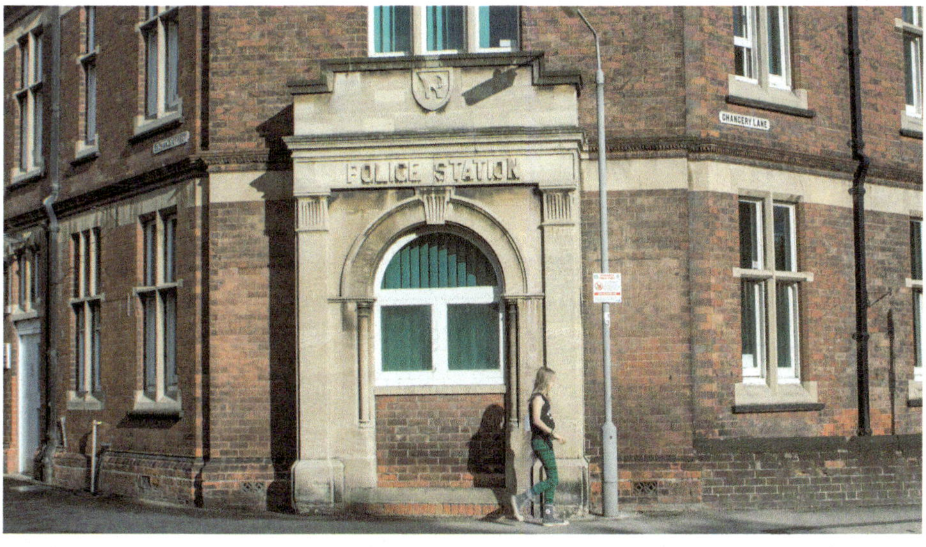

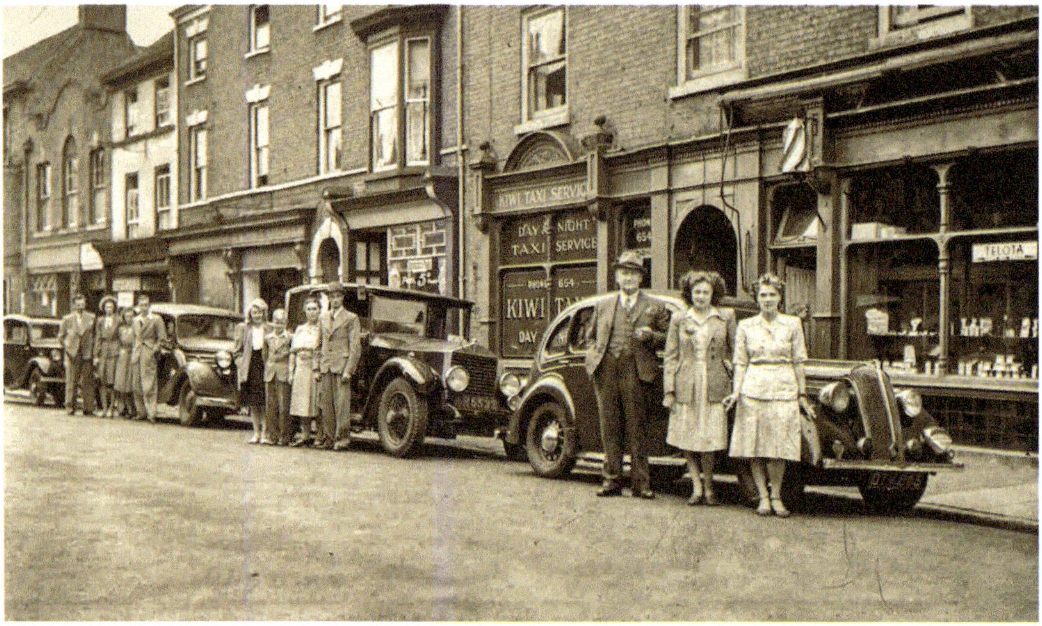

Row of Taxis on Grove Street, 1947

Retford has a number of thriving taxi services. They no longer gather here as seen in the old photograph but in the taxi rank next to what will soon be the newly refurbished and reopened White Hart Hotel. The modern Grove Street has large pavements with young trees. Some people still find this an inviting place to park, so it is difficult to get a photograph of Grove Street without any traffic.

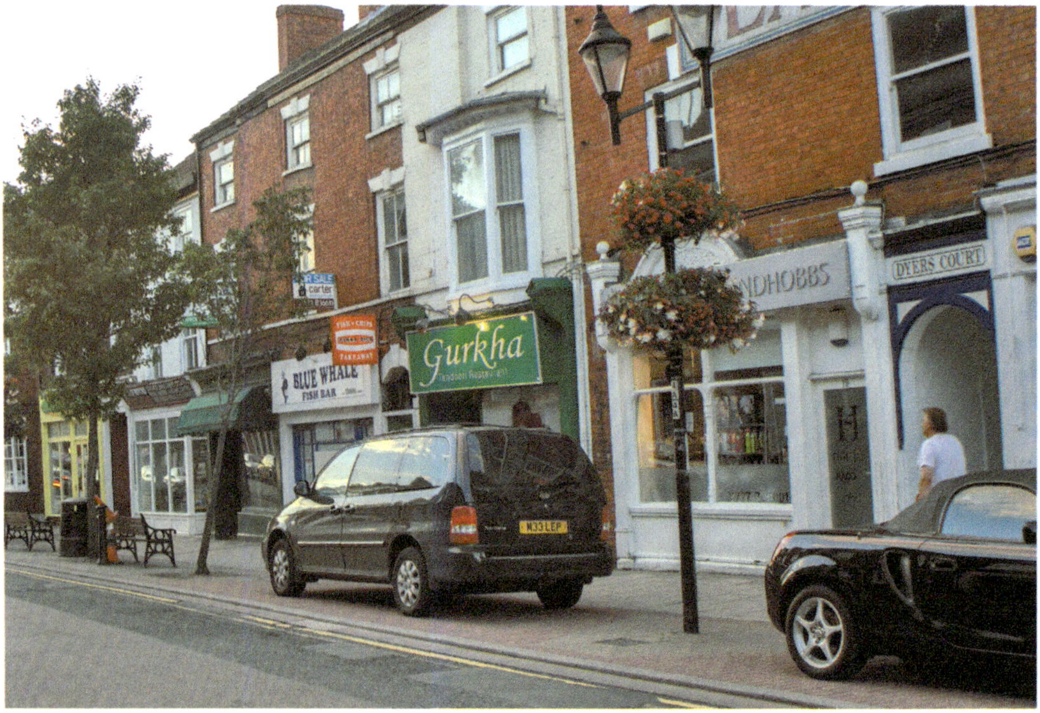

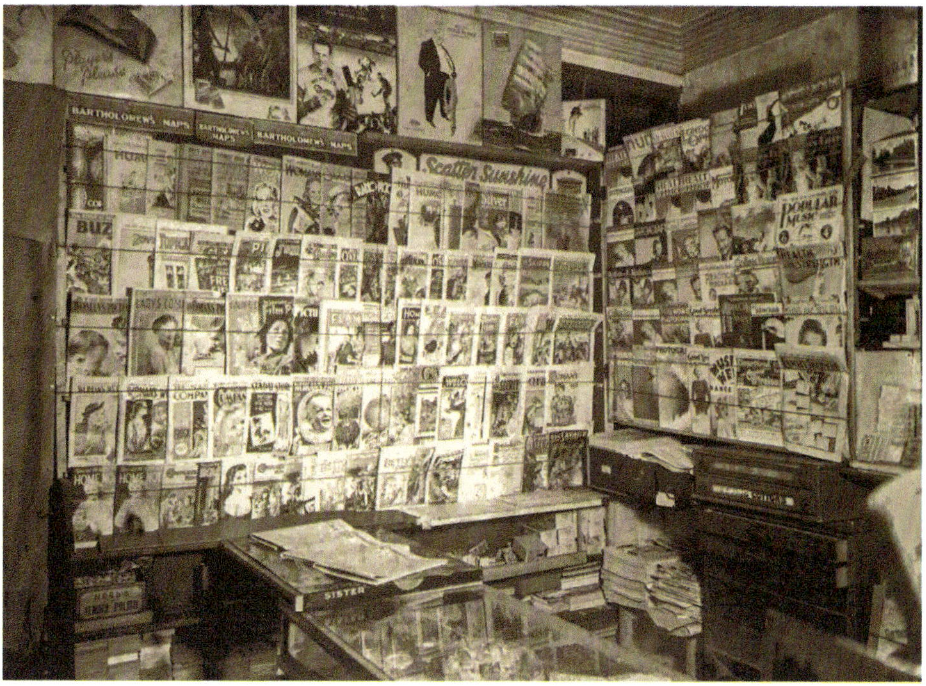

Bowskill's Shop, 1933

Billy Bowskill's shop sold comics, sweets and you could always get a firework. At the rear of the shop was a children's play area, which now has been converted into flats. Bowskill's was a very popular shop with children *en route* to school, and it was a sad day when it finally closed down in the 1980s. Today the premises are a thriving modern hairdressing salon called Reflections and the employees talk fondly of the Billy Bowskill days.

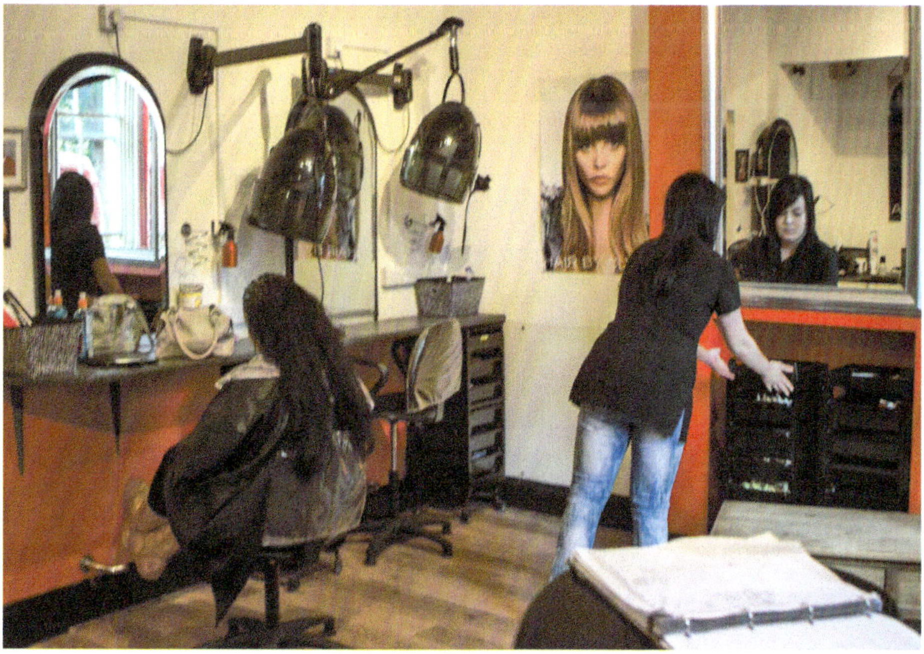

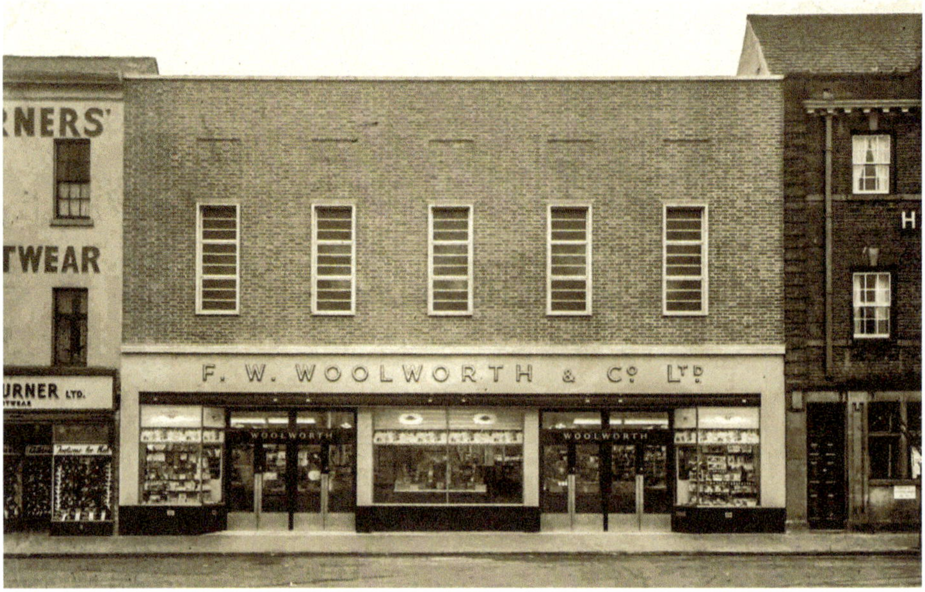

Woolworth's, 1956

This shop needs no introduction as most of us grew up around a Woolworth's or have heard of the Woolworth family. Today the shop is a competitively priced clothing and household goods store falling in line with the new shops taking over in Retford. People in the town argued that a Marks & Spencer's may have been more welcomed than another bargain supermarket, but it never happened and more old buildings were knocked away for the latter. Retford currently has four major supermarkets and numerous smaller ones. The day of the independent family grocer and butcher is seriously under threat – in fact the town grocer is no more. Maybe town planning should consider community spirit when making their important decisions.

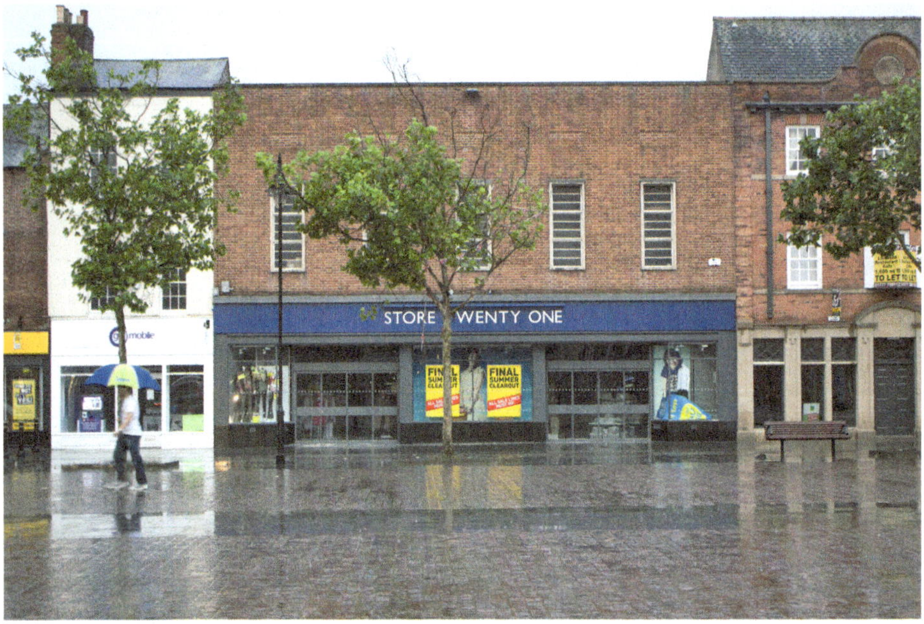

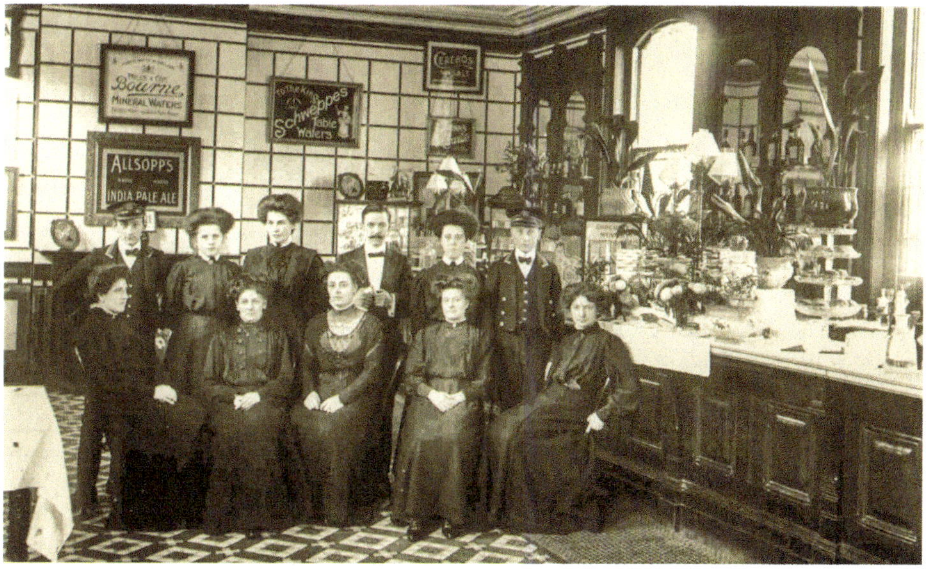

Retford Railway Refreshment Staff, 1910

The first railway into Retford was the Sheffield & Lincolnshire Junction Railway, which opened on 16 July 1849, and the Great Northern Railway line from Doncaster arrived on 4 September the same year. The former buffet and first class dining room on Platform 1 are currently used as clubrooms for the Bassetlaw (North Notts) Railway Society. The club has installed wonderful display of local railway images in the windows of the rooms and Retford station hosts some marvellous old black-and-white photographs and their modern equivalent. Michael Palin of Monty Python fame recalls frequently visiting Retford station as a youngster for trainspotting as it was in easy reach of his home town Sheffield, and provided access to legendary locomotives like the *Flying Scotsman,* running on the East Coast Main Line of the former LNER. Retford train station still holds its historic charm and is definitely worth a visit, and being only 168½ miles north of King's Cross it was and still remains a very popular and pretty station.

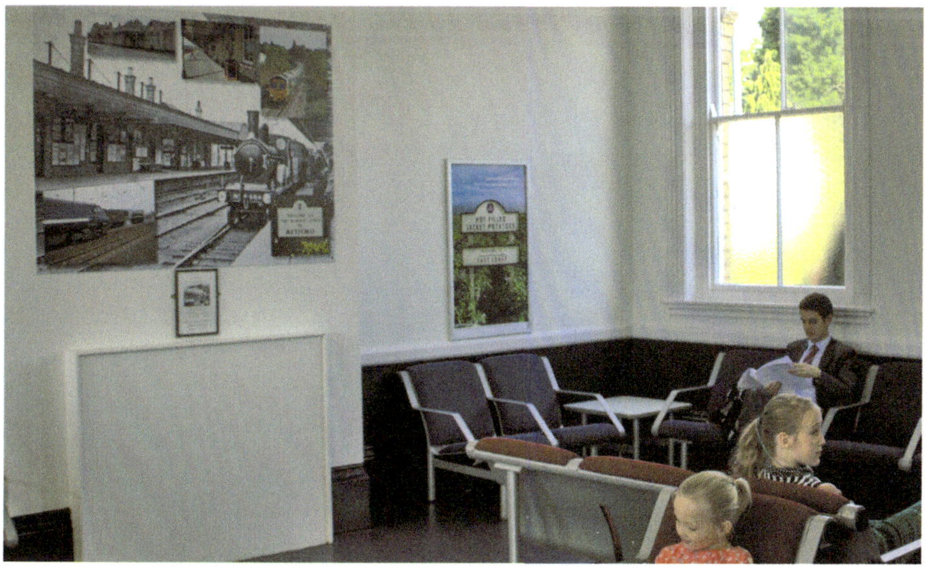

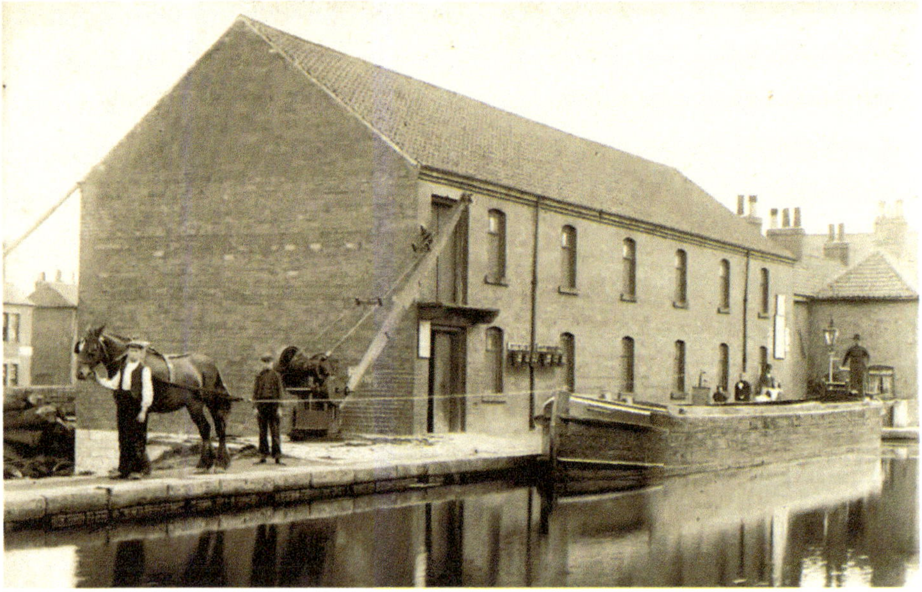

Wharf Road Dock House, Chesterfield Canal, Wharf Road, 1910

The *Gentleman's Magazine* of 1777 observed that the Chesterfield Canal was 'already of prodigious advantage to the neighbouring country in conveying limes, coals, and other heavy articles, which are now carried at about one fifth part of the usual price of land-carriage and altogether as expeditious'. Retford's population doubled from 5,999 in 1801 to 12,340 by 1901, and the town also saw the introduction of new technologies with the Northern Rubber Company in 1871. The factory's proximity to the junction of two important railways and the Chesterfield Canal helped it prosper. This traffic ceased about 1962. Towards the end, all the working boats on the Chesterfield Canal were horse-drawn. The building has since seen many changes, one being the Broken Wheel Nightclub – the organisers were Eddy Law and his wife Pat, who held popular soul nights in the small, but atmospheric, establishment. Currently the old dock house is up for sale.

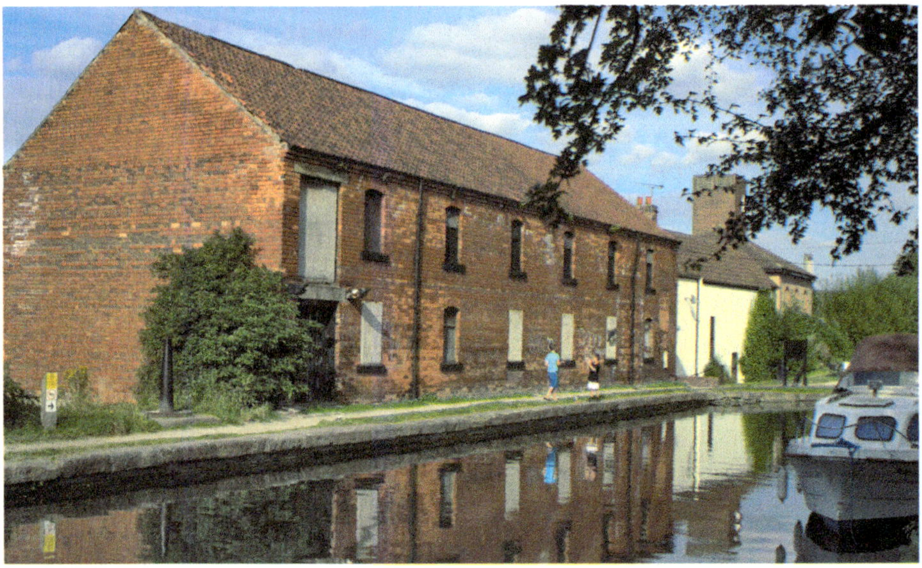

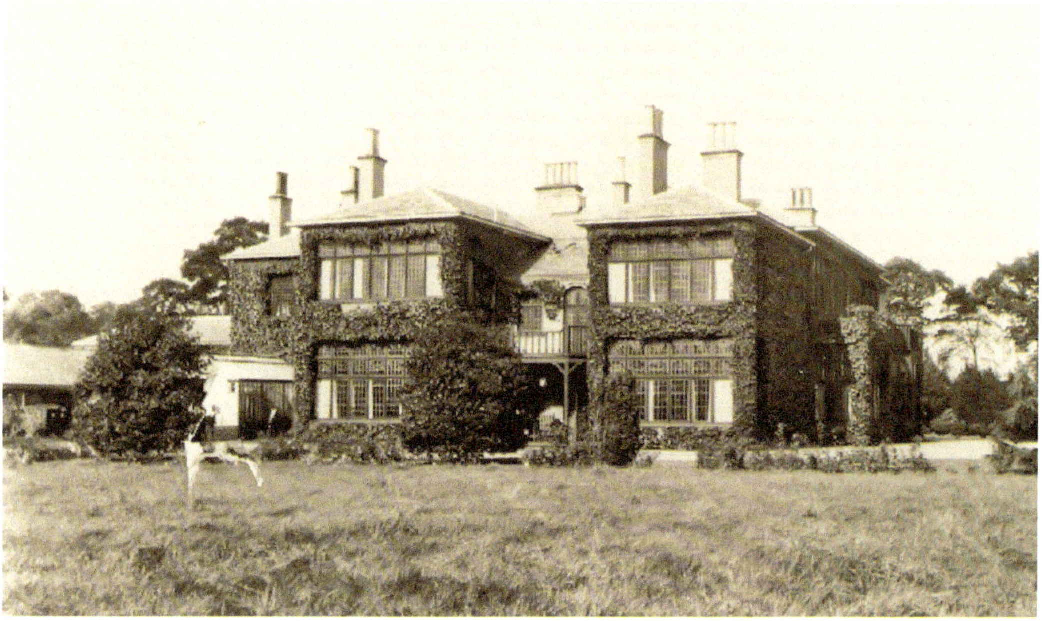

Ordsall Hall, 1910

Ordsall Comprehensive School was situated on Ordsall Road. In 2007 it merged with the King Edward VI Grammar School to become Retford Oaks High School in a new complex built on a greenfield site. Following its closure, the school buildings and the old hall were demolished. The site was used for a new post-16 centre and a swimming baths for Retford. The old hall was built in 1820 and was used as part of the school for sixth-form studies and music lessons. It was surrounded by majestic landscape and gardens. Now 190 years of history have been built over by a contemporary sports centre.

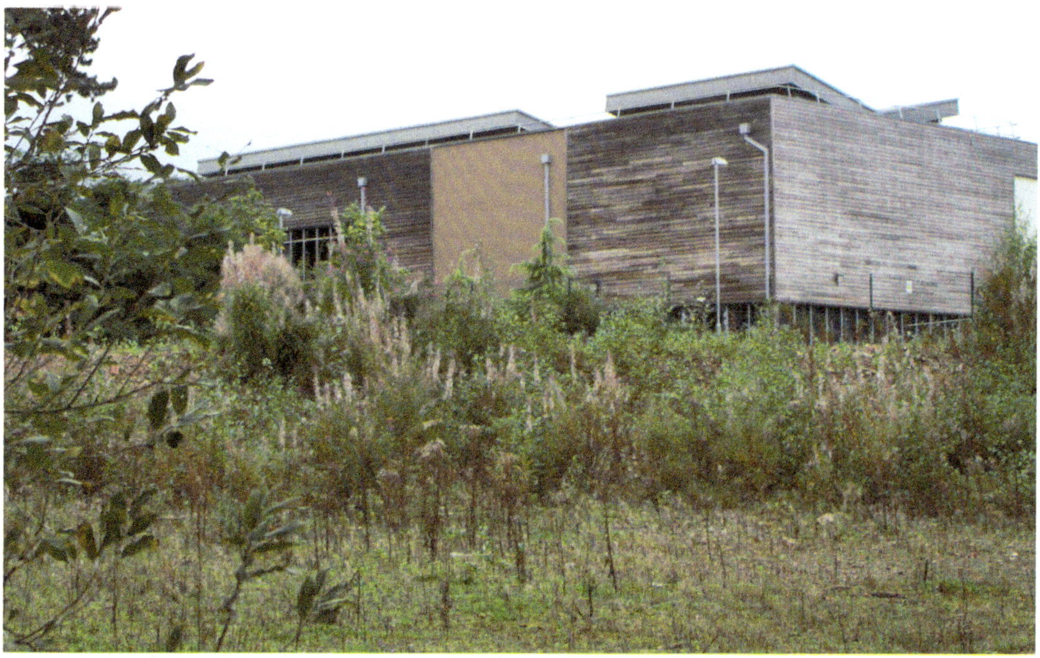

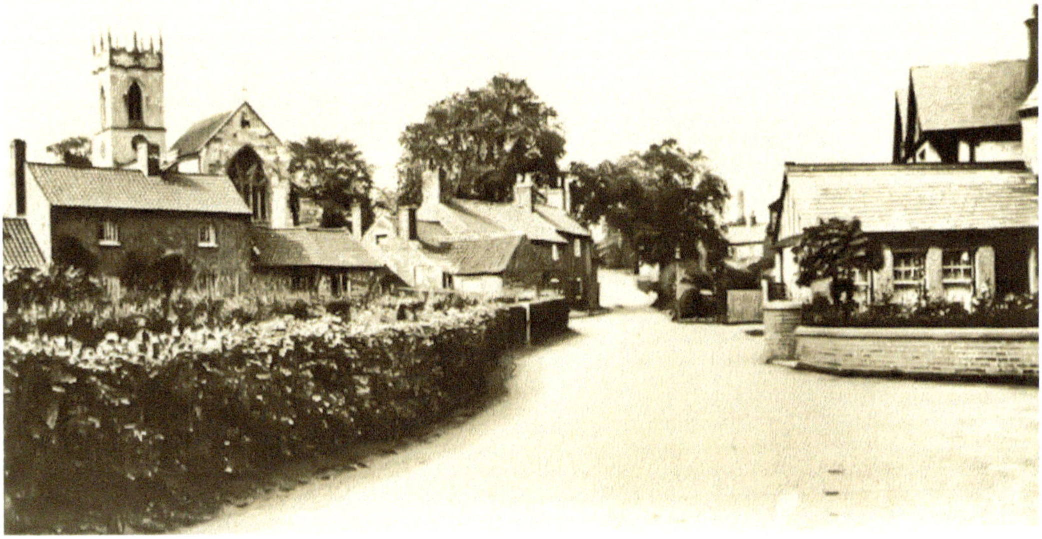

Ordsall, 1920

Here we have Ordsall village with All Hallows church and the Gate pub on the right, Stephen Hemsworth was parish clerk of Ordsall, and landlord of the Gate Inn. The village of Ordsall is a suburb of the town, divided from Retford by the River Idle and the railway. In the Domesday Book of 1086, the name of the village is 'Ordeshale'. For centuries the parish of Ordsall consisted of the village and two small hamlets, Thrumpton and Whitehouses. The population in 1801 was just over 500; in 2001 there were over 4,000 residents in Ordsall.

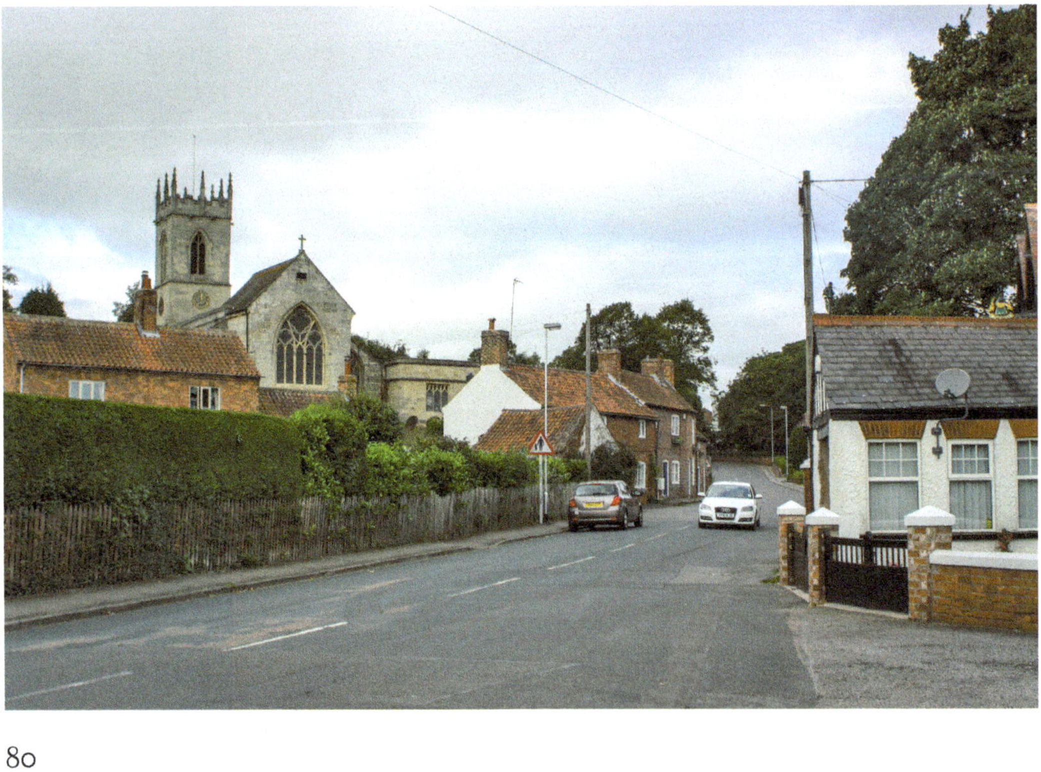

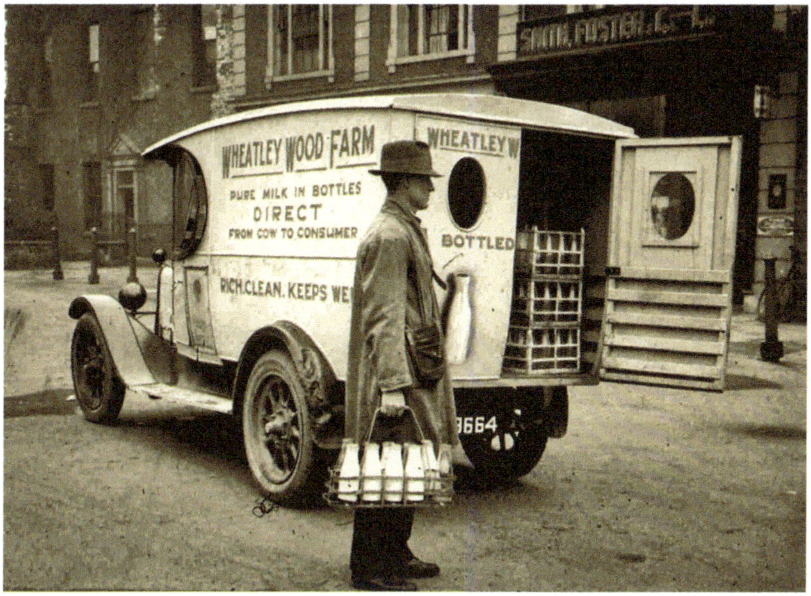

Wheatley Wood Farm Milk, 1929

Wheatley Wood Farm milk van driver Mr Horrocks in the town square. He would deliver glass bottles door to door. Carole Tasker of Wheatley Farm informed me that they do not have a dairy or even cows anymore. The dairy was bought by the Tasker family from Martin Horrocks in the fifties and the dairy closed. Wheatley Wood now farms about 450 acres but no livestock. Their main crop is strawberries, which Wheatley is famous for and most Retford locals have enjoyed!

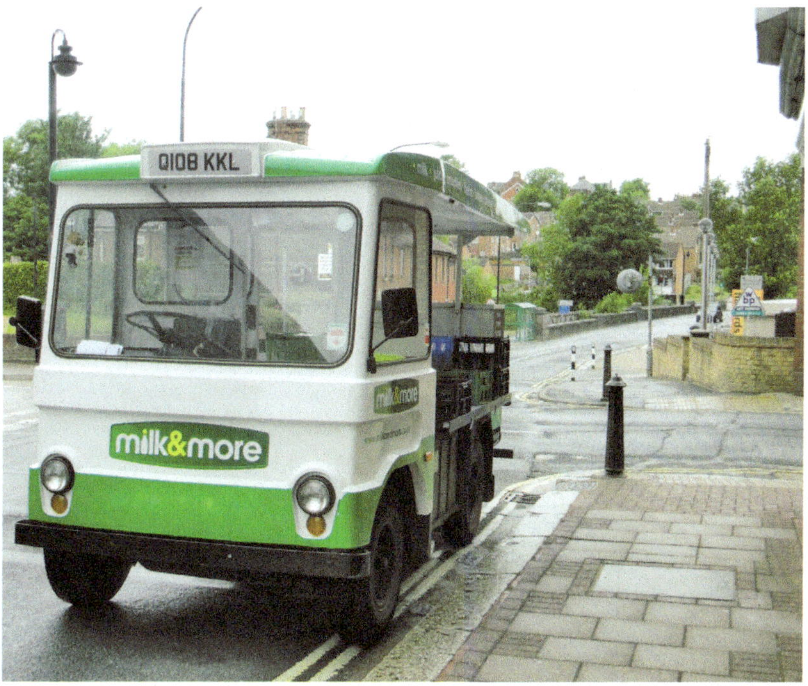

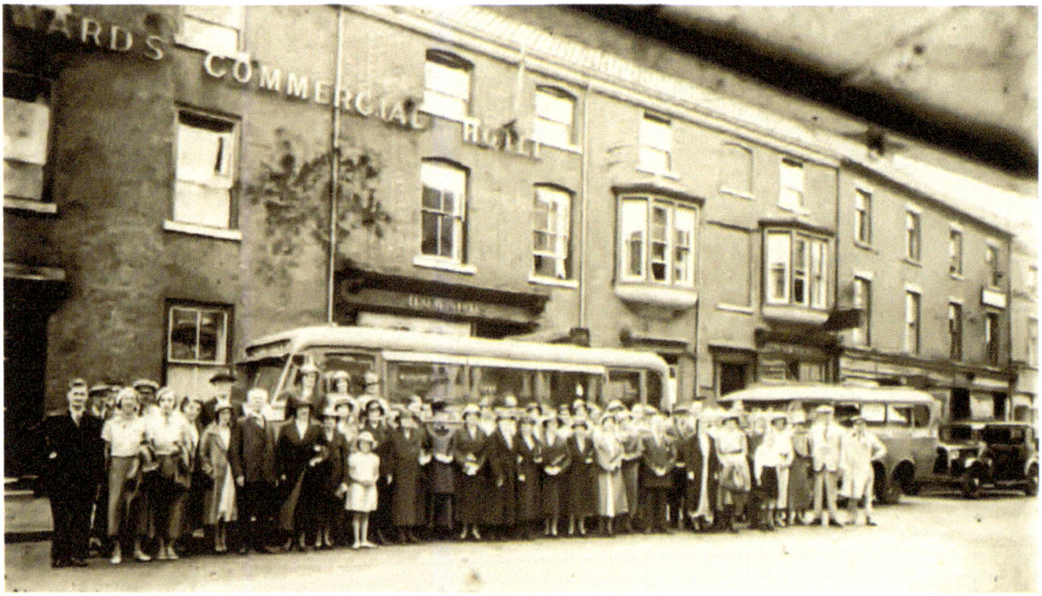

Howards Community Hotel, Grove Street, 1935

In the old photograph we see a coach parked outside the Howards Hotel. The principal streets of Newgate (Grove Street), Carr Hill Gate (Carolgate), Churchgate or Kirkgate, and Bridgegate radiated out from the square. Retford's population increased over the twentieth century. In 1901 there were 12,340 inhabitants and road congestion in Retford had become an issue as early as the 1920s when calls were made for the construction of a bypass. By the 1950s it was a chronic problem and relief only came when the A1 was opened to the west of the town in the 1960s. A bypass was constructed around the town centre in the 1970s. Grove Street remains a wonderful street to walk along and glance upwards to enjoy the Georgian windows and Victorian structures.

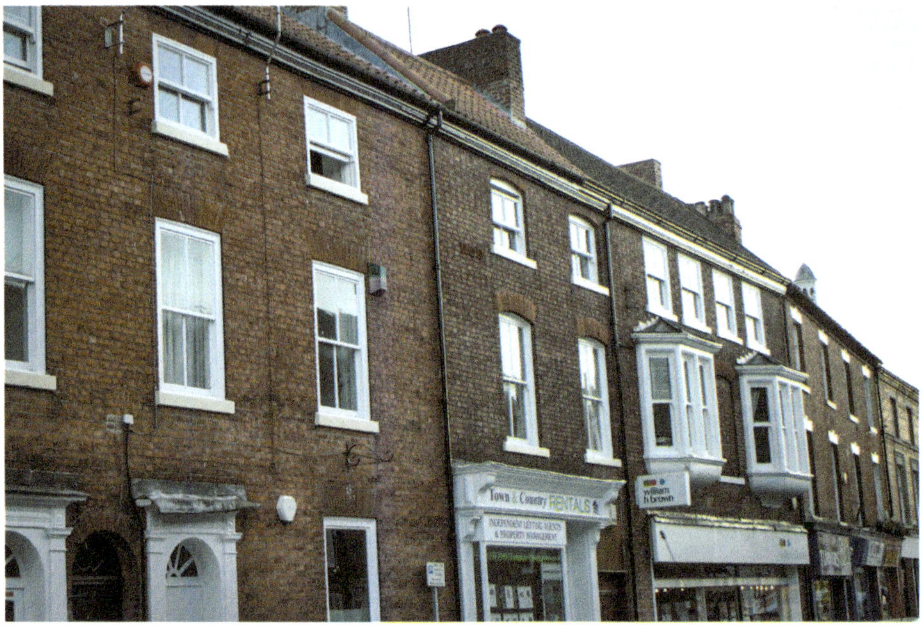

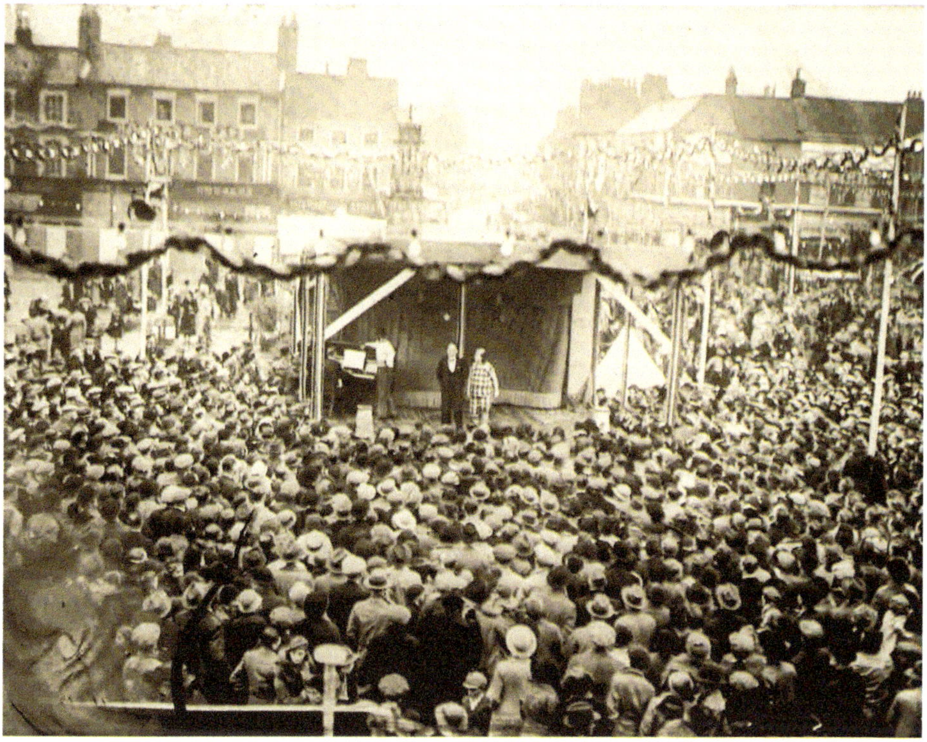

Peace Celebrations, Market Square, 1918

The signing of peace at the end of June 1918 meant that celebrations were fixed for Retford and around the country celebrations took a host of different forms: convicts at Parkhurst prison on the Isle of Wight were given a holiday and extra rations including plum pudding. The elders from the butter market told me how their parents all had a note through the post and all were to meet in the market square for 'an announcement'. They talk of how they were hanging on to the coats of their parents as excitement and celebrations took hold of the town. After the war, the population of Retford swelled, with hundreds of people coming into the town.

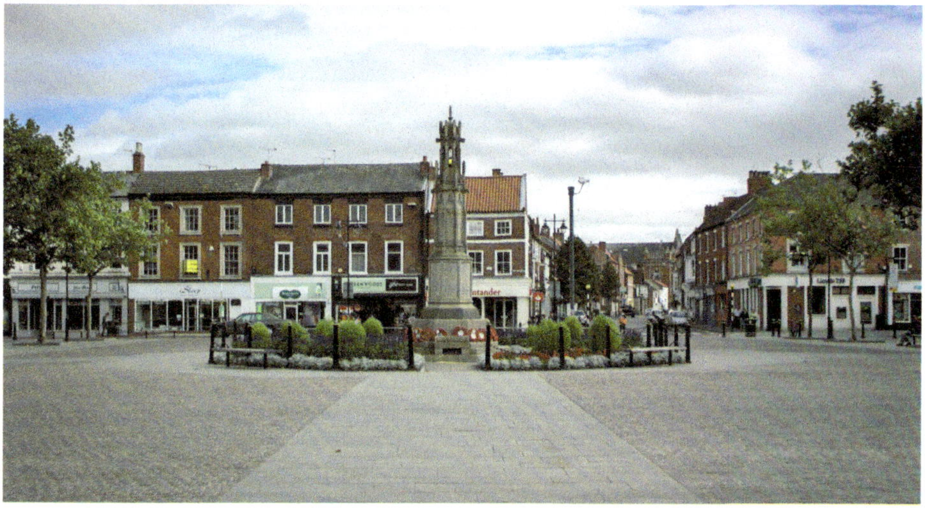

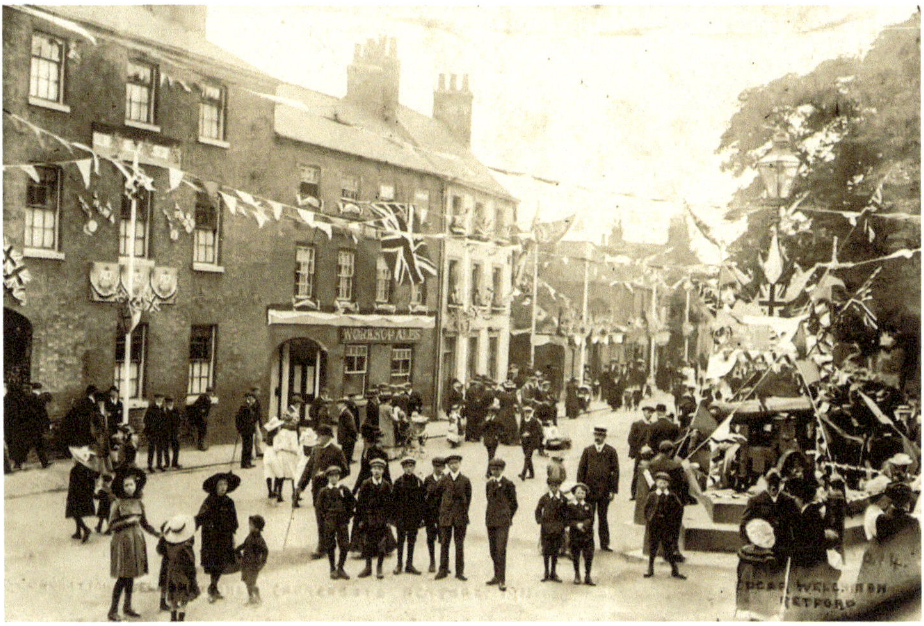

The Cannon Square, 1911

Retford really celebrated the Coronation of King George V. So many of Edgar Welchman's old photographs are of Retford people decorating their streets or having parties and lighting up their houses, even sending candles down the canal for the festivities. There's one thing Retford people know how to do and that is enjoy themselves! Here in the old photograph there are local people celebrating outside the Vine pub, which still serves as a public house, and waving flags around the cannon and St Swithun's church. The cannon was captured from the Russians during the Siege of Sevastopol at the end of the Crimean War in 1856.

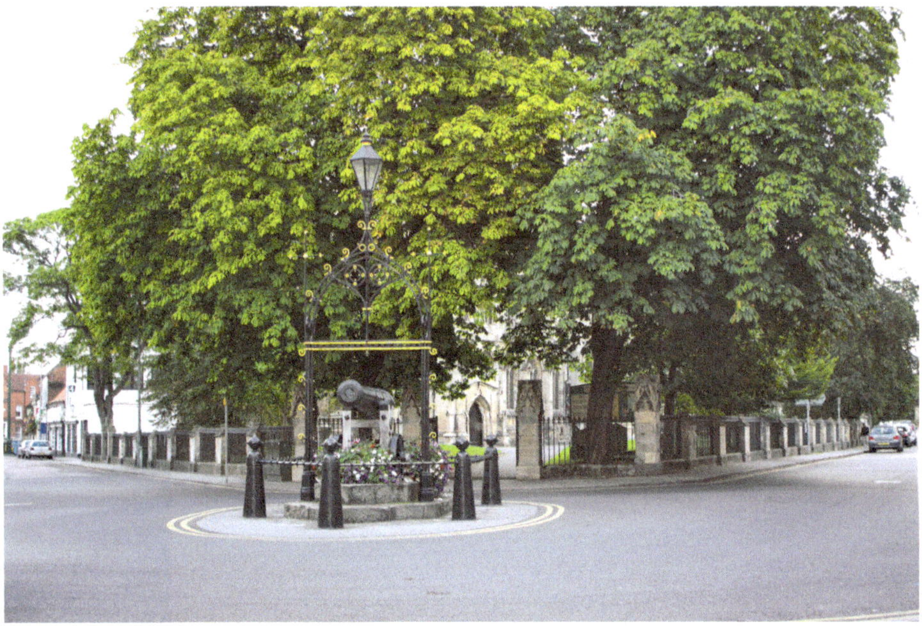

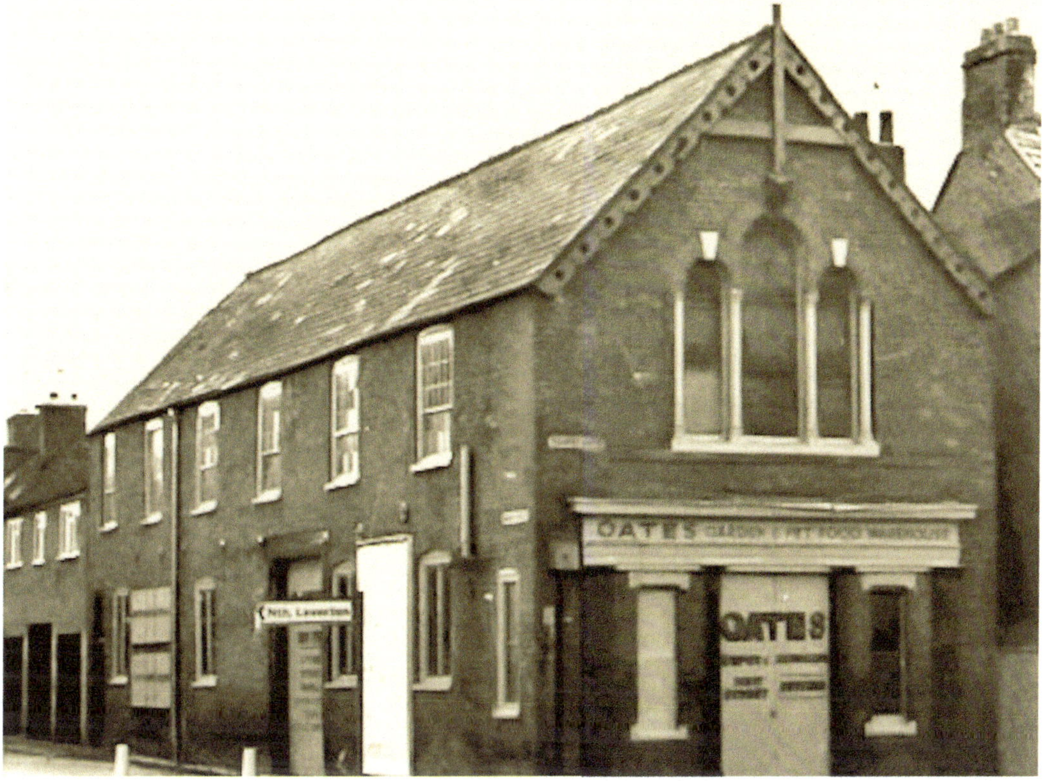

The National School, Corner of Chapelgate and Union Street, 1970

Built in 1813, this is an example of earlier pre-state education for the children of workers, organised by the church or other voluntary societies, and superseded in 1870 by the Forster Education Act, which introduced national and local school boards. John Shadrach Piercy moved to Retford in 1822 to take up the post of master of the National School on Chapelgate; he became parish clerk for East Retford, and journalist on several local newspapers. His life was also touched by scandal in 1852 over accounting irregularities while acting as assistant overseer of the poor. He was forced to resign. He died after a long illness on 22 June 1868 and was buried in Ordsall churchyard. The building now flourishes as Pine Furniture of Retford.

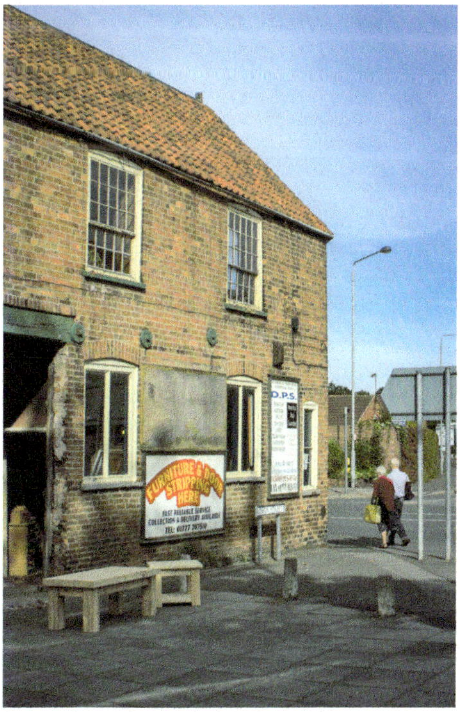

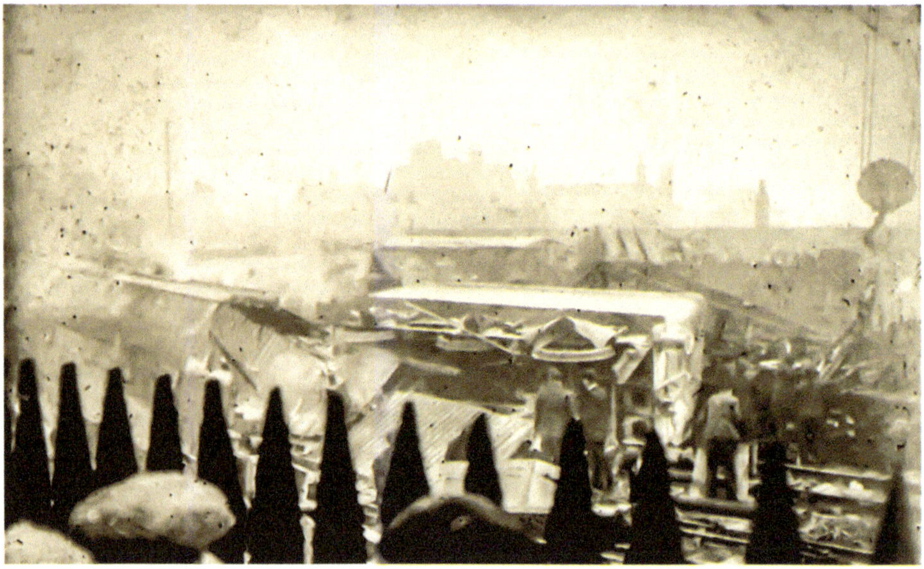

Railway Accident, Retford Station, 1923

On 13 February 1923 a No. 146 mail train (Aberdeen sleeping car express), travelling at high speed, collided with the rear of No. 101 goods ('A' class) train as it was backing at a slow speed to clear the points giving access to the up-platform. The driver and fireman of the express, as well as a locomotive inspector who was travelling on the footplate on duty were killed. The conductor of the express fortunately escaped with serious cuts, whilst seventeen passengers and five railwaymen travelling as passengers suffered minor injuries, bruises, and the effects of shock. Talking with the elders who meet weekly at Retford butter market, I was informed that one of the deceased was a Mr Zaccaria, who had come over to England as a refugee. They said the money from the accident ensured a secure future for the Zaccaria family, who had settled in Retford.

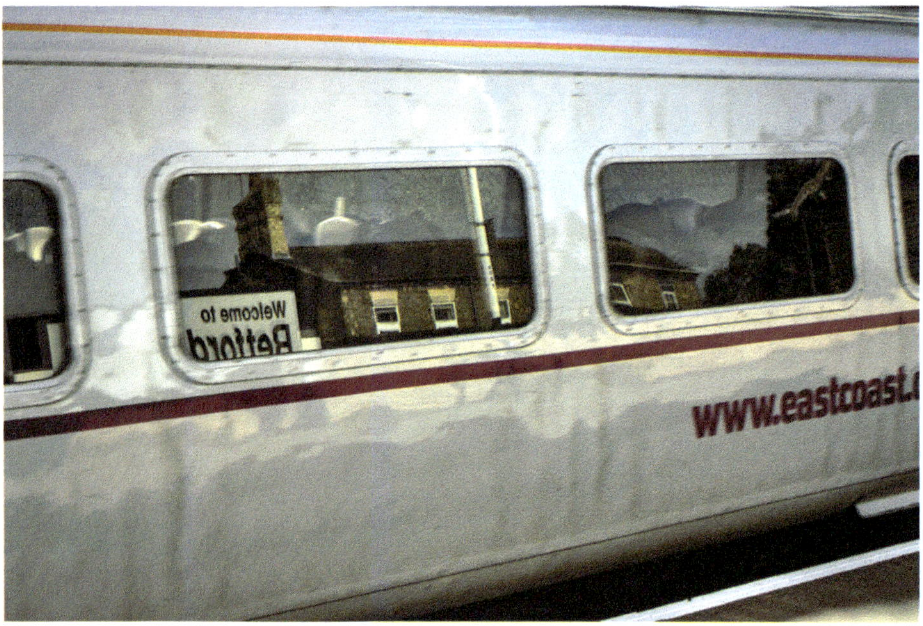

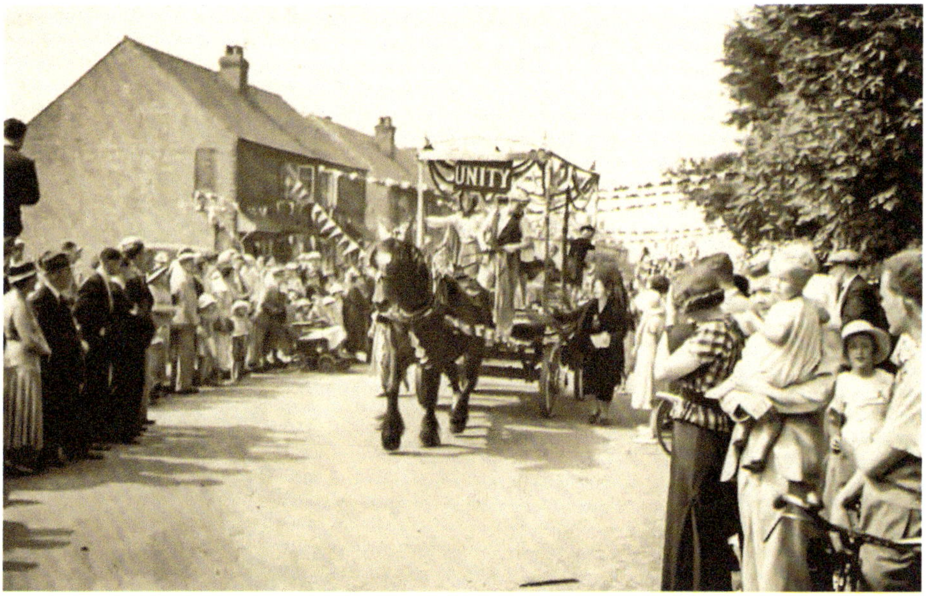

Hallcroft Carnival, 1923

Retford's population swelled over the twentieth century but not as greatly as it did during the preceding century. In 1901 there were 12,340 inhabitants; by 2001 this had increased to 22,000. The spread of Retford's housing stock was a key hallmark of the interwar period. Building on the Hallcroft estate started in 1920. Major private developments (North Road estate, Welham Road to Tiln Lane area, Grove Coach Road to Bracken Lane area, Babworth Crescent, etc.) have been completed since the Second World War. Traditional industries in Retford have, however, declined in recent years with long-established companies such as Jenkins Newell Dunford (engineering) and Bridon Ropes (wire) closing. Like so many other small towns, Retford is now overshadowed by large supermarkets and the service industries.

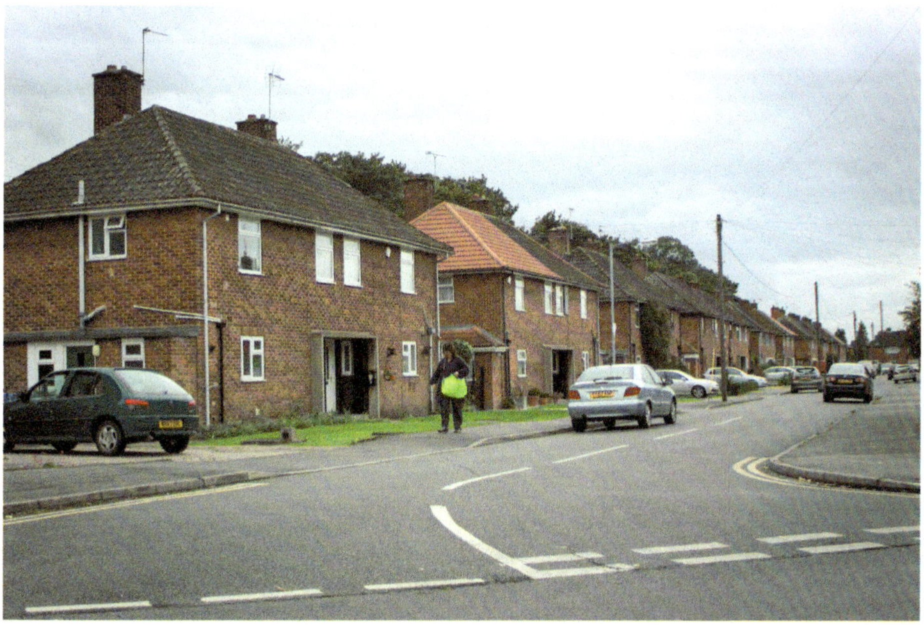

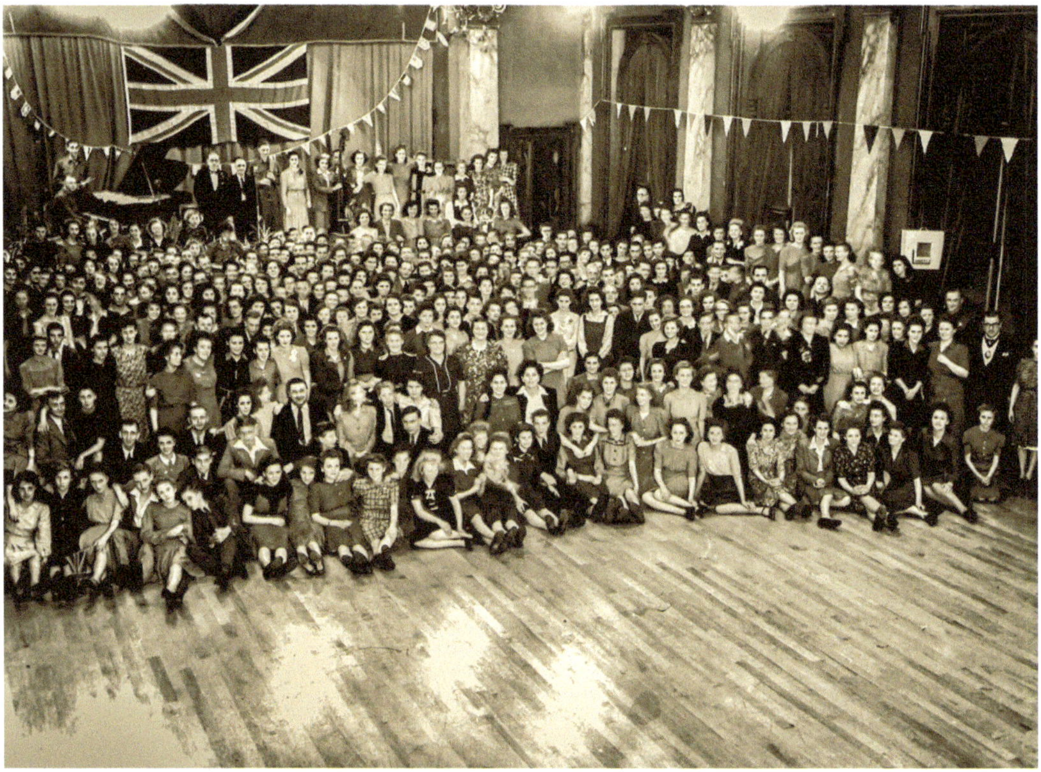

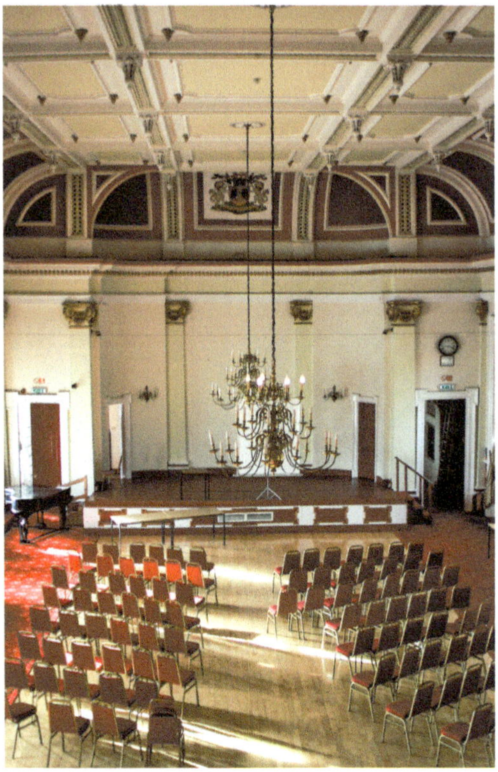

Retford Town Hall, 1940

The 'Victorian Romanesque' town hall on the south side of the market square was designed by Bellamy & Hardy of Lincoln and built by Thomas Hopkinson, a local building contractor, in 1866-68. It is built of brick but faced in Bath stone with plinths and columns in Mansfield stone. Here we have a dance for employees at Clark's Dyeworks Ltd, Hallcroft, Retford, in Retford town hall. Peter Thorpes, who is the current caretaker, kindly took me around the hall, which is still very much in use, and up to the wonderful clock tower. He described how the crystal chandelier – the second most expensive in the country – was presented to the town hall in 1954, and ten years ago its value stood at £250,000.

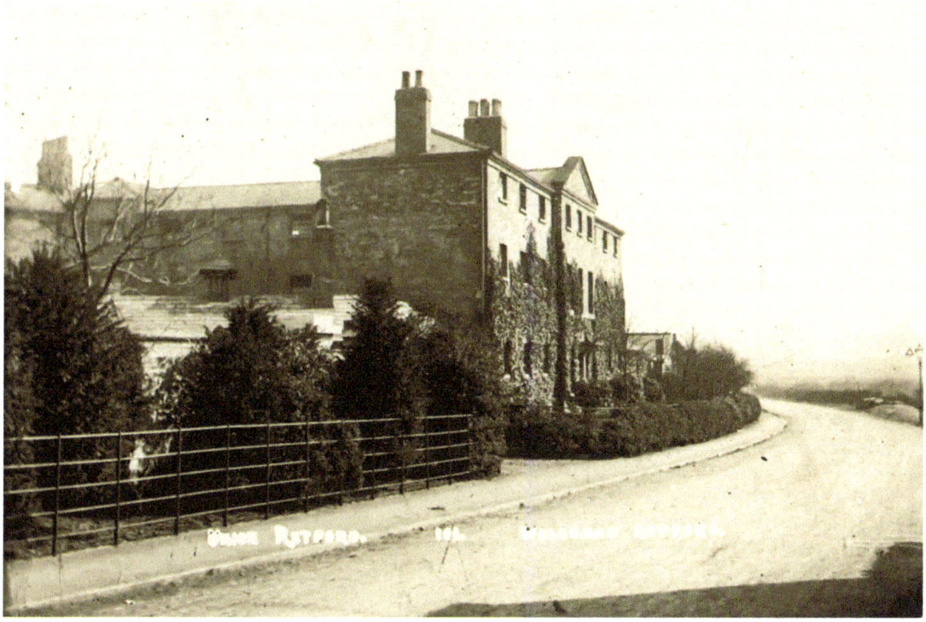

The Union Workhouse, 1910

East Retford Union Workhouse at the top of Spital Hill was erected in 1830–38 for 200 inmates in what was then open countryside. It cost £45,000 and was designed by H. J. Whitling, whose design was a variation on the model hexagonal plan published by the Poor Law Commission in 1835. The first master and matron were Joseph Cheaten and his wife, both aged sixty-seven, who continued in office until 1857. The punishment at the workhouse for acts of 'indecency' and 'absconding' was solitary confinement and bread and water for three days. The ladies were forced to have their hair cut and were not allowed to wear hats for three months. In 1948 it became a care home for the elderly and was demolished in 1970. Now the area is a housing estate.

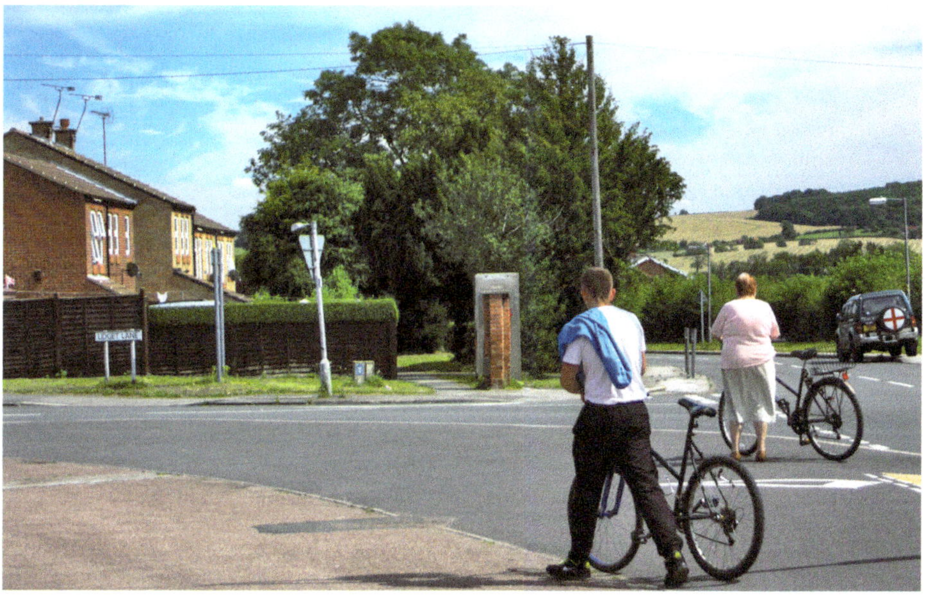

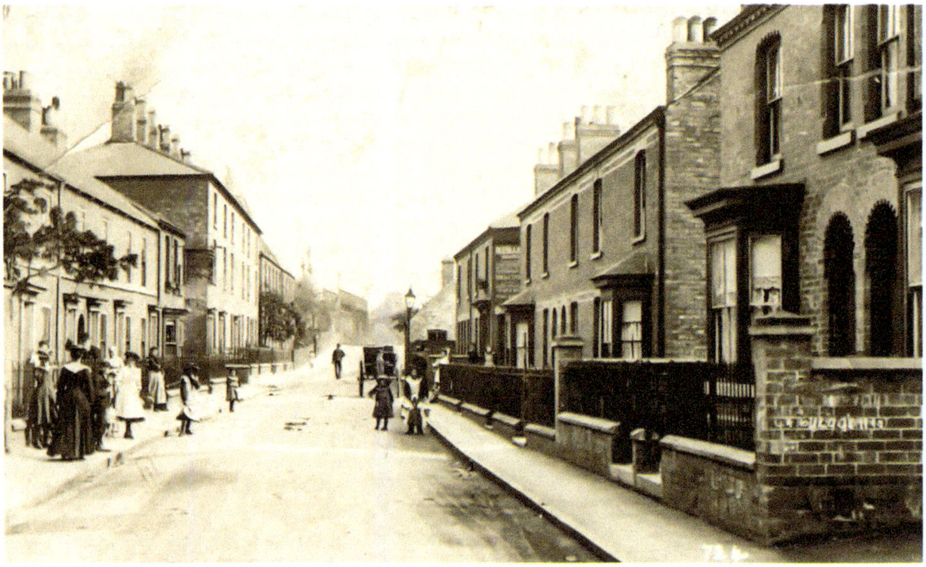

Thrumpton Lane, 1910

The old shop on George Street still exists as a shop, which is something in an area that has seen much transformation since the introduction of the railway on 16 July 1849. I recall being sent to the bottom of the street by my grandparents, which seemed miles away, to fetch a bag of sweets. The sweetshop is now a pet shop, but I bet it is just as thrilling for a young adventurer. The old iron railway bridge can just be seen in the distance in the old photograph taken by Mr Edgar Welchman of Retford. The house to the left was to become the Northern Rubber Works, which brought much employment to the residents of Thrumpton and neighbouring streets. Any local will talk fondly of hearing the 5 p.m. foghorn to signify the close of a workday. Today this area is thriving with new housing and lots of young families due to its close proximity to all the good schools, the train and bus links and the town centre with all the local amenities such as Kings' Park.

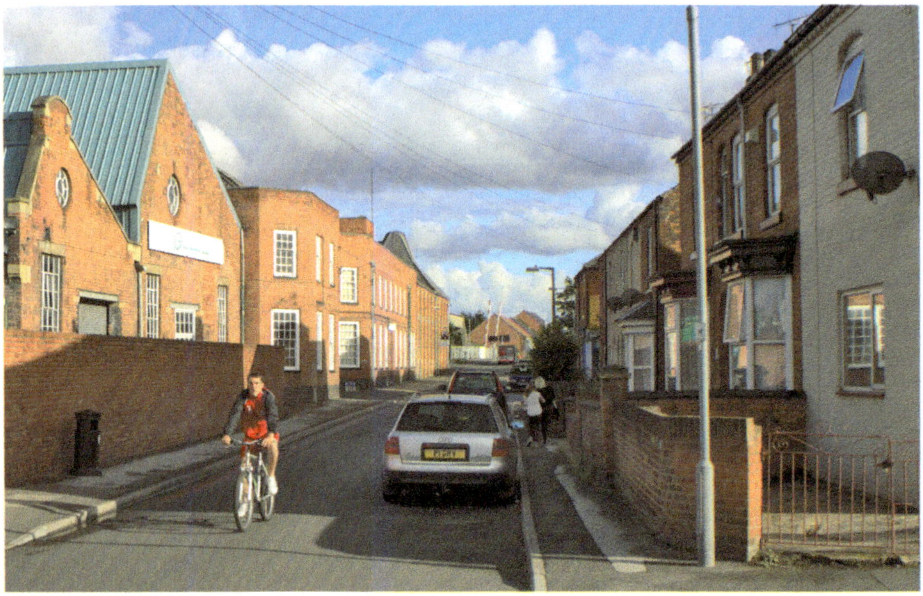

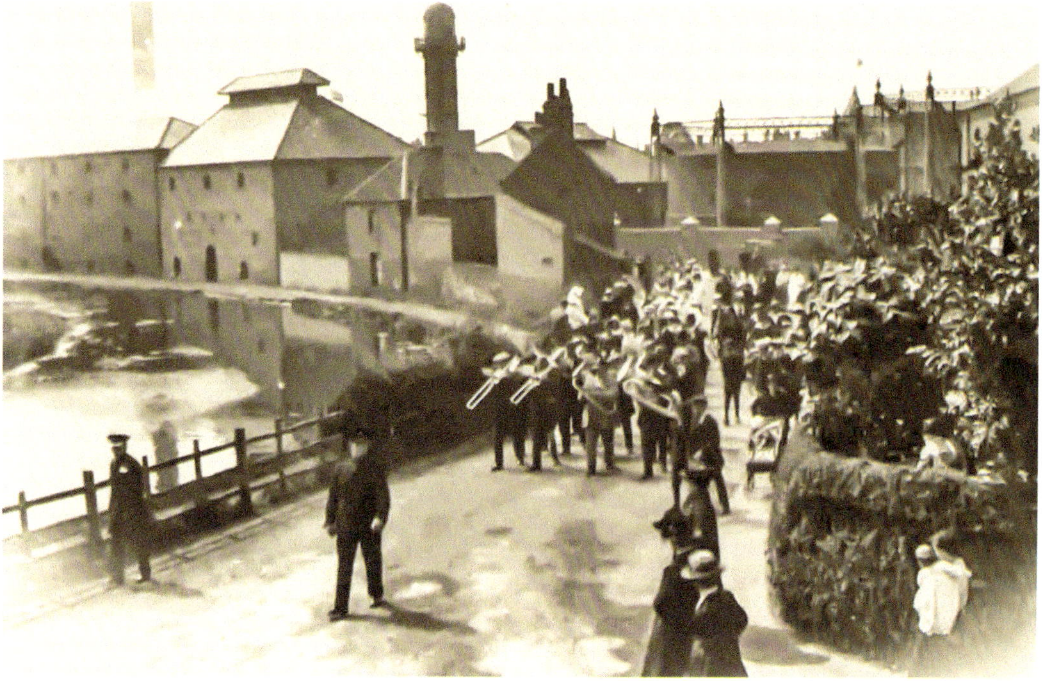

Grove Mill, Raglan Road, Gasholder, 1910

T. James Brindley designed the Chesterfield Canal, on which work started in October 1771. The canal was completed in 1777. It used to link Shireoaks and Worksop to Retford, and it ran for 46 miles, contained sixty-five locks, sixty-nine bridges and two tunnels. Its chief purpose was to transport coal from Derbyshire pits. Grove Mill dates from 1838 and has functioned as a malt kiln and flour mill. Today it is a popular snooker hall and a Grade II listed building. In fact, Retford has several mills that were next to the bridges, and over time were used for fulling, grinding corn and papermaking. The gasholder is no longer there.

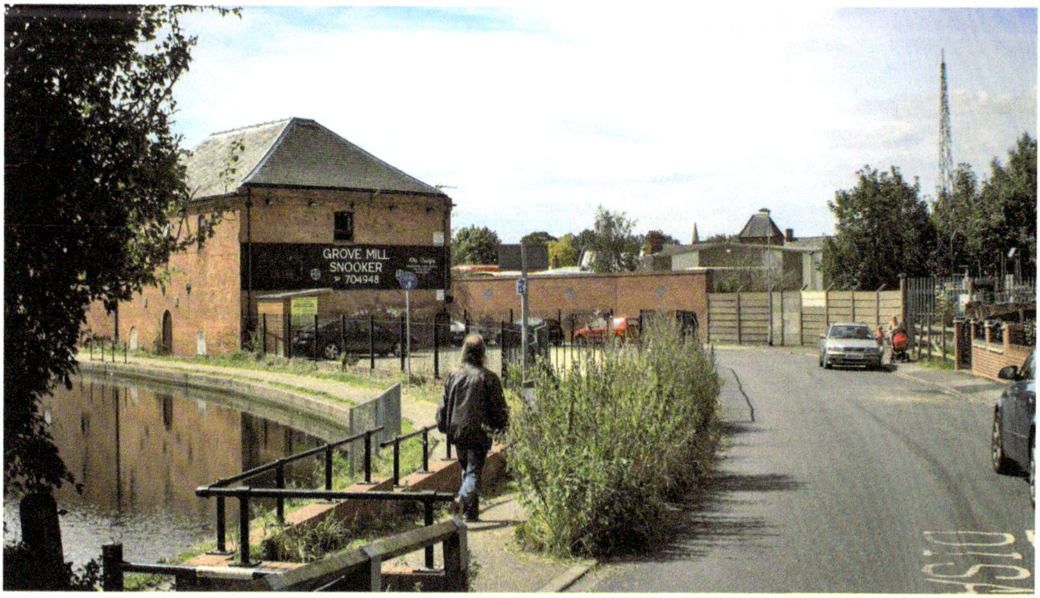

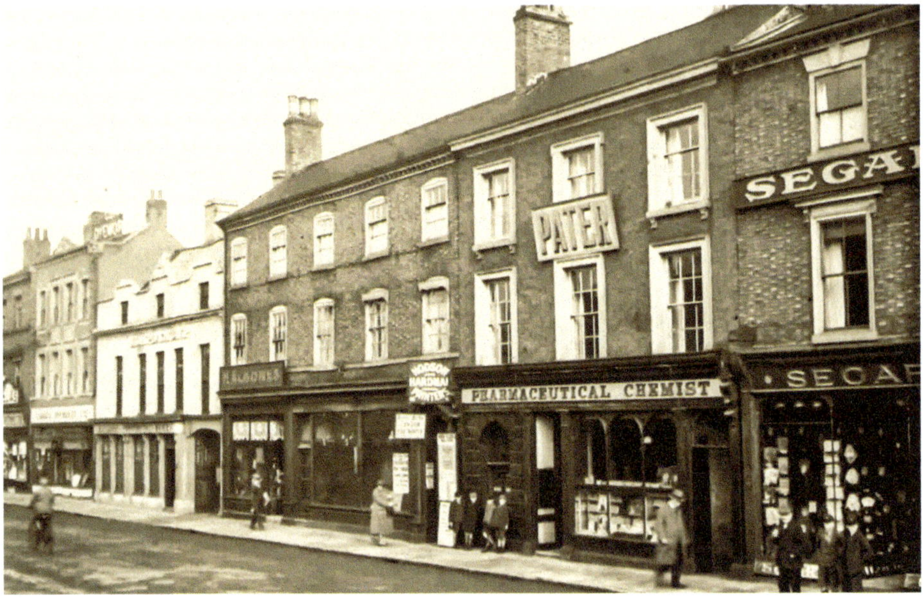

Carolgate Corner, Market Square, 1931

Retford boasts an attractive spacious square and market place. It is neat and elegant with shops laced around its edge. The Great North Road, in a kind of circuitous direction, ran through the centre of it; when journeying northward, the traveller has the market place to the right, and the square to the left. The old town hall, which stood upon the same ground as the present one, was erected in 1389, and pulled down in 1754. About 130 years ago the market place was unpaved, and a ditch, or common-sewer, was open from north to south, by the side of which stood live old trees; in consequence, however, of the ill effects which the noxious fumes arising from the hole had upon the health of the inhabitants, it was ordered to be covered in, the trees were taken away, and the market place paved in a regular manner. No fear of that now as thousands have been spent on a new market square.

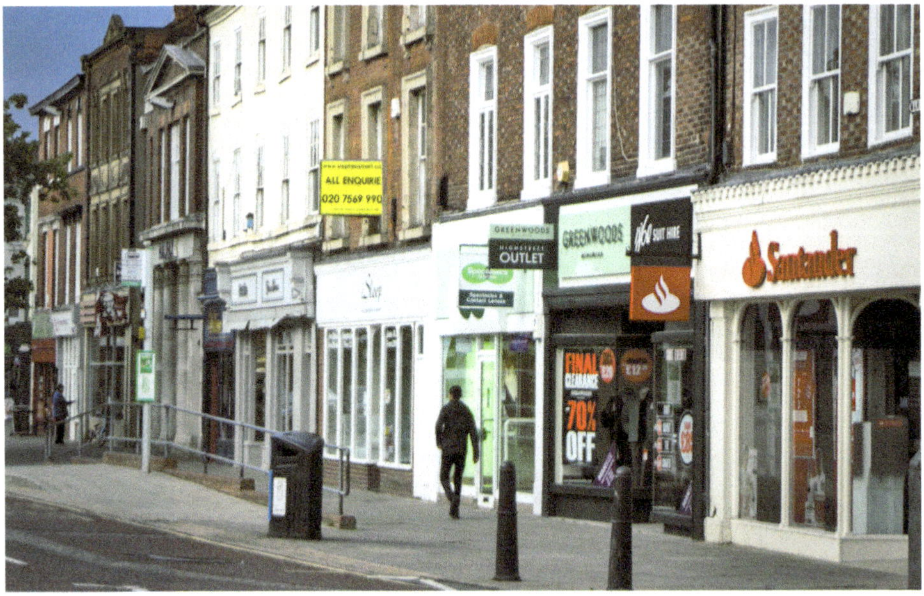

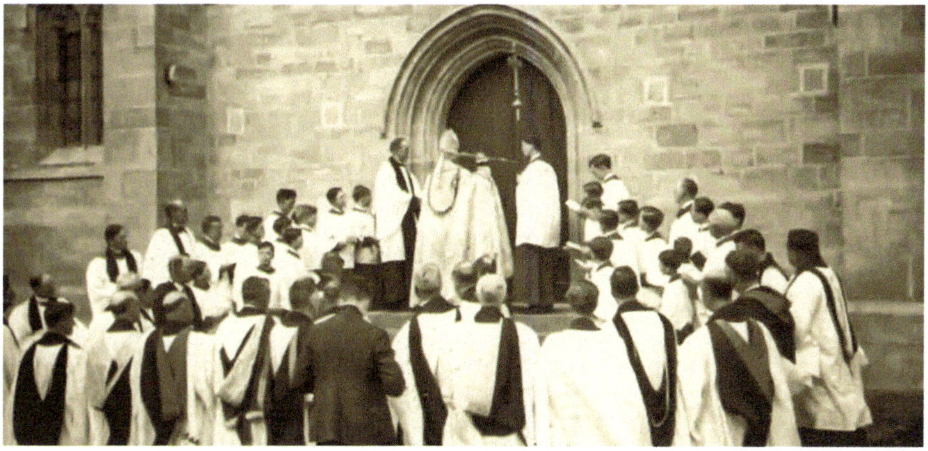

St Alban's Church, 1931

In the 1880s South Retford's population had grown rapidly and the parish's mission room in Albert Road was no longer adequate. In 1893 the rector, Samuel Stothert, proposed the building of a church in south Retford, but apart from a few committee meetings nothing then came of the suggestion. When Revd Dr Walter Stott came to the parish in 1896 he regarded the matter as urgent. Over the next eleven years he was the driving force in the creation of a new church. The poor, it was argued, did not come to church because there were not enough places for them. The missionary response was to build more churches. In May 1898 it was resolved to form a syndicate to purchase the Holly Mount Estate. They bought the estate, marked off a site 71 feet wide by 240 feet long, and sold off the remainder, enabling them to convey the property earmarked for the new church to the church committee free of charge. Yet despite this strong start completion of St Alban's church, hampered by inadequate funds, was to take three decades. For 100 years the church of St Alban's has faithfully served the people of south Retford. Those days are now coming to an end in two ways: the world has changed and has moved away from widespread and active Christian adherence, and then on 7 August 2008 police arrested three teenage boys in relation to the fire at St Alban's church. The beautiful building now stands in ruins and its future is uncertain.

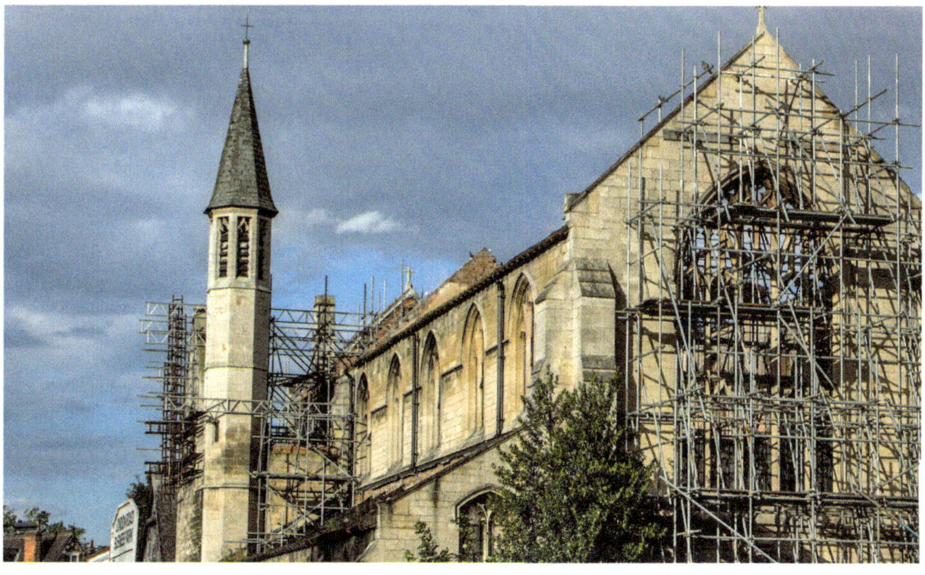

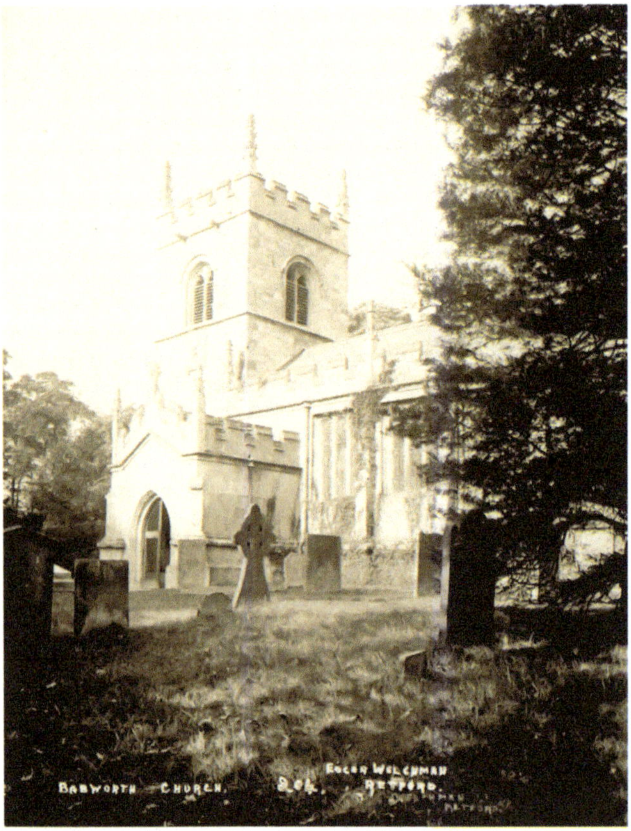

Babworth Church, All Saints, 1910

Babworth parish church, All Saints, is so quaint and is surrounded by beautiful greenery. The church is around 900 years old. It is a small structure with a tower steeple with three old bells (to which were added three newly cast bells in the late 1950s) and a clock, a nave, chancel and a porch. Most of the building dates from the fifteenth century. The chancel and sanctuary contain furniture by Robert Thompson (noted for his mouse trademark). In early spring the church is surrounded by a spectacular display of snowdrops, which the public is free to visit. In 1674 it became the property of the Wortleys, from whom it was purchased by John Simpson Esq.

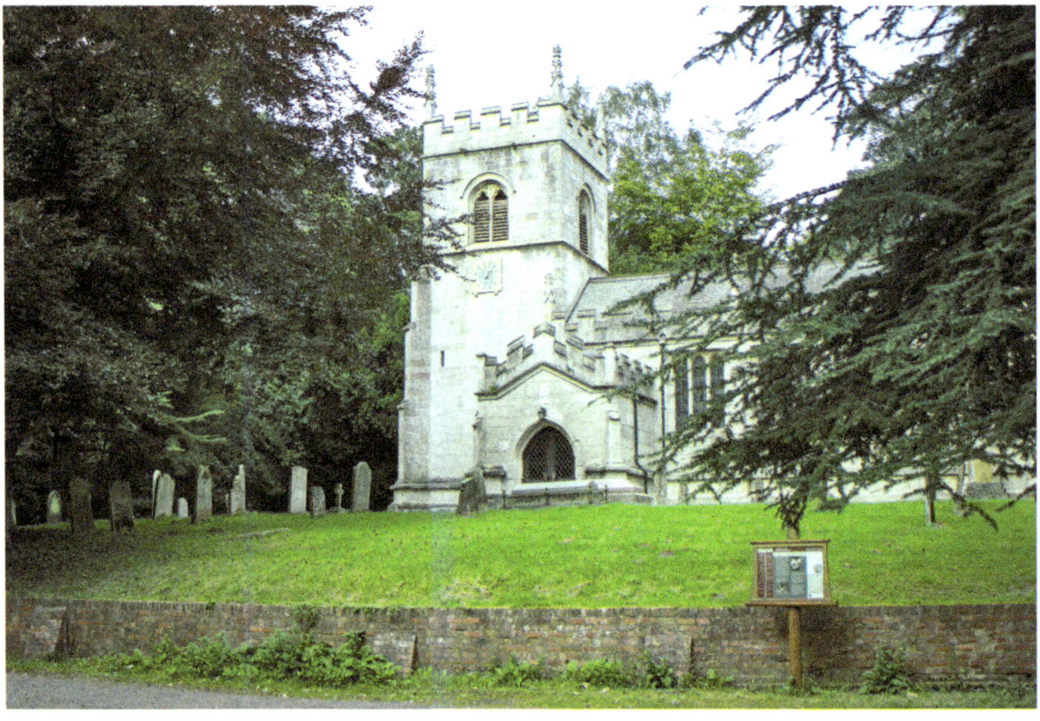

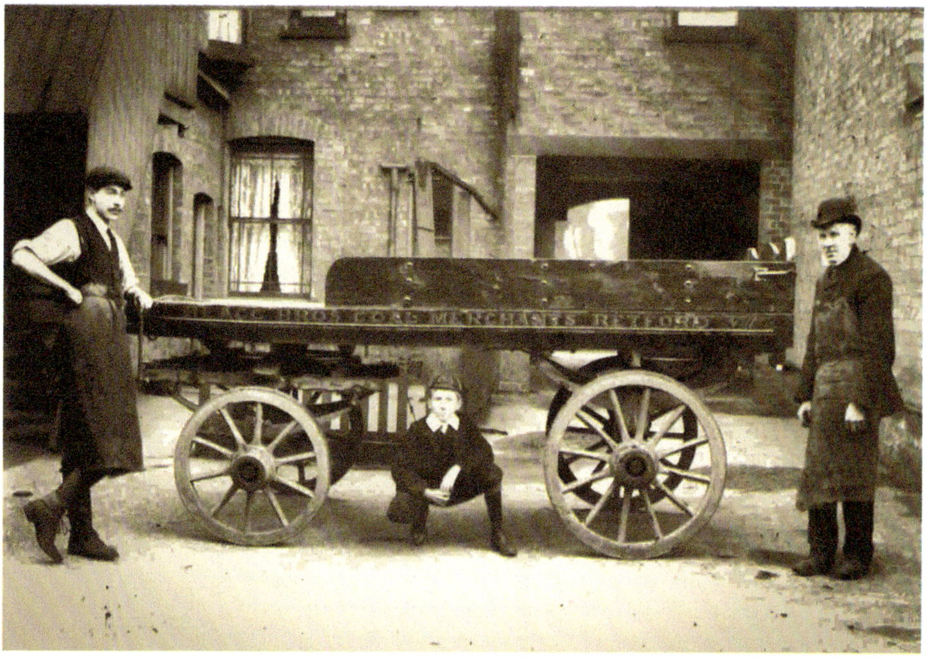

Blagg Brothers Coal Merchant, Union Street, 1900

The modern photograph is in the rear yard of the original Blagg Brothers coal business. Mrs Stokes of Union Street kindly invited me into her home so I could stand where Edgar Welchman would have stood to take the old photograph back in 1900. Mrs Stokes said that it was her great-grandfather who owned the coal merchant's, and the garage door to the right on the modern photograph was the old stables. Union Street is a wonderful street in Retford. It still manages to retain a beautiful charm as it keeps one foot proudly rooted in the history of Retford.

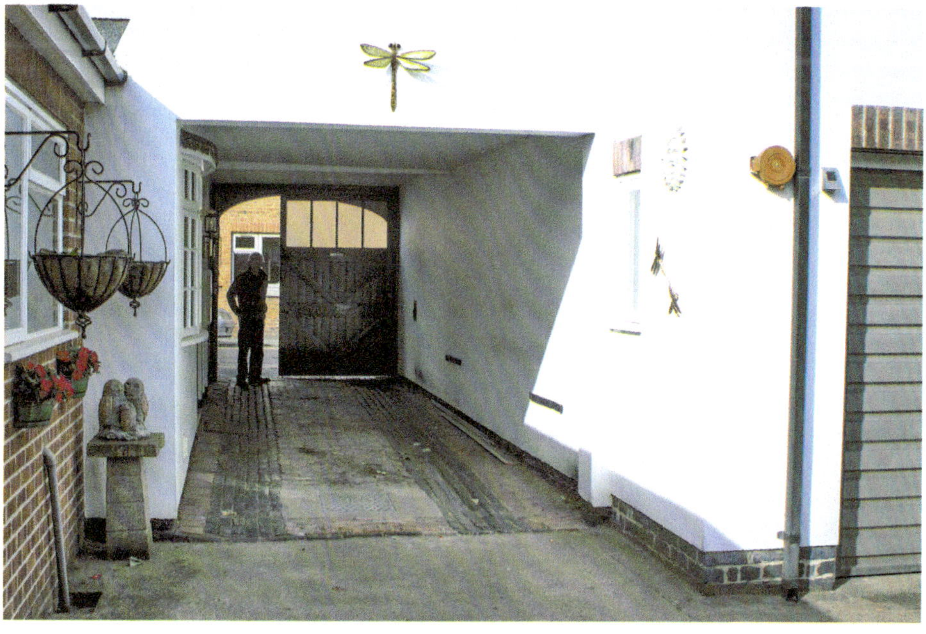

Acknowledgements

I have produced this book with the help of the Bassetlaw Museum. Without their kind permission to reproduce their old photographs, this book would not have been possible. My gratitude lies undoubtedly with Edgar Welchman, whose 4,000 images, taken by professional photographers Edgar Welchman & Son of Grove Street, Retford, between 1910 and 1960, have been lovingly sifted through in hope of creating the best possible interpretation of Retford through time. Thanks also to all the ladies and gents from Retford butter market, who meet weekly in the town hall for a cup of tea and a chat, for their wonderful and exciting memories of yesteryear. Thank you to Peter Thorpe, the caretaker of Retford Town Hall, for his kindness; to Helen from Bassetlaw Museum for putting me on the right track when I strayed; and to Roy Reville of Union Street, and Norma and her son from Spa Common, who all opened their homes, embraced my random questions and welcoming my curiosity. Last but not least, I would like to say thank you to my family – my husband Simon, and my children Nina and Zoe – who have been led down one alleyway after another on what they thought was yet another dog walk while I collated the ninety-two contemporary images for this book. Thanks also to Amberley Publishing, of course, for trusting me to complete this project.

Research was conducted by using the following websites: www.bassetlaw.gov.uk; www.bassetlawmuseum.org.uk; www.eyemead.com; www.chesterfield-canal-trust.org.uk; www.le.ac.uk/ucas/publications/document/40nottspmedi-000.pdp; www.macearschive.wordpress.com; www.nottsheritagegateway.org.uk; www.nottinghamshirehistiry.org; www.nottinghamshirepolice.co.uk/about/history; www.orsdallparish.plus.com; www.retfordretained.co.uk; www.retfordtoday.co.uk; www.retfordwheelers.co.uk; www.signalboxes.com/babworth.php; www.squidoo.com/Retford; www.visionofbritiain.org.uk; www.westretford.co.uk/histiry/html; www.wikipedia.org; www.workhouse.org.uk/eastretford.

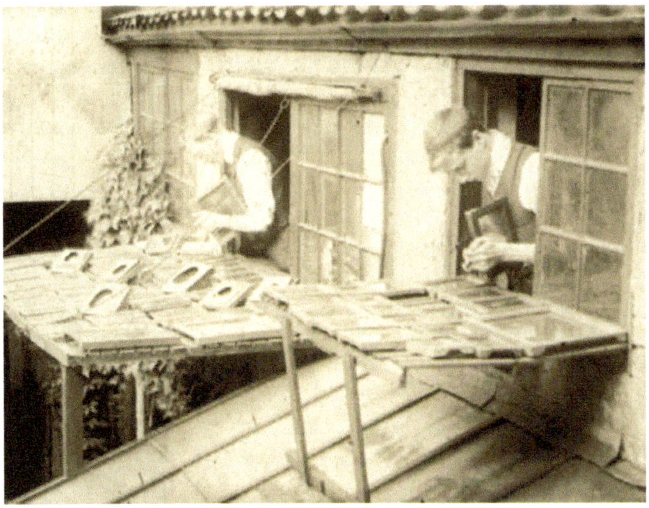

Edgar Welchman at work.